GRAPHIC DESIGN & PRODUCTION TECHNOLOGY

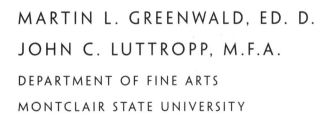

MARTIN L. GREENWALD, ED. D.

JOHN C. LUTTROPP, M.F.A.

DEPARTMENT OF FINE ARTS

MONTCLAIR STATE UNIVERSITY

UPPER MONTCLAIR, N.J.

Prentice Hall

Upper Saddle River, New Jersey 07458

Library of Congress Cataloging-in-Publication Data
Greenwald, Martin L., 1943–
    Graphic design and production technology /
    Martin L. Greenwald, John C. Luttropp.
        p. cm.
    ISBN 0-13-017445-9
        1. Printing. 2. Graphic arts. I. Luttropp, John E. II. Title.
Z244 .G844 2001
686.2--dc21

                                                    00-041666

Publisher: Dave Garza
**Director of Production
and Manufacturing:** Bruce Johnson
Acquisitions Editor: Elizabeth Sugg
Developmental Editor: Judy Casillo
Editorial Assistant: Lara Dugan
Managing Editor: Mary Carnis
Manufacturing Manager: Ed O'Dougherty
Production Editor: Denise Brown
Interior Design and Composition: John Luttropp
Art Director: Marianne Frasco
Cover Design Coordinator: Miguel Ortiz
Cover Design: John Luttropp & Miguel Ortiz
Printing and Binding: Victor Graphics
Cover Printer: Victor Graphics

Prentice-Hall International (UK) Limited, *London*
Prentice-Hall of Australia Pty. Limited, *Sydney*
Prentice-Hall Canada Inc., *Toronto*
Prentice-Hall Hispanoamericana, S.A., *Mexico*
Prentice-Hall of India Private Limited, *New Delhi*
Prentice-Hall of Japan, Inc., *Tokyo*
Prentice-Hall Singapore Pte. Ltd.
Editora Prentice-Hall do Brasil, Ltda., *Rio de Janeiro*

The authors wish to extend their appreciation to the experts who provided valuable comments and suggestions for this text in the course of its development: Gary Coll, University of Wisconsin-Oshkosh; Dr. Lenore D. Collins, Rhode Island College; Robert Ferro, Pittsburg State University.

This book was produced using Adobe Illustrator 8.0, Adobe Photoshop 5.5, QuarkXPress 4.1 with final output in Adobe Acrobat 4.0. The type families used are Adobe Daily News and Adobe Avenir. The cover uses Penumbra and Shelly Allegro Script. The book was composed on an Apple Macintosh G4. Scanning was done with an Epson Expression 636 Professional scanner.

Portions of this book were previously published under the title: *Graphic Communications: Design Through Production,* Delmar Publishers, Inc., 1997.

10 9 8 7 6 5 4 3 2 1
ISBN 0-13-017445-9

Contents

Graphic Design and Production Technology:

A Note from the Authors

In many disciplines, subject matter undergoes little, if any change from year to year. However, those areas affected by technological change should undergo content review and analysis at frequent intervals. Graphic design and the production technologies have been affected by technological change and related computerization as much, if not more, than any other sector of the industrialized economy.

Graphic Design and Production Technology has been tailored to the needs of students in the visual arts and technology-related disciplines. For the graphic designer, familiarity with the options available to bring a design to completion is invaluable. For the production technologist, first-hand knowledge of the design process allows for more sensitivity to the creative elements of the printed page, an aspect often overlooked in technical training programs where emphasis stresses function rather than underlying form. The development of a mutual understanding and respect on the part of each enhances the performance and accomplishments of both.

With respect to these objectives, the following are highlights of the organizational strategy of *Graphic Design and Production Technology*.

The Problem Solving Design Model

The creation of any graphic design piece is really a solution to a specific communication problem. Problems are best solved in a methodical way that incorporate a step-by-step approach, enabling not only a full understanding of the problem but researching all of its related aspects in order to come up with the best solution possible. Problem solving strategies are not new, but have undergone a rebirth in recent years. Students can use the graphic design problem-solving model to define, research and solve a variety of design and production problems.

Comprehensive Coverage of Each Step in the Design and Production Process

From producing thumbnails to post-press finishing techniques, this text highlights the stages that the graphic designer must master to become not only an effective communicator but knowledgeable about all of the processes needed to bring a design concept to completion.

Examination of Techniques Used to Digitize and Manipulate Data

Strategies and techniques related to data input and manipulation available to the graphic designer and production technician is constantly changing. While specific techniques applied to input and digital editing will change as software and hardware are continually upgraded, it is the knowledge of the concepts that underlay these techniques that is most important. *Graphic Design and Production Technology* highlights and

XV

emphasizes these concepts to help provide the designer and technologist with a broad-based conceptual foundation.

An Overview of the Historical Context of Graphic Communications

It is not enough to simply know about design. A good designer understands and appreciates the role of design and communication within the world community, and how that role came to be. *Graphic Design and Production Technology* provides an overview and examination of some of the events that highlight humankind—from the first creative expressions that appeared on cave walls in Europe, to the design and production of microprocessor circuitry and high-speed computers.

Web Design Basics and Multimedia Concepts

An increasing number of graphic designers are applying their talents towards Web and multimedia projects. In *Graphic Design and Production Technology* we offer an introduction of how pages for the World Wide Web are put together, as well as the steps involved in designing computer interactive multimedia titles. The emphasis here is on design concept and production techniques to provide a foundation for further explorations in specific applications related to Web and multimedia design.

Culminating Experiences for the Student

These projects back up and reinforce lessons and exercises in the text. Coupled with an Instructor's Supplement, these projects are designed to build on the concepts presented in the text with an eye towards enhancing student understanding as well as providing a foundation for portfolio development.

Preface

The use of computers has revolutionized not only the processing of information and the graphic arts industry, but also the educational institutions that offer programs focusing on these technologies. Until a few short years ago, company newsletters were routinely sourced out to businesses called service bureaus which handled all of the design, typesetting, and printing functions. Today, with the advent of affordable computer technology and powerful software packages, much of this work, including the printing, can easily be handled in-house.

Until recently, expensive color scanners were required to separate an original color photograph into the four separate color separation negatives necessary for printing the picture. However, using current technology, color pictures from the family vacation can be transferred from digital camera flash memory cards directly into a computer or onto a compact disc. From there, the pictures can be imported into a photographic manipulation program where they are modified and personalized. The pictures can either be printed on a high-resolution color printer, displayed on the family television set, or output to a digital typesetter or color copier for further processing or printing. Advances in digital photography now allow us the flexibility of selecting either conventional or digital cameras, both of which are in easy-to-use, point-and-shoot formats.

To keep up with the almost unbelievable pace of technological innovation affecting both graphic designers and printing technicians, curricula, equipment, and courses within the graphic arts must be continually updated. Computers purchased just two years ago are stretched to the limits of their memory and processing capabilities when running current software packages. Second- and third-generation software-driven typesetters have been obsolete for more than ten years. Level I Postscript® typesetting equipment strains to recognize the command structure of current Postscript® command strings. Early obsolescence is hastened by ongoing advances in computer operating systems and platforms, the continuing evolution of central processing chip technology that has passed the 1,000 MHz cycle level, and 1,000-fold increases in disk drive capacities. Many new computers no longer come factory-equipped with conventional floppy disk drives. Hard drive systems thought to be rock-solid in performance and technological sophistication are driven from the marketplace by ever-smaller, faster, and more efficient drive technologies. Sophisticated software application programs currently have memory requirements that were thought to be impossible only a year or two ago.

Many of the courses in graphic design and production techniques taught on both the secondary and post-secondary levels have evolved into two distinct categories: those that focus on creative, graphic design-oriented activities, and those that focus on production-oriented activities. The shortcomings of this course approach are obvious. Students educated with a strong background in the creative arts know little of what happens to a design when it leaves the drawing board or computer screen;

students with strong technical backgrounds in production-related programs are weak in many of the creative aspects of design and layout strategies.

Within business and industrial settings, these weaknesses are often manifested as a lack of communication among different levels in the design and production process. For example, when engineers design a product that encounters difficulty in some stage of manufacturing or production, the design engineer needs to talk to the production technologist to solve the problem. If the technologist and engineer are familiar with each other's tasks, communication between them is easy and the problem-solving process can proceed. Similarly, when graphic artists, graphic designers, and printing technicians have a working knowledge of both the design and production ends of the communication process, then the entire process is streamlined. In this environment, the graphic designer or production technologist is, by virtue of his or her comprehensive knowledge base, a more valuable employee. Also, due to the influence of the computer and associated software programs in virtually every aspect of business, a measure of graphic arts training is increasingly required for all employees, regardless of their specific job titles. People in human resource relations and training, management, and quality control technology all need to know how to get the printed message across in an effective, efficient manner.

Given this dichotomy of traditional education in the graphic arts, the purpose of this text is to bring together the areas of creative graphic design and production technologies under a single instructional umbrella. Ideas and concepts are presented and followed from the initial inception of a job to the printed and finished product.

Graphic Design and Production Technology has been tailored specifically to the needs of students in the visual arts and technology-related disciplines. For the graphic designer, familiarity with the options available to bring a design to completion is invaluable. For the production technologist, first-hand knowledge of the design process allows for more sensitivity to the creative aspects of the printed page, an aspect often overlooked in technical training programs where the emphasis stresses function rather than the underlying form. The development of a mutual understanding and respect on the part of each enhances the performance and accomplishments of both.

Within this framework, the authors have carefully avoided what they consider to be in-depth coverage of areas and skills that would ordinarily fall under the auspices of more traditional texts directed toward training printing production personnel. Also, there needs to be a recognition on the part of both graphic designers and production technicians of the profound effect and influence that digitization will have on the communication technologies in the near future and how this influence will affect the direction of instructional programs. Traditional technologies at both the design and production levels will continue to undergo many changes in the coming years. Educational programs will need to stay abreast of these changes. More importantly, students educated within this constantly changing technological landscape will need to be adaptable. The philosophy that guides this text is the belief that knowing how and where to find information, rather than memorizing information, is the key to a successful future in the workplace.

An additional key point in the philosophy of this text concerns the placement of traditional skills and technologies within the framework of an ever-changing technological landscape. Technological advances continue to gain strong footholds in the traditional printing production areas; the old labor-intensive methods are beginning to disappear. This raises the question, "Why learn old technologies and outdated production methods?" There are several answers to this question. The first and most important answer is that knowledge of, and experience with, the foundations of basic technological processes gives the technician and designer insights into modern processing techniques they would otherwise not have.

This text therefore begins with an introduction to graphic communication design and production, highlighting a description of the creative input and production technologies that form the graphic communication process.

It has been said that the second part of the history of the world and the arts began with the invention of printing. An historical perspective of the development of the graphic communication technologies is examined in Chapter 2, from early communication techniques in the form of primitive cave and wall paintings, to the development of moveable type and the sophisticated computerized systems that make possible the simultaneous publication of the same printed page throughout the world.

Chapter 3 investigates the principles of basic typography, from type families through a variety of typesetting systems. The creative design process is covered in Chapters 4 and 5. Chapter 4 highlights the steps in designing a project and focuses on the design process from a problem-solving perspective. The graphic design process is separated into distinct, manageable components, beginning with the definition of the problem. It then moves through the development of budget and schedules, to critique, design refinement, and then, final project review. Chapter 5 looks at the creative elements involved in graphic design. From the selection of proper column formats to the use of presentation graphic, design elements that are responsible for successful visuals are presented, with examples of what to do and not to do. Chapter 5 also deals on an in-depth basis with color as a design element. From the selection of colors to the differentiation between spot and process colors, the reader is given a broad perspective in the consideration of color as a creative design element.

Chapter 6 examines the fundamentals of computer graphics. The types of graphic design software programs that are available, along with the basic skills that are required to get the most out of these programs, are presented. After data have been digitized, what then? Chapter 6 looks at the basics of electronic page composition and layout. The digital revolution holds the promise of a future with only limited use of chemical photography based on traditional film processing. To the graphic designer and printing technician, the process of turning digital information into a finished page takes place primarily through the use of electronic page composition or layout programs. Readers will see how text, graphics, and design from a variety of sources come together on the computer screen in a format that is ready for the printing press. This material is covered in a generic manner, enabling the transfer of concepts from one computer program to another.

What are digital data? What makes digital data different from other types of information? These questions and others are answered in Chapter 7, which focuses on how original copy is digitized, manipulated, edited, and then output. The technology of scanning line, continuous-tone, and color copy is examined in relation to the scanning process. Also, because compact discs and digital versatile discs have assumed a major role in graphic and video production processes, both CD-ROM and DVD formats are examined in detail. The role and operational characteristics of digital presses and duplicators are examined in this chapter as well.

Chapter 8 examines traditional photographic imaging, with an emphasis on large-format graphic arts process cameras used in the production of line and halftone negatives, as well as combination page camera work. In addition to conventional chemical-based photographic techniques, direct-to-film procedures of computer output directly to an imagesetter, which is ready for plating, are covered as well.

Chapter 9 details stripping and platemaking procedures. Beginning with rough and finished sketches, our discussion moves through the assembly and combination of the basic elements of a mechanical layout to the procedures used to make presensitized photo-offset plates. Direct-to-plate technology involving the use of laser-sensitive plate material exposed in either platesetters, imagesetters, or directly on the printing press is also covered in this section.

Chapter 10 begins with tips on designing a job for the press room, including job specification sheets and related considerations that enable a production run to proceed on schedule and with a minimum of unexpected delays. An introduction to offset printing, examining the oil and water principle as the concept foundation for understanding the offset printing process, is a focal point of this section. The offset printing process, from press adjustments to hints for successful press operation are covered in detail. From traditional offset printing, our discussion moves to newer digital printing presses and the special considerations involved in digital reproduction techniques. Also, a variety of post-press finishing and binding techniques is presented.

Chapter 11 presents several culminating experiences for students: the production of newsletters, display advertising, catalogues and brochures. Using examples of student's work produced over a period of several years, the common elements of the design and production process that link these experiences are examined, along with a series of alternative schemes that emphasize the wide variety of options available in both design and production techniques.

Chapter 12 presents the art and technique of successful Web page designing. This chapter uses Web design techniques based on software applications that utilize both easy-to-use interfaces as well as traditional HTML programming codes that maximize control over all aspects of page design and interaction.

Chapter 13 highlights the fundamentals of computer interactive multimedia design and production techniques. How do you set up branching options for a computer program? How are text, graphics, and animation produced and combined to make interactive presentations that literally jump off the screen? Techniques to accomplish these tricks, from the initial storyboarding of a project that forces the developer to organize and sequence all material, through the final road testing and production of the finished program, are covered in this chapter.

Finally, we wish to emphasize that we did not design this text as a comprehensive graphic arts textbook. The material in this book focuses first on the basic processes of creating a design and then on what is involved in reproducing it. Thus, this text should be viewed as an introduction to a complex and constantly changing field.

Acknowledgments

The authors wish to extend their appreciation to the experts who provided valuable comments and suggestions for this text in the course of its development: Gary Coll, University of Wisconsin-Oshkosh; Dr. Lenore D. Collins, Rhode Island College; Robert Ferro, Pittsburg State University.

We'd also like to thank Geoffrey W. Newman, Dean, School of the Arts at Montclair State University for his continuing support in the development of our outstanding Graphic Design program, from which this book was developed.

Personal thanks go out to our partners, Reesa Greenwald and Lynda Hong, who graciously put up with us while we spent long hours in front of our computers when we should have been with them.

Chapter 1 INTRODUCTION TO GRAPHIC DESIGN AND PRODUCTION

Chapter 1 INTRODUCTION TO GRAPHIC DESIGN AND PRODUCTION

Identify the Major Printing Processes

Understand Digital Printing and Copying Techniques

Examine the Principles of Nonimpact Electronic Imaging

Understand Computer Technology and Peripheral Devices

Provide an Overview of Employment Opportunities within the Graphic Arts and Production Industries

■ INTRODUCTION

The major objective of this book is to demonstrate how images are creatively designed and reproduced, emphasizing the relationships between processes and technique. The master key in the process is, of course, the computer. Affecting every area of modern society, computers have totally and completely changed the graphic arts in fewer than fifteen years—less than a generation! People who were working at jobs that existed for almost 100 years had to be either retrained, or were out of work practically overnight.

All at once, tools for designing and imaging were available to everyone. However, tools can only function with the creative inputs of talent and skill tempered with the right attitude. The objective is to understand how the tools match up to the creative and skillful input of information. With this in mind, Chapter 1 serves as an introduction to, and foundation for, concepts, processes, and terminology that are examined in greater detail throughout this text. We begin with an overview of the major processes of printing. Although the ways in which things have been printed have historically been classified into distinct and familiar categories, those categories, like everything else in the graphic arts, are changing.

The classification of printing processes depends on both the physical relationship of the printing to the nonprinting areas of some type of master material as well as how that image is transferred from the master to the reproduced copy. Our overview begins with an examination of the traditional printing processes and moves on to the newer nonimpact laser and electronic technologies. Included in this overview are the processes of waterless offset, digital printing and copying, and the variety of techniques available for outputting computer-generated images.

This overview is not meant to be all-inclusive. Rather, it serves as a basis for examining the graphic design and print technologies that make up the fascinating world of the graphic arts.

■ THE MAJOR PROCESSES OF PRINTING

For purposes of this text, the major printing processes have been classified as follows: relief printing; gravure printing; lithography or planographic printing; nonimpact electronic imaging; dry offset or waterless printing; along with digital printing and copying techniques. Each of these major processes and adaptations is described in more detail.

Relief Printing

Relief printing is the oldest method of printing, dating from about the eighth century, A.D., at which time the Chinese pioneered printing from relief, or raised, images that had been cut into wooden blocks. In this process, the image area is raised above, or in relief from, the nonimage, or nonprinting areas. This process is illustrated in Fig. 1.1.

Although the fundamental process of relief printing has remained virtually unchanged, the techniques have been subjected to numerous technological enhancements over the years. Handcarved wooden blocks gave way to replica-cast type, foundry type and photoengravings, and finally, machine-cast lines and pages. Whether the type or illustrations were set by hand or machine, relief printing continued to be the dominant printing process until the middle of the twentieth century.

The traditional process of setting type by hand uses foundry type. Foundry type consists of individual letters, numbers and figures of type manufactured from an alloy of lead, tin, and antimony, in a foundry dedicated to type casting. When setting type, the individual letters are placed next to one another in a device called a composing stick. The letters are set upside down and backwards in the stick, to eventually make up individual lines of text. The separate lines are then assembled to make up the completed page. A type case, which holds one complete font of type including letter spaces and special characters, is seen behind a composing stick, used to set type by hand, illustrated in Fig. 1.2. Having set a page of type by hand, the historical implications and appreciations of the process will remain with you forever.

The invention of the Linotype by Ottmar Mergenthaler in 1887 made it possible to assemble text automatically rather than by hand. Using a Linotype machine, complete lines of text are cast onto a single slab of lead called a "slug" (see Chapter 2 for more details on the invention and impact of the Linotype machine). Individual "slugs" from the Linotype are assembled to form complete pages of text. Graphics can be incorporated into the page using zinc or magnesium line cuts for the illustrations and photoengravings for the halftone pictures. In a line cut or photoengraving, the nonimage, or nonprinting, areas are etched

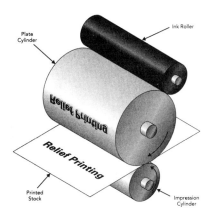

FIGURE 1.1:
The relief printing process

FIGURE 1.2:
Handset type

below the surface of the image areas using an acid bath to etch the zinc or magnesium plate. Figure 1.3 shows a zinc line cut used for printing illustrations in the relief process.

FIGURE 1.3:
Zinc line cut

One type of the relief printing process is known as *flexography*. Flexography uses rubber plates for image transfer. The image areas on the rubber plates are raised in relief from the nonimage areas. Flexography is a commercially well-established process, widely used for printing items such as paperback books, labels, plastic and glass packaging materials, etc. Flexography's use is also increasing in the printing of newspapers. Recently developed water-based flexographic inks dry on the surface of porous newsprint, avoid the fuzzy edges and graying of the sheet that sometimes occurs when using traditional offset inks. The overall quality range of flexography is somewhat lower than that of high-quality offset printing. Rubber-based flexographic plates are illustrated in Fig. 1.4.

Gravure Printing

FIGURE 1.4:
Rubber flexographic plate mat

The gravure process is also known as *engraving, intaglio,* or *etched printing.* The image to be printed is cut into, or engraved below, the surface of the printing plate. During printing, the plate is first inked entirely over its surface. Ink is deposited both within the image area grooves, or cells, that have been cut into the plate, as well as the nonimage areas of the plate. After inking, the plate is scraped across its surface with a doctor blade that acts as a squeegee to remove all ink on the plate surface. What is left is the ink that was deposited in the etched grooves. When the plate comes into contact with a sheet of paper, ink from the image areas is lifted from the etched grooves onto the paper. Different line shades and effects can be achieved by varying both the depth and width of the groove, or engraved lines on the plate. The gravure process is depicted in Fig. 1.5.

The best known application of the gravure process is in the printing of the supplement sections in the Sunday newspapers that contain most of the color advertising and the comics. This section is sometimes referred to as the *rotogravure section,* named after both the process and the high-speed presses used to print the

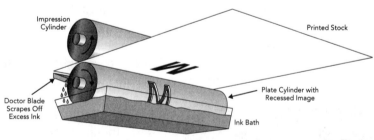

FIGURE 1.5:
The gravure process

supplement. Because of its clear line transfer capabilities, gravure has many applications within both the larger commercial printing and art reproduction markets. The familiar wedding invitation and business card, with their raised-print letters is one example of this process. A raised printing effect can also be achieved by a process known as *thermography,* which uses special resin-based powders. These powders are applied to freshly printed sheets of paper which are then heated to fuse the powder and form a raised image (see Chapter 10 for a detailed discussion on thermography.

Engraved printing is used to produce specialty items that require fine line details; the printing of money and stamps are typical examples.

Commercial gravure presses can print up to 200,000 impressions of a multi-page signature per hour (see Chapter 9 for a detailed discussion of setting up signatures). This results in equivalent press runs of several millions of copies in a standard eight-hour work shift.

Lithography (Planographic Printing)

Lithography is a chemical-based printing process in which both the image and nonimage areas are located on the same plane, or height, on the printing plate. Because of this, lithography is also known as *planographic printing,* or *planography.* The chemical-based properties of image transfer in lithography distinguish it from the relief and gravure processes which rely on the physical separation of the image and nonimage areas on the printing plate.

Based on the chemical principle that oil and water don't mix, lithography was developed by Alois Senefelder, a Bavarian playwright. Classic lithographic reproduction enables the printer/artist, working on a stone, to reproduce all hand-drawn lines with a very high degree of accuracy. The lithographic stone has to be prepared in reverse so that it is the mirror image of the finished print. Preparing the image in reverse is necessary because, during the printing process, the stone prints directly onto a sheet of paper. A stone prepared with a reverse image will therefore produce a right-reading picture. When preparing the litho stone, the artist uses special grease-based inks and liquid media. Note the prepared litho stone and preparation materials in Fig. 1.6. Commercial lithography is covered in greater detail in Chapter 10.

FIGURE 1.6:
Litho stone
(Courtesy The Smithsonian Institution)

To print from a litho stone, the stone is first watered down. The grease-based image on the stone then repels water and the stone absorbs the water in the nonimage areas. When ink is next applied to the surface of the stone with an ink roller, the ink adheres only to the drawn image on the stone. The still-wet areas of the stone repel the ink.

After inking, a sheet of paper is placed on top of the inked stone and pressure is applied over the paper by a platen, or pressure plate, on the printing press. Under pressure, the image is transferred from the inked stone to the paper.

Another form of lithography, known as *offset printing,* was discovered by an American papermill operator, Ira Rubel, in his plant in Nutley, New Jersey. Noting the quality of the images that printed onto a rubber blanket that backed up in the impression cylinder on a direct image lithographic press, Rubel worked with transferring the image from the plate to a blanket, and then onto the paper. Quite by accident, offset printing was born in 1895! The process of "offsetting" the image to an intermediate transfer surface results in prints with a softer tone than those achievable with direct lithography. Offset printing also enables stones, or printing plates, to be prepared as positive rather than negative images. Rubel's early offset press is pictured in Fig. 1.7.

Lithography has historically enjoyed wide application as both an artistic and a commercial medium throughout the world. The nineteenth century lithographs of Currier and Ives, along with the well-known posters of the French artists Jules Chéret, Henri de Toulouse-Lautrec, Edgar Degas, and Edouard Manet are perhaps the finest expressions of the lithographic art form. As a commercial process, offset lithography currently accounts for just under half of all printed material.

By the 1950s, offset lithography had gained wide acceptance and became the dominant printing process in the world, eclipsing the centuries-old process of relief, or letterpress printing. The development of high-speed, multi-color offset presses such as the six-color unit pictured in Fig. 1.8 have printing speeds of 15,000 impressions per hour (iph) and can print on both sides of the sheet during a press run, a process known as *perfecting*. Many of the high-speed presses are fed from a roll rather than from individual sheets of paper and are known as web presses. A web feeder on a four-color press is highlighted in Fig. 1.9.

Specific skills and techniques applied to the traditional offset printing process are highlighted in detail in Chapter 10.

We now move on to examine a recent adaptation of the offset process that eliminates the use of dampening solutions to differentiate the image and nonimage areas of a print. This process is called *dry offset* or *waterless offset* printing.

Dry Offset (Waterless) Printing

As noted earlier, the traditional process of offset lithography relies on a careful balance of ink and water, delivered to the printing plate, to produce quality printed images. A modification of the wet offset process works without the use of a dampening solution to prevent inking the nonimage areas and is known as dry offset, waterless, or *dryography*. Although used primarily in large-format offset presses, dry offset is continually being adapted for use in smaller presses as well.

Dry offset takes place on conventional offset presses in which the ink delivery system has been modified by replacing the standard ink rollers with hollow-core rollers coupled to a water-

FIGURE 1.7:
Rubel offset lithographic press
(Courtesy The Smithsonian Institution)

FIGURE 1.8:
Six-color sheetfed press
(Courtesy SIRS Mandarin, Inc.)

FIGURE 1.9:
Web feeder on a four-color press
(Courtesy SIRS Mandarin, Inc.)

based temperature control unit. The temperature controller precisely monitors and controls the surface temperature of the ink rollers to between 80° F and 86° F. Dry offset inks have a higher viscosity than do conventional offset inks, but their viscosity begins to drop at temperatures below 86° F.

The waterless process requires the use of specially designed offset plates. Waterless plates incorporate a layer of ink-repellent silicone that is sensitive to ink vis-cosity. The silicone layer resists ink deposits in the image areas of the plate, based on the viscos-ity of the ink. Ink viscosity is in turn controlled by the temperature of the ink, which is main-tained by the temperature control unit. Multicolor dry offset presses use a temperature-controlled roller system in each of the color printing heads. Temperature regulation of the printing ink replaces, from an operational stand-point, the use of a dampening solution to con-trol the adhesion of ink to the image areas on the printing plate. Figure 1.10 illustrates the tem-perature control system logic of a typical water-less offset press. Figure 1.11 shows the cross-section of a waterless offset plate.

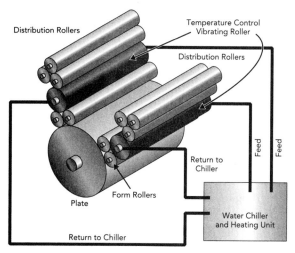

FIGURE 1.10:
Temperature control system logic of a waterless press

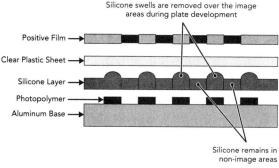

FIGURE 1.11:
Cross-section of waterless plate

Other than the hollow-core rollers on the ink system and the temperature control unit, the remainder of the dry offset process is identi-cal to traditional offset printing. After inking the plate, the image is transferred from the plate to a blanket cylinder, and from the blanket cylinder onto either a sheet or web of paper. The elimi-nation of water from the printing process results in less press preparation time (called *makeready*) than in the conventional offset technique. Also, since there is no need to adjust dampening and ink system balances, less paper is wasted in set-ting up the press, resulting in greater quantities of final printed copies.

Some of the advantages of waterless offset over conventional offset are:

- Faster makeready times on the press
- Greater color consistency and higher print quality due primarily to greater dot control
- No fountain solution to dilute and otherwise cause the typical halftone dot to spread
- Less paper waste due to faster makeready times
- Less environmental impact in the plant due to elimination of plate processing chemicals and alcohol-based dampening fountain solutions

Some disadvantages of waterless offset compared to conventional offset are:

- High conversion costs from wet to dry offset
- High cost of waterless plates compared to wet offset plates
- Current limitation of long-run capability of dry offset plates used on web-fed presses

Waterless offset continues to grow in use throughout the industry. Because of quality advantages, particularly in the area of controlling halftone dot spread, waterless offset can be expected to continue to make significant inroads into the conventional offset's traditional markets in the coming years.

■ DIGITAL PRINTING AND COPYING TECHNIQUES
Background

Traditional offset printing will soon be entering its second one-hundred years. In contrast, digital printing presses were first introduced to the marketplace around 1994. Since that time, digital presses and copiers have slowly established a firm niche in the communications marketplace. As of this printing, digital printing technology accounts for just under 10% of all printed products. This share of the marketplace is estimated to grow to around 20% within the next ten years. This growth will come primarily at the expense of traditional offset printing, whose marketshare is estimated to shrink from around 50% of all printed products to less than 40%. Shrinking market-shares for both gravure and letterpress will also contribute to digital's increasing market penetration. In this section we'll take a closer look at the technology, benefits, and cost comparisons of this rapidly growing segment of the graphic arts. From a technical stand-point, digital printers fall within the classification of nonimpact imaging systems, which are discussed in the next section of this chapter. However, because digital presses are competing head-to-head with conventional printing processes such as offset, letterpress, gravure, and screen printing, digital techniques are highlighted separately.

The advantages of digital printing over traditional printing technologies are primarily in the areas of reduced time, materials, and labor required in production. Although somewhat simplified, the workflow associated with the two major production technologies in Fig. 1.12 highlights this comparison.

The Technology of Digital Color Presses (DCPs)

Digital printing's market niche resides primarily in its ability to produce low-cost, short-run, high-quality color prints. The slow, 3-page-per-minute color copier of the past has given way to high-speed digital color presses and copiers capable of output speeds in excess of 4,000 impressions per hour.

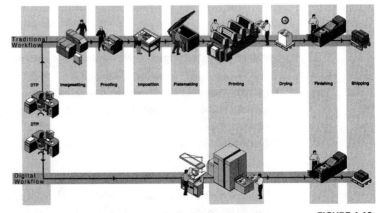

FIGURE 1.12:
Comparison of traditional and digital production workflows
(Courtesy Canon USA, Inc.)

FIGURE 1.13:
Digital print engine
(Courtesy Canon USA, Inc.)

The heart of most digital systems is a four-color—cyan, magenta, yellow, and black, or CMYK—high-resolution, toner-based, print engine that produces offset-quality images as shown in Fig. 1.13. Additional colors can be incorporated into the print engine for printing spot colors.

The standard digital print engine supports a web of paper that is 12.6 inches wide; the larger-format version of the print engine can support a 20-inch wide web of paper, capable of printing two sides of the sheet at once (also known as *perfect printing*).

The toner is fused to the paper using a heat source contained in the print engine. Some presses incorporate a second heating, or fusion unit, to increase the color saturation of the toner, while imparting a glossy finish to the toner.

Because the entire printing process is digital, neither film nor plates are used in image production. This eliminates not only the film and plating steps associated with conventional offset printing, but the labor and material costs associated with these operations. Original artwork and text are digitized by either scanning or file creation using conventional and proprietary desktop publishing and image manipulation software and are stored in digital format. When ready to print, the files are sent to a raster image processor (RIP). The RIP separates the images into the four process colors (CMYK), as well as the required dot patterns for each color.

Once the job has been "RIPped", the RIP sends images of each of the pages to the press individually. Since the pages are sent to the press one at a time, the press can vary the images on different pages, a feature referred to as *variable-printing*. There is a variety of variable job software applications available from press vendors and general software providers.

The RIP sends the digital images directly to the press, where the images are separated into component colors. As the press receives the digital images, it pulls the web of paper first through a conditioning unit and then into the actual print tower of the press. In the standard four-color press, there are eight photoconductor drums for printing both the front and back sides of the paper. Digital presses reproduce images using either a laser light source or a light-emitting diode (LED). The light source exposes images onto the photoconductor drums which then place charges on them. The light sources are variable, which enables them to vary the intensity of the electric charge on each drum. The intensity of the charge determines how much toner is picked up by the drum and deposited onto the paper as it passes through the print head.

As the paper web moves through the printing head, each toner color is added on top of the previous color to form the complete color image at a resolution of 600 dots per inch (dpi). Because of the press' ability to vary toner in relation to the charge on the drum, the effective resolution of the image is about 2,400 dpi.

On the output side of the press, the paper goes to a *sheeter* where it is cut into individual sheets, then on to a stacker for further finishing operations. Most digital presses are capable of printing on a wide range of paper stocks, including transparencies and polyesters and coated and uncoated paper stocks.

■ MARKET APPLICATIONS FOR DIGITAL PRINTING

Currently, digital presses and copiers excel in three market segments: low- to mid-volume office applications, variable data printing, and short-run color output.

Office Printing

Modern office printing requirements are bringing more and more color into office correspondence, business presentations, short-run mailings, and sales handouts. Although office copiers have been around for a long time, the capabilities of the new generation of high-speed networked copiers are impressive. The copier shown in Fig. 1.14 is capable of printing 24 full-color pages per minute (ppm) on paper sizes up to 11 x 17 inches.

FIGURE 1.14:
Canon Color Copier 2400
(Courtesy Canon USA, Inc.)

Machines such as the copier in Fig. 1.14 are capable of running independently, or, within an office intranet where each person has access to the copier through their desktop computer. The finishing options on these machines includes stapling, hole-punching, stitching, and a variety of folding.

Variable Data Printing

Customized printing applications, sometimes referred to as variable data printing, have always been one of the strengths of digital presses and copiers. Since each page is sent individually from the RIP to the press's print engine, information can be inserted or removed on the fly at machine-rated print speeds. This process is illustrated in Fig. 1.15.

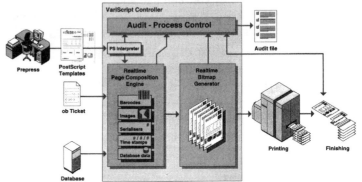

FIGURE 1.15:
Variable data printing technology
(Courtesy Canon USA, Inc.)

Direct mailings, for example, can include not only different names and addresses, but specialized content designed to appeal to different customer profiles. Consider the possibility of adding spot color to a document that highlights the negative balance on a customer's bill. Marketing materials such as cover letters, job proposals, and other related materials can be targeted to customer preferences, job categories and titles, etc. Graphics can also be interchanged so that illustrations that are used to appeal to one group of customers can be changed when the material is sent to a different demographic group.

Everything from credit card statements to utility bills and investment portfolio statements will soon be printed in full color and will include marketing and promotional information linked to the purchasing habits and interests of the customer. Sales handouts can be customized to reflect the priorities of different types of buyers. A market analysis, for example, may reveal that the customer base of a particular company is split on their concerns regarding price and product integrity. The vendor can generate sales materials that stress both advantages of their product that appeal to each of the different types of customers. Although these statements and materials appear personalized, they are in fact, "customized," since similar offers and information go out to many people. However, the effect of all this is very personal, and marketers are betting on this technique to increase business through the "personal touch."

Short-Run Printing Applications

Digital printing presses excel in short-run color printing; that is, press runs between 1,000 to 5,000 impressions. There's little doubt that high-quality color output not only attracts attention but is an effective sales tool as well. Digital printing represents a fundamental break from traditional offset, once the only way to produce full-color printed materials. By eliminating film and plating steps in the printing process, as well as the associated labor and material costs, and coupled with the ability to generate and print from digital files, digital presses are ideally suited for short-run color applications. Short-run printing using traditional offset presses is expensive because of the system makeready costs, including the preparation of negatives and platemaking procedures. Although traditional offset still holds a significant edge in color stability, quality, and cost effectiveness for long runs, the short-run market is profitable and growing. As a proven commodity, many jobs that were printed as long press runs can now be broken up into smaller, digitally-produced jobs. This minimizes the need to order large quantities of a product, and then warehousing the excess until the remainder of the copies are needed. Ordering smaller quantities also adds flexibility to the entire process, since changes in products, prices, etc. can be incorporated into the printing of future copies of the job, keeping information and inventory up to date.

In addition to short-run printing, printers are increasingly using their digital presses as color proofing options for long-run traditional offset jobs. Indications are that digital color proofs get high marks in color accuracy. All of these markets will continue to grow as the industry continues to undergo a slow, but inexorable, shift to digital printing technology.

■ DIGITAL PRINTING EQUIPMENT OPTIONS

There are three ranges of digital options: low-end, mid-range, and high-end. A typical low-end color printing solution is the combination of a color laser copier driven by a software RIP, which is either embedded into the copier or supplied as a separate unit. These systems are limited in productivity, and paper sizes are usually restricted to letter, legal, and tabloid. The print quality of these systems, while described by many professional printers as "pleasing," cannot achieve consistent high-quality color reproduction: output is usually limited to 10,000 to 15,000 copies per month.

Mid-range solutions are significantly higher in price than their low-end counterparts. However, the productivity and quality of these systems are impressive. Bigger, more complex, and faster than entry-level units, their capabilities include duplex printing, handling a wide range and quantity of paper stocks, and greater speed and higher quality to handle most medium-range on-demand printing requirements. These high-speed copiers are marketed as alternatives to the more expensive digital printing presses. These systems can usually print full bleed tabloid

FIGURE 1.16:
Mid-range color copier
(Courtesy Canon USA, Inc.)

(11 x 17 inch) jobs using oversized sheets with duty cycles of about 30,000 copies per month, Fig. 1.16 (a full bleed is an image that extends to the edge of the printed sheet, with no margins).

High-end, state-of-the-art digital printers feature either web or sheetfed duplexing presses based on dry and liquid toner print engines. The Xeikon® digital press shown in Fig. 1.17 features a web-fed duplexing, or perfecting, print engine outputting at 600 dpi, which is capable of outputting 25 double-sided tabloid (11 x 17 inch) sheets per minute.

The Xeikon® uses LEDs to charge the photoconductor drum. Figure 1.18 illustrates a cross-section of the major press components. Figure 1.19 highlights the location of the dry toner cartridges and the paper travel path through the print head of the press.

A somewhat different technique from the Xeikon® is used with a Risograph® digital press (Fig. 1.20).

The Risograph® incorporates a high resolution scanner built into the press. As the original copy is scanned, signals are sent from the scanner to a thermal head that burns holes in a master material. The holes in the master material match up to the light and dark areas of the original. Figure 1.21 illustrates the components of the Risograph® digital press.

Once the master has been produced, removal of the previous master (if any), and loading of the new one is fully automatic. During the printing process, ink from an ink cartridge is forced through the screened master, similar in many respects to conventional silk screen printing.

The Risograph® prints one color in a single pass. To print additional colors, ink cartridges stored below the press are changed, and the paper is again fed through the press to print each additional color.

We have described only a select few digital printers from among the great number of different types of digital printing presses currently available. The variety of technology variations and adaptations of the digital printing process will continue to proliferate in the coming years.

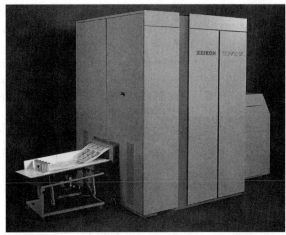

FIGURE 1.17:
Xeikon® Press
(Courtesy Xeikon America, Inc.)

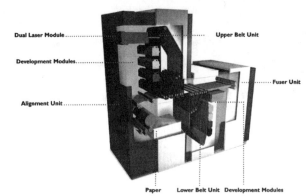

Dual Laser Module · · · · · · · · · · · · · · Upper Belt Unit

Development Modules · · · · · · · · · ·

· · · · · · · Fuser Unit

Alignment Unit · · · · · · · · · · · · · ·

Paper   Lower Belt Unit   Development Modules

FIGURE 1.18:
Xeikon® Cross-section of components
(Courtesy Xeikon America, Inc.)

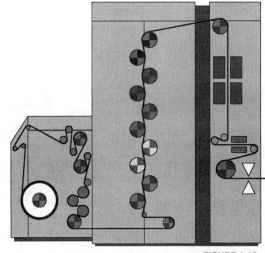

FIGURE 1.19:
Paper travel path through Xeikon®
(Courtesy Xeikon America, Inc.)

FIGURE 1.20:
Risograph® digital press
(Courtesy Riso, Inc.)

NonImpact Electronic Imaging

Nonimpact copy reproduction was born with the invention of electrostatic printing in 1938 by Chester Carlson. This process later became known as Xerography®. The nonimpact segment of the communications industry accounts for increasingly larger market shares as technology results in increased processing power and output capability.

The technologies of digital printing and nonimpact imaging are not mutually exclusive. In fact, these distinctions are made by the authors within the framework of nonimpact printing processes, more from the point of view of market application than from technical differences. Digital printing presses are, for the most part, nonimpact printers. In this section, we will examine that segment of nonimpact imaging that deals more with low-volume applications in addition to some of the more technical aspects of the technology.

• Photocopy Processing

No process exemplifies nonimpact image copying better than the traditional photocopy machine. The photocopy process appears, on the surface, to be deceptively simple. An original document is placed on a glass surface. When a button is pressed, the glass table, or an exposure light, moves back and forth, scanning the original document with high-intensity light. At the same time, a sheet of paper is picked up from the paper feed tray, sent through the machine, and comes out the opposite end with the copied image.

During the operation of the photocopier, there are actually eight separate processes occurring in rapid succession. Figure 1.22 illustrates the machine components incorporated into the typical photocopier processor.

Original tray · Image scanner · ADF unit · Cylinder · Load roller
Thermal print head · Write roller · Master roll
Master disposal box · Master removal unit · Pickup roller · Scraper roller · Separator
Paper feed tray · Guide roller · Timing roller · Pressure roller · Suction unit · Paper receiving tray

❶ First Paper Feed Area: Feeds single sheets of paper to the Second Paper Feed Area via the Scraper Roller, Pickup Roller, and Stripper Unit.

❷ Second Paper Feed Area: Controls the vertical print position and feeds paper to the print cylinder via the Timing and Guide Rollers.

❸ Print Area: Uses the Pressure Roller to press paper against the master on the Cylinder. The Cylinder rotates the Pressure Roller, raises it to the Cylinder, and prints an image on the paper.

❹ Paper Ejection Area: Separates the printed paper from the Drum, and transports it onto the Paper Receiving Tray.

❺ Cylinder Section: Supplies the Cylinder surface with Ink from an ink bottle.

❻ Master Disposal Area: Separates a used master from the Cylinder and disposes it into the Master Disposal Box.

❼ Image Scanning Area: Carries an original and scans it with the Image Scanner and converts the image information into digital data.

❽ Master Making Area: Makes a master with the Thermal Print Head.

❾ Carrier and Clamp Area: Feeds the prepared master material to the Cylinder, loads it on the Cylinder, and cuts it to an appropriate length.

FIGURE 1.21:
Components of Risograph® press
(Courtesy Riso, Inc.)

In the following discussion of the photo-copy process, refer to Fig. 1.22 to identify the specific machine components.

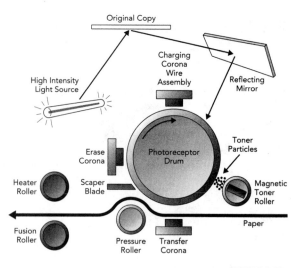

1. Main Charging Process: During main charging, the surface of the pho-toreceptor drum is exposed to a high, positive electrostatic charge from the corona wire.

2. Image Exposure Sequence: In exposing the original copy, light is reflected from the original, off a mirror, and onto the surface of the drum. The drum is made from a photoresistive material (selenium, for example). The drum loses its electrical charge when it is exposed to high intensity light, and retains its charge at lower intensities of light. White areas of the original copy (the nonimage areas), reflect more light onto the drum than the image, or dark areas of the original. Therefore, the light, nonimage areas of the original leave those corresponding areas of the drum with little or no electrical charge. Conversely, the dark, image areas of the original leave those areas of the drum with a static charge. After being exposed to reflected light from the original, the drum is left with what is known as an *electrostatic latent image*. This image is an exact duplicate of the original copy, but in electrostatically charged form, which is invisible to the eye at this point in the process.

3. Development of the Visible Image: As the drum continues to rotate, it pulls toner particles from a toner roller assembly. Photocopy toners are available in either powder or liquid form. Toner particles, which are made up of carbon and resin particles, are carried on the toner assembly by small iron particles within a magnetic field on the roller. Only the toner particles transfer to the drum from the toner roller. The toner adheres only to the electrostati-cally charged image sections of the drum.

4 – 5. Transfer and Separation: Transfer of the image from the photore-ceptor drum to a sheet of paper is accomplished by first passing the sheet of paper through an electrostatic charge given off by the transfer corona wire. The paper retains this electrostatic charge, which then attracts the toner from the drum onto the paper. After the image has been transferred, the paper is mechanically separated to prevent it from sticking to the drum. After separa-tion, the paper enters the image fixing section of the copier.

6. Image Fixing: In the fixing section of the copier, a band of heat and pressure is applied to the paper. Heat applied to the toner particles softens the resin around the carbon particle. Pressure between an upper and lower roller forces the toner particle into the paper, resulting in a permanent, undistorted copy of the original image.

7. Charge Erasure: To prepare the drum for the next copy sequence, the charge on it must be erased. To accomplish this, the drum is exposed to an electrical charge that lowers its static charge. Although a few toner particles still adhere to the drum at this point, the remaining latent image is very weak.

8. Cleaning: Toner is deposited on the developer roller, because the electrostatic attraction of the developer roller is greater than the charge left on the image roller after the roller has been erased. The drum is now clean, and ready to process a new image.

Modern photocopy machines are able to print in excess of 6,000 copies per hour in either black and white or color, and can incorporate a variety of finishing processes, depending on the options supplied with the particular machine.

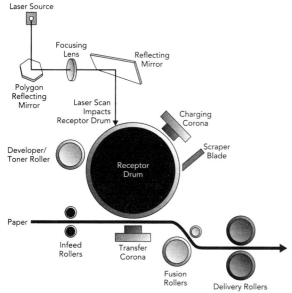

FIGURE 1.23:
Components of a typical laser printer

• Laser Printer Technology

The output quality from high-resolution laser printers virtually matches the output quality from traditional photo typesetters and digital imaging systems. Although laser printer development is based in part on the photocopy process, laser printers must also be able to interpret instructions from a computer. Computer instructions are then translated into the movement of a laser beam exposure unit, precisely moving paper through the machine which then results in a high resolution image. Figure 1.23 illustrates the major components of a typeset-quality laser printer. Note the similarities in the processing technology of the laser printer and the photocopier.

The laser printer uses a device called a *print engine* which is similar in operating principle to the photocopy developing unit. The heart of the print engine is the photoconducting, light-sensitive cylinder, also referred to as the drum. This drum is similar in concept to the photoconductor drum in the photocopier.

The image in a laser printer is exposed line by line using a focused, narrow laser beam. The laser beam reflects off a mirror on to the drum. The laser flashes on and off, creating a series of dots that eventually make up the completed image. The laser exposes the paper line by line while advancing the paper for each new exposure line.

As with the photocopy process, the pattern of charges created by the laser beam leaves an electrostatic latent image on the drum. Toner particles are attracted to the image areas of the drum that will print black. Some printers use a write-black system in which the dots on the drum that represent the image areas in the original copy are sensitized and print black. In a write-white system, the laser beam alters the charge on the drum in the nonimage areas only. Laser printing consists of six separate steps: charging the drum; removing the charge from the non-printing (white, or nonimage areas) of the drum; developing the latent electrostatic image; transferring the image to paper, fusing the image; and cleaning the drum.

Laser printers can reproduce images in either black and white or color. When outputting in color, the output speed of the printer is slower than when printing in black and white.

First-generation laser printers used a paper advance of 1/300 inch, resulting in a 300 dpi resolution. Three hundred dpi laser printers are not typeset quality since their output, on close examination, shows ragged edges on letters and illustrations. Second-generation laser printers produce 600 dpi output on the low-end of the market. High-resolution typeset-quality laser printers deliver image resolutions greater than 2,000 dpi that rival digital typesetters.

Figures 1.24, 1.25, and 1.26 compare the output of a variety of laser printer resolutions. The type in each of the three illustrations has been enlarged 300 percent to better show the quality of the images.

Note the ragged edges of the 300 dpi type in Fig. 1.24, making this level of quality unacceptable as camera-ready copy in most typesetting and graphic design work. Contrast the edges of the type in Fig. 1.24 with those in Figs. 1.25 and 1.26. The quality of the output at 600 dpi in Fig. 1.25 is better, although still unacceptable for quality graphic reproduction. Not until output reaches 1,200 dpi, (Fig. 1.26) do the edges of both type and graphics reach minimally acceptable camera-ready standards. The graphic designer should keep in mind that output resolutions of between 2,500 and 4,000 dpi, delivered by high-quality image setters, are a pre-requisite for all high-quality graphic design work.

• Electron Beam (Ion Deposition) Imaging

Electron beam (EB) printing is also referred to as ion-deposition imaging. This technology is used in high-performance,

FIGURE 1.24:
300 dpi laser printer output
(enlarged 300%)

FIGURE 1.25:
600 dpi laser printer output
(enlarged 300%)

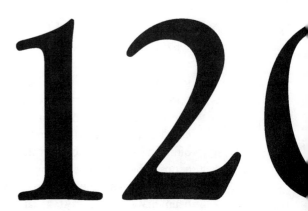

FIGURE 1.26:
1,200 dpi laser printer output
(enlarged 300%)

high-speed printing applications. Electron beam printing is a simpler process than that used in laser printers since fewer steps are involved in exposing and developing an image. Compared to the six-step process of conventional laser printers, EB printers use only four steps to produce an image: generating the image on the drum with electron beams; developing the image; transferring and fusing the image onto paper; and cleaning the drum. The components of an electron beam printer are illustrated in Fig. 1.27.

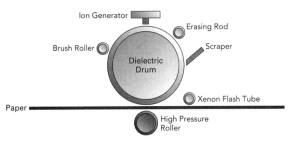

FIGURE 1.27:
Electron beam printer

The heart of the printer is an electron beam cartridge using high voltage and frequency to fire a stream of electrons at a rotating dielectric drum. The control grid of the printer determines when the beam is turned on. In this way, electrons on the drum form a latent image that attracts toner away from the toner assembly and on to the drum.

EB printers use a cold fusion process in which a static electric charge draws toner particles onto the paper. A high-pressure roller then fuses the toner particles to the paper. This toner transfer and fusion process is more efficient than the heat fusion process used in conventional laser printers. Because of this, an ordinary scraper bar is used to remove excess toner from the drum. Following the fusion process, an erasing rod removes any remaining image from the drum and prepares the printer for the next copy. Cold fusion does not produce as strong a bond between the toner and paper as does heat fusion. Because of this, cold fusion images do not hold up well to rough handling.

FIGURE 1.28:
Wide format ink jet printer
(Courtesy SIRS Mandarin, Inc.)

Ink Jet Printers

Ink jet printing technology continues to grow in popularity in a variety of printer formats. Inkjet technology and printers are now the norm for desktop, wide-format, and color-proofing printers. Figure 1.28 shows a 600 dpi wide-format (36-inch) four-color printer.

There are several different adaptations of ink jet technology ranging in price and capability. Continuing advances in ink jet technology have resulted in significant price decreases accompanied by increases in resolution and print quality. When ink jet printers were first introduced to the marketplace, four-color printers were the standard. Printers with 6- and 8-color print heads are currently available that produce photo-realistic pictures for only pennies per page. We'll take a closer look at some of the varying technologies within the ink jet classification.

• Continuous Ink Jet Printers

Continuous ink jet printers are high-end devices capable of producing photographic quality prints at a relatively low cost per page. In continuous ink jet technology, a pump forces a continuous stream of ink through a nozzle under constant pressure. This produces very fine ink droplets at the rate of more than one million per second. When used in color proofing and general printing applications, the four color process inks—cyan, yellow, magenta, and black—in addition to spot color inks, are supplied in continuous streams through the print nozzles. This process is shown in Fig. 1.29.

Drop-On-Demand Printing

Drop-on-demand technology is found in many ink jet printers used for producing color proofs prior to printing. Two major technologies are used in drop-on-demand printers: liquid thermal/bubble jet and solid ink jet systems.

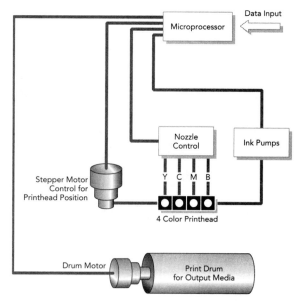

FIGURE 1.29:
Continuous ink process

• Liquid Thermal/Bubble Jet Printing

Bubble jet printers incorporate dozens of very small nozzles in the print head. An electrical current passing through a small resistor heats ink in a tiny tube. Heat from these elements vaporize water in the ink which causes many bubbles to form and fuse into a larger bubble. As the bubble expands, pressure inside the printing nozzle pushes the ink droplet onto a sheet of paper (Fig. 1.30).

After ink has been pushed from the nozzle, the ink bubble contracts, which lowers the pressure in the printing head, drawing in more ink to repeat the bubble cycle. This process takes place several thousand times each second and is precisely controlled to produce very high-quality prints.

FIGURE 1.30:
Bubble jet printer

• Solid Ink Jet Printers

Solid ink jet systems are also referred to as *phase-change ink jet printers.* The term "phase change" refers to the fact that the ink starts out in solid form and changes to a liquid during actual printing.

In this process, ink is supplied in solid form, resembling crayon sticks. During the printing process, the ink in the stick is heated and quickly melts. The print head travels across the paper, spraying ink droplets onto the paper. The ink quickly solidifies on the paper with little or no smudging. Solid ink printers are versatile and can print on a variety of paper stocks and transparent media.

Wax Thermal Transfer

Wax thermal printers were typically used for prepress color proofs, desktop publishing, and business presentation applications. Advances in liquid ink jet printers have taken over significant parts of these markets. Wax thermal printers use print heads that contain an array of individually controlled tiny heating elements. The elements in the print head melt a ribbon coated with a wax-based color ink. The ink then transfers from the ribbon onto specially coated paper stock. In most wax printers, each color prints in a separate pass of the print head; the paper is repositioned for each pass of a different color on the print ribbon.

Dye Sublimation Thermal Transfer

Of all the printers described, dye sublimation printers are capable of producing the most photographically realistic output. The coloring agents in these systems are contained in a plastic film or solid ink transfer ribbon. The print head contains thousands of tiny heating elements, each of which can produce up to 256 different temperatures. The hotter the temperature, the more dye is transferred from the film ribbon to the paper during printing.

In dye sublimation printing, varying amounts of dye are transferred to a specially coated paper stock based on the temperature of heat delivered to the print head. When the dye is heated, it changes from a solid to a gas in a chemical process called *sublimation*. When the gaseous dye comes into contact with the specially coated paper, it changes back into a solid. By precisely controlling the amount of heat, and thereby the amount of dye transferred to the receiving paper, the intensity of each color dot can be precisely monitored. The different color dyes are deposited on top of one another for full-color process and continuous-tone printing.

Many advances have taken place in dye sublimation printers. Currently, 2,400 dpi dye sublimation printers are available for under $500.00, a printing technology that only three or four years ago would have cost the consumer over $25,000.

Advances in ink jet technology will continue to deliver greater color accuracy and image representation, and, coupled with its printing speed and reduced cost per page, will continue to heavily influence all forms of computer image output.

■ COMPUTERS AND PERIPHERALS
The PC and Graphic Arts

An examination of any up-to-date textbook on graphic arts, graphic design, or production quickly reveals that the computer is the central input and output tool of the industry—remove the computer and the printing presses stop! What is obvious to those involved in the industry for more than fifteen years is that this computer revolution and refocusing of the industry has taken place in less than a generation.

Prior to the introduction of the Apple Macintosh® in 1984, typesetting was done on phototypesetters using code-intensive front ends to input text. Data storage was limited to 8-inch floppy disks, and type fonts were stored on plastic discs that had to be loaded into a typesetter, one-at-a-time, to change not only fonts, but type sizes and styles as well. Illustrations were prepared on film; mechanicals, consisting of illustration board on which all of the illustrations and type proofs were pasted in place, were the norm for setting up pages for conventional, chemical-based photographic processing and platemaking.

Computer-based technology creates obsolescence in less than a year, not for the sake of continued sales alone, but to bow to advances in processing power and system capabilities. Keeping skills, techniques, and abilities up to date in this technological landscape is akin to swimming upstream—you have to keep swimming just to keep from moving backward! Within this context, we'll examine PCs and peripherals.

PC Platforms, Publishing, and the World Wide Web

When the IBM PC® was introduced in 1981, it had little competition in the marketplace. Apple computers were installed in many schools, the IBM PC® was aimed at the business market, and, the home computer market, except for some Radio Shack Model TRS 80s, was virtually nonexistent. The introduction of the 128K Macintosh® forever changed not only the computer marketplace in general, but the graphic arts industry in particular.

Many graphic artists, designers, and publishers took to the Mac immediately: No arcane string of commands to enter or operating system to deal with—just click on an icon and the machine responded. During the ensuing years, although computers have changed, graphic designers and production personnel remain largely Macintosh-oriented. There are indications that the Mac may be losing its dominance in this arena as inroads are made by PC-based machines running Windows NT® as well as by Unix workstations with dedicated scanners and other processor-intensive applications..

The Macintosh presently enjoys about an 80% market share among corporate designers, illustrators, graphic designers, commercial photographers, advertising agencies, and small publishers. A legacy of this magnitude is hard to change. This installed base, coupled with the Mac's ability to manage color (the ability of the computer to predict accurately printed colors) will likely keep the Mac in its dominant, creatively-based publishing role. Regardless of the specific PC platform used in any area, graphic designers and other creative personnel and production technicians entering the field today should be versed in both the Mac and PC platforms.

One change affecting computer platform choice is a move into the arena of Web publishing. Since the Web is a virtual, and not an actual printing press, color management and type control are not as significant on the Web as they are in the graphic arts. Because activity on the Web is largely in the PC environment, publishers moving toward Web publishing are likely to switch their computer platforms from Macintosh to PC-based systems.

In the recent past, it was relatively easy to classify computers as either PCs (desktop systems), workstations, and dedicated systems. Because almost all system components are now virtually interchangeable, these categories are no longer mutually exclusive. PCs can operate either as stand-alone units, or, with the addition of network cards and a phone cable, they can be connected via a network to function as individual workstations, using instructions and software from a central file server. Connecting a computer to a scanner, platesetter, or imagesetter turns the PC into a dedicated system. However, as long as the network cable remains attached, the computer can be instantly transformed back to an individual workstation or stand-alone system. Given the flexibility of PC system design and available peripherals, old categories and classification systems are no longer appropriate.

Front and Back Ends

Regardless of the computer system and its function within any system, the computer terminal or desktop unit (the front end) converts information from the computer and outputs this information to a printer, imagesetter, or platesetter (the back end). Other peripheral devices, such as scanners, digital cameras, etc. are detailed in Chapter 7.

Imagesetters

Of all components in the publishing environment, the imagesetter is probably the most important. The imagesetter had its roots in early-generation phototypesetting machines. These early typesetters were part computer and part photographic exposure unit and were able to output text only. They had to be loaded with specific type fonts for the job before they could generate text.

An imagesetter contains two separate processing units that convert the data sent from the computer into a printed image. The first of these units is a processing computer that converts the text and graphics from the computer into a page description language. The page description language then tells the second unit, the RIP, whether to print the text, lines, and graphics onto either a sheet of film, paper, or a printing plate. In most configurations, the imagesetter and the RIP are supplied as two separate units. This arrangement allows the end user to update either the RIP or the imagesetter separately as improvements in processing technology become available.

FIGURE 1.31:
Imagesetter with external RIP
(Courtesy SIRS Mandarin, Inc.)

Imagesetters can output to photographic paper, photographic negatives, or plate materials, ready for the printing press. Figure 1.31 shows an imagesetter with an external RIP. In this illustration, the RIP is located on the floor between the two sections of the imagesetter.

Imagesetters fall into one of two operating configurations: capstan and drum-type systems. These configurations are discussed next.

• Capstan Imagesetters

Capstan imagesetters are known as "roll-fed" devices. The standard imagesetter uses a laser diode to expose light-sensitive paper, film, or plate media. The media is housed in a light-tight cassette. During the imaging process, the media moves from its light-tight box over a laser diode exposure unit and into a take-up cassette. A series of transport rollers keep the media under tension and moves it from the supply to the take-up cassette as the imaging is taking place. Early capstan devices were known to apply enough pressure on the media to distort or stretch it slightly, causing registration, or image alingnment, problems. These problems were eliminated in later capstan drives. Figure 1.32 shows one type of capstan used on imagesetters.

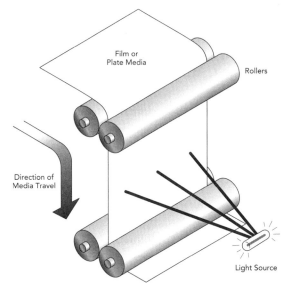

FIGURE 1.32:
Capstan drive imagesetter

• Drum-Type Imagesetters

Drum-type imagesetters differ from their capstan counterparts in both media exposure and transport through the unit. During the imaging process, media is fed from a supply roll onto a drum where it remains during the exposure sequence. Drum-type units are configured as either internal or external exposure. On internal exposure units, the media must first be cut, then held in place on the inside of the drum during the exposure sequence. On external drum units, the film is cut and held on the outside of the drum during exposure. In both internal and external designs, the drum rotates at high speed as the imaging head moves across the drum. Figure 1.33 shows an external drum design; Fig. 1.34 illustrates an internal drum unit.

Both capstan and drum-type imagesetters are in widespread use throughout the industry. Drum-type units are the system of choice over capstan units in shops where most of the work is for generating separation negatives that will be used for producing high-end color reproductions.

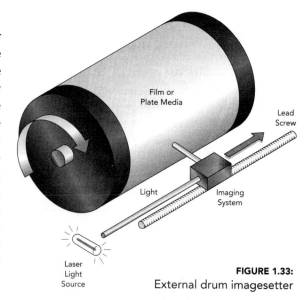

FIGURE 1.33:
External drum imagesetter

Light Sources

Several different light sources are used for media exposure in imagesetters. Among the most popular are helium/neon lasers, argon lasers, laser diodes, and LEDs. Each of these light sources requires a different type of paper, plate, or film media; they are not interchangeable.

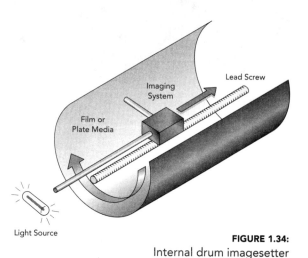

FIGURE 1.34:
Internal drum imagesetter

Raster Image Processors

The raster image processor, or RIP, interprets data from the computer and sends this information to the imagesetter. In this interpretive process, the RIP describes the content of all images and text in the job, communicating with the imagesetter as to how to record these data as a series of dots on the film, paper, or plate material. The RIP is made up of two separate components, the RIP interpreter and the renderer. The interpreter uses image data directly from the computer and encodes them for use by the rendering section of the RIP. The renderer controls the actual operation of the imaging system.

Low volume printing businesses producing short books, pamphlets, etc., will have different needs from large book publishers or integrated printing plants that specialize in full-color, long-run printing. Given the wide variety of imagesetters available, the key to success is to match the imagesetter to its end use.

Page Description Languages

Information must be interpreted in order for a printer to take the text and graphics generated on the computer and properly place this information onto the printed page. For example, the printer must know how far down from the top of the paper to begin setting the first line of type, as well as where the various elements of a graphic display or photograph will appear. Computer programs that contain these commands are called *page description languages* (PDLs).

When personal computers first began to be widely used for in-house printing and publishing in the middle 1980s, output was restricted by first- and second-generation daisy wheel and dot matrix printers. Although daisy wheel printers gave the page a finished appearance for text, their output was limited to the fonts available on the interchangeable wheels; they had no graphics imaging capabilities. The Diablo 630 daisy wheel printer established the first widely used printer control language, which told the printer which letter to print and when to print it.

Dot matrix printers offered more flexibility than their daisy wheel predecessors. Because they defined a smaller grid on the page, which could be printed either black or left white, the printer had the ability to print not only text, but graphic images as well. The printer languages that controlled the action of the pins in the matrix printing head grew far more complicated than the original Diablo printing protocols. Computers, for the first time, were now able to create shapes, graphs, and different type styles. The output quality of these pages was poor by today's standards and imaging took a long time—simple black and white line drawings could take several minutes to compose and print.

The introduction of the first Hewlett-Packard Laserjet® printer was accompanied by a corresponding page description language known as its *printer control language* (PCL). Despite advances in computer technology, typesetters were still chained to specific output devices and their PCL languages until the introduction of the PostScript page description language by Adobe Systems in 1985. PostScript uses mathematical algorithms to describe each typeface and graphic element on the page. Drawing commands within PostScript enables the computer-processing of arcs, lines and Bezier curves, and text. The versatility of PostScript was first demonstrated in 1985 when the Linotype Corporation, in partnership with Adobe Systems and Apple Computer Corporation, demonstrated the same PageMaker file simultaneously outputting to a 300 dpi Apple LaserWriter® and a linotronic imagesetter at 1,270 dpi and 2,540 dpi. Revisions to a variety of page description languages are on-going, and Adobe's PostScript and revised *portable document format* (PDF) language now dominate the prepress industry.

■ EMPLOYMENT OPPORTUNITIES IN GRAPHIC DESIGN AND THE PRODUCTION TECHNOLOGIES

Explosive technological developments within the graphic design and communications industries enable increasing opportunities for employment. Small- to medium-sized businesses employing fewer than 25 people dominate the graphic design and production industries. Corporate employment is focused in the areas of in-plant printing and creative design. Many corporations that house in-plant printing facilities take in outside printing jobs in addition to the parent corporation's printing needs to increase profits and help make the printing operation self-supporting. Depending on geographical location and specific job descriptions, union membership might be a pre-requisite for employment. For example, businesses in large, urban areas might require union membership for skilled tradespeople whereas smaller businesses in suburban or rural areas might not.

Employment within technical areas such as graphic design and computer-intensive applications usually requires some type of college-level training. Basic training is available either at community colleges or vocational training centers in which design and printing technologies are incorporated into the curriculum. Programs in technology education and specializations within the fine arts curricula of most four-year colleges offer numerous courses in graphic design, commercial illustration, related fine arts, and printing production coupled with high-level computer applications. Middle- and upper-management level positions usually require a four-year baccalaureate degree that provides experiences in both the technical and business aspects of design and printing. Educational institutions that incorporate apprenticeship and job training components, such as internships or cooperative education, enable students to experience real-world work situations during their education, and are a valuable addition to traditional classroom instruction.

There are also numerous trade and industrial organizations with chapters throughout the world, whose main purpose is to promote professional opportunities within the graphic design and printing disciplines. Appendix I contains a comprehensive list of professional associations within these areas that are an excellent source of information concerning job and educational opportunities. In addition, check out the web sites recommended in Appendix II for additional job-related information.

■ SUMMARY

This chapter introduced the reader to the basic concepts and processes within the graphic design and production areas. Since the invention of moveable type more than five hundred years ago, printed communication has relied on four basic reproduction processes: relief printing from a raised image, gravure printing from a recessed image, the chemical process of lithography, and stencil printing, exemplified by screen-process technology. Added to this list by virtue of computerization, is a fifth graphic reproduction process—electronic digital printing.

The middle of the twentieth century witnessed offset printing's rise to dominance at the expense of both gravure and relief printing processes. With the emergence of digital reproduction, this mix will eventually change as digital technologies make significant inroads into the traditional methods of image reproduction.

Employment will continue to expand in response to technological advances taking place within the graphic design and printing industries.

■ SUGGESTED STUDENT ACTIVITIES

1. Undertake a printing project that demonstrates the basic methods of image reproduction. Each of the five basic methods of image reproduction should be represented: relief, gravure, planographic, stencil, and digital.

   A. Prepare either a linoleum block or wood block print and reproduce the image on a proof press. If a proof press is not available, the image can be reproduced using pressure applied by hand, in a paper cutter, or similar process.

   B. Produce a gravure print using the process of dry-point engraving. Prepare an original line drawing, and place the line drawing beneath a sheet of flexible plastic. Using an old dental tool or scratch tool, engrave the print and print the image on an engraving press.

   C. Prepare a litho print using a tracing paper and a photo offset printing plate. An original drawing is prepared on tracing paper using black india ink. The plate is then exposed in a platemaker, using the tracing paper and india ink to take the place of conventional film. Develop the image, wet the plate and ink it up. Pull a plate proof using suitable pressure to transfer the image from the plate to a sheet of paper.

   D. Using available materials, prepare a small silk screen frame using crinoline and cardboard. Stencils can be cut from craft paper. Ink can be either thinned offset or letterpress ink.

   E. Prepare an image in either black and white or color and reproduce it using a suitable photocopy machine.

Chapter 2   THE DEVELOPMENT OF GRAPHIC COMMUNICATIONS

Chapter 2 THE DEVELOPMENT OF GRAPHIC COMMUNICATIONS

Understand Modern Day Communications Technology in Historical Context

Develop an Appreciation of Prehistoric Art and Communication Techniques

Understand Mass Communication and the Impact of the Printed Word as Facilitated by the Invention of Moveable Type

Provide and Overview of the Development of Printing in North America

Understand the Invention of Moveable Type and the Development of the Transistor as Two Major Enabling Developments in Human History

■ INTRODUCTION

The history of communications, from the early use of handdrawn pictures on cave walls to represent things or ideas to complex digital communication and information processing systems, is a study of the development of human technology. It is an ever-increasing sophisticated system of manipulating and controlling the environment around us in order to satisfy human wants and desires. For purposes of this text, our examination follows humankind from their beginnings as hunters and gatherers through the development of agricultural systems, which for the first time, allowed for permanent settlements. Enabled by the invention of the plough, farmers were able to grow surplus food for the first time. Surplus food set the stage for production-based economies. The development of modern complex digital technologies that enable instantaneous communication of thoughts, ideas, and information can be traced back to the first communication technology: pictures drawn on cave and cliff walls.

The casual examination of any particular technology or technological development at first may appear to be based on an isolated event or discovery, and in fact, sometimes they are. We can all visualize the genius inventor or scientist in the laboratory, at work for years to perfect a particular device or idea. Closer examination reveals however, that in most instances, the development of any device or invention is built on the work of those who came before. Each development, each act of genius, whether by accident, good fortune, or purely by mistake, often sets the stage for the events that follow, enabling future advances and achievements.

Within the area of humankind's ability to communicate, two achievements in this technological landscape stand out as landmark events in human history: the development of the printing press and moveable type by Johann Gutenberg in 1455 and the invention of the transistor in 1948 by Bell Laboratory physicists Walter Brattain, John Bardeen, and William Shockley.

The printing press, in conjunction with the development of moveable, replicacast type, set the stage for the spread of literacy throughout the world. These events, in effect, built the foundation for what later would come to be known as mass communication. No longer the exclusive domain of the rich and privileged, every person now had access to books and to the power of words and ideas.

The discovery of the transistor clearly marks the beginning of a shift in the direction of human history. While there are many remarkable developments that have accompanied the evolution of the computerization of every facet of human existence, the transistor enabled the development of electronic miniaturization which has forever changed both the nature and the direction of political and social events.

Graphic Communication Timeline

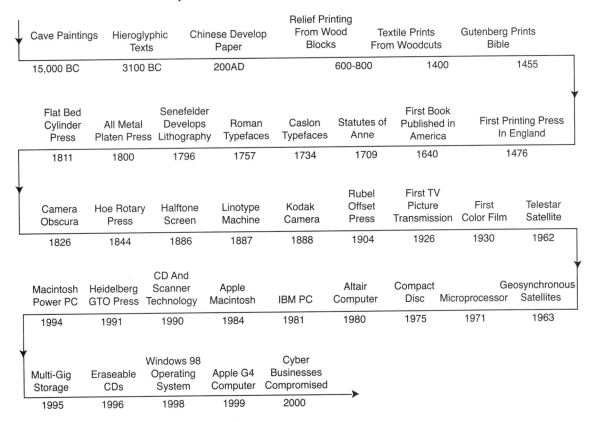

Cave Paintings	Hieroglyphic Texts	Chinese Develop Paper	Relief Printing From Wood Blocks	Textile Prints From Woodcuts	Gutenberg Prints Bible
15,000 BC	3100 BC	200AD	600-800	1400	1455

Flat Bed Cylinder Press	All Metal Platen Press	Senefelder Develops Lithography	Roman Typefaces	Caslon Typefaces	Statutes of Anne	First Book Published in America	First Printing Press In England
1811	1800	1796	1757	1734	1709	1640	1476

Camera Obscura	Hoe Rotary Press	Halftone Screen	Linotype Machine	Kodak Camera	Rubel Offset Press	First TV Picture Transmission	First Color Film	Telestar Satellite
1826	1844	1886	1887	1888	1904	1926	1930	1962

Macintosh Power PC	Heidelberg GTO Press	CD And Scanner Technology	Apple Macintosh	IBM PC	Altair Computer	Compact Disc	Microprocessor	Geosynchronous Satellites
1994	1991	1990	1984	1981	1980	1975	1971	1963

Multi-Gig Storage	Eraseable CDs	Windows 98 Operating System	Apple G4 Computer	Cyber Businesses Compromised
1995	1996	1998	1999	2000

FIGURE 2.1
A timeline of communication technology

In this chapter, we look at some of the events in the evolution of communication technology that help to place our current position in historical perspective. A timeline of some of the major events that chronicle the development of communication technology is highlighted in Fig. 2.1.

Figure 2.1 illustrates some of the highlights of the development of communication technology over a period of 35,000 years. This timeline features selected events and is not meant to be all-inclusive. Rather, it shows an increasingly sophisticated development in the nature of how people communicate with one another. We'll take a closer look at these developments, starting with some of the earliest documented images left by our ancestors: early cave paintings and pictographs.

■ PREHISTORIC ART AND WRITING

The study of communication technology begins more than 35,000 years ago during the Paleolithic period. Paleolithic art took the form of crude drawings and paintings made on clay. This period of art lasted until approximately 10000 B.C. The existence of artistic ability on the part of primitive cultures was largely dismissed until the discovery of cave paintings at Altamira, Spain. As more and more caves were dis-

covered with increasingly sophisticated discovery techniques and changing ocean water levels, Stone Age art was authenticated. The subject matter of most of the drawings focused on animals of the period, including bison, wild cattle, and goats, to finger drawings and hand imprints. The paintings were made by mixing readily available natural colorants such as manganese, iron oxide, charcoal, and blood with vehicles such as animal fat or natural juices and fluids. This mixture was then painted onto a clay tablet or cave wall, using either a stick or a brush. Typical of these is the cave painting from Spain, shown in Fig. 2.2, the subject of which is a deer hunt.

FIGURE 2.2:
A deer hunt as seen by early cave dwellers in Spain
(Courtesy American Museum of Natural History)

Cave paintings are sometimes referred to as *pictographs,* which literally means "writing with pictures." Because it would take too many pictures to represent complicated ideas or long messages, pictographs are limited in their ability to communicate only simple messages.

The art of cave painting led to the development of rock painting, a tradition that continued through the Mesolithic (Middle Stone Age) period, the Neolithic (New Stone Age) period as well as the Bronze and Iron Ages. These images range in date from about 10000 B.C. to 4000 B.C. Different styles of rock art have been found all over the world. The greatest concentrations of this art form have been discovered in Europe and the Saharan and Libyan deserts in Africa. North and South America also contain rock face and cave painted walls as well.

■ HIEROGLYPHICS

Pictures and symbols that represent ideas, objects, and symbols in a formalized writing system are known as *hieroglyphics*. The term hieroglyphics comes from the Greek "hieroglyphika grammata" which means "sacred carved letters." More far-reaching than the Greek definition, hieroglyphic texts deal with many more subjects than those that were simply religious in nature. Although many hieroglyphic texts have been deciphered, many remain a mystery, undeciphered due to insufficient information necessary for proper analysis. The major key to deciphering ancient Egyptian hieroglyphic texts came with the discovery of the Rosetta Stone. The stone contains a decree issued in 196 B.C., written in three languages: Greek, Egyptian hieroglyphics, and Demotic (a cursive evolution of hieroglyphic text and symbols). The stone was eventually deciphered by a French scholar, Jean Champollion, in 1822. Keys from the stone have been used to decipher most of the hieroglyphic texts to date, although, as stated earlier, many mysteries remain. The Rosetta Stone is on permanent display in the British Museum in London, England.

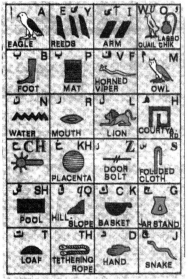

FIGURE 2.3
Some common Egyptian hieroglyphic symbols

Hieroglyphic texts evolved from simpler forms of pictorial art as various societies developed increasingly complex writing systems that were necessary to keep up with their development. Hieroglyphic texts are composed of *ideograms*; that is, each sign or drawing represents some object or concept that is derived from the graphic. Many hieroglyphic texts are also phonetic and represent basic grammatical expressions. Although sophisticated ideas can be represented in this type of writing system, it requires many ideographs to communicate a message. For example, both the Chinese and Japanese systems of writing, which still contain ideographs, each require more than 10,000 symbols. Figure 2.3 illustrates some of the basic Egyptian hieroglyphic symbols, along with their letter and symbolic counterparts.

■ THE ALPHABET

The evolution of hieroglyphic texts eventually led to the invention of letters. The use of alphabetic writing began to appear in Egypt around 3000 B.C. The Phoenicians are generally thought to have developed the system of representing sound with written symbols—the basic alphabet. The Phoenicians were trading widely throughout the Middle East around 1100 B.C. and were known to have imported papyrus for writing. It is likely that they adopted Egyptian alphabetic letters for their own alphabet as well.

By the fourth century B.C., the Greeks had adopted and modified the Phoenician alphabetic system and added vowels to the alphabet. The Greeks reversed the facing of some of the letters, as the Phoenicians wrote from right to left and the Greeks write from left to right. The Greeks also changed the names of some of the letters as well. The Romans later took the Greek alphabet and adapted it to their own language. The Roman alphabet has remained largely unchanged and is what we continue to use today.

■ THE DEVELOPMENT OF PAPERMAKING

The development of an efficient and inexpensive system of making paper as well as printing from moveable type began to converge during the fourteenth and fifteenth centuries A.D. These developments lay the foundations for the spread of literacy throughout the world.

When human beings first began to experiment with communicating ideas with drawn images, any material that could be used to draw, paint, or carve on could be used as a writing tablet. Cave and rock walls gave way to clay and wooden tablets. Clay and wood were eventually replaced with natural materials such as papyrus. Most Egyptian hieroglyphic texts are printed on papyrus, which remained in widespread use throughout Europe into the twelfth century A.D. Parchment, made from animal skins was also used extensively for writing until paper made from interlaced plant and cloth fibers replaced it.

The process of making paper is credited to a Chinese court official named Tsai Lun, about 105 A.D. The Chinese were able to keep the process of papermaking a secret for more than 500 years. Eventually, knowledge of the process spread, and by the sixteenth century paper mills were established throughout much of Europe. The process of papermaking at this time was a manual one. Linen and wood was reduced to a pulpy mass by suspending these ingredients in a solution of water. A wire mesh screen could then be dipped into the pulp vat. When the screen was removed, it contained a thin layer of pulp across the screen. As water drained through the screen, the linen and wood fibers bonded together to form a sheet of paper. The sheet could then be pressed and dried. The manual papermaking process was slow and restricted the amount of paper available for printing. A mechanized process would be needed to supply increasing amounts of paper that would be needed to feed the printing presses of the day.

The mechanized process for making paper was developed in 1798 by a Frenchman, Nicolas Robert. Robert's papermaking machine used an endless wire mesh screen that ran between two drive rollers. The screen vibrated as it moved, and was fed a mixture of watery pulp from a vat. The vibration of the screen helped remove the excess water from the pulp and allowed the water to drain through the screen. The pulp fibers locked together as they moved down the screen forming an endless web of paper. The paper web was then sent through a series of rollers to establish uniform thickness and surface finish. This process was further refined by the Fourdrinier brothers, who built the first commercially successful papermaking machine in 1804 in England. Modern papermaking machines still bear their name as well as a remarkable resemblance to the original Fourdrinier papermaking machines.

■ THE PRINTED WORD

Until a process for mass producing the printed word was developed, information was accessible to the relatively few people who could afford handprinted or handscribed manuscripts. Both block printed and handscribed materials had severe limitations. Wooden blocks used for printing had to be carefully handcrafted and each block represented only a single book page. The printing presses of the time were modified from wine presses and used heavy pressure against the block to print the page; pressure which eventually flattened out the block, rendering it useless. As an alternative to block printing, handscribed manuscripts were expensive since scribes were in short supply and demanded high wages for their craft.

Fifteenth-century Europe was poised for the invention of moveable type and mechanized printing. The process of papermaking had developed to the point where it was now cheaper and more readily available than either parchment or papyrus. Relative affluence, a by-product of European recovery from the bubonic plague a century earlier, resulted in an abundant supply of linen for papermaking. It was at this point in history that Johann Gutenberg offered his landmark invention to the world.

The invention of moveable type and the printing press is attributed to Gutenberg, a German goldsmith. Gutenberg's great contribution to civilization lies in his development of a method to produce moveable, easily replicated letters of type. Gutenberg's early attempts at printing used wooden letters that were held together in lines by running a wire through a hole drilled at the base of each piece of type. With the lines of type held in place within a frame, pages could be printed. However, the wooden type quickly wore down, and Gutenberg moved on to experiment with other materials for type. Drawing upon his skills as a goldsmith, Gutenberg introduced the process of replica-casting individual pieces of type. In the replica casting process, each letter of the alphabet is carved in relief to form a master letter punch. This master is then used to punch the letter into a brass mold. Type is then cast, one letter at a time in the matrix. The mold is designed to be reusable, so many letters of type can be cast from the same mold, each identical to the other. This process was an early forerunner of the principle of interchangeable parts. The type metal used was an alloy of lead, tin, and antimony, and it is still used today to cast what little metal foundry type is used in special-purpose printing applications.

FIGURE 2.4:
The Gutenberg press

Gutenberg adapted the wine presses of the day for use in printing pages of both type and illustrations. He also developed a printing ink that was formulated to adhere to the type metal alloy because ink that was used to print from this new type had to be different from the inks that were used to make prints from wood blocks. The basic design of the Gutenberg printing press is illustrated in Fig. 2.4.

The Gutenberg bible, also known as the 42-line bible (because of the number of lines of text on each page), was published around 1455. This bible, more than 1300 pages long, was printed two pages at a time, by hand, on Gutenberg's first-generation printing press. Historians question whether the bible was actually published by Gutenberg or by Johann Fust and Peter Schoffer. Fust and Schoffer took over Gutenberg's press and materials after Gutenberg defaulted on the repayment of the loans to them. The bible was published during this period.

Despite what can be regarded as a milestone achievement in the history of technology, Gutenberg later abandoned printing in the 1460s and died in 1468, still heavily in debt. Yet, Gutenberg's invention led to the spread of knowledge and literacy throughout Europe by enabling the distribution of inexpensively produced books.

First-generation type designers were busy at work throughout Europe following the development of moveable type and mechanized printing. One of the most famous type designers was a Venetian, Aldus Manutius, a printer who pioneered the production of inexpensive books that could be easily carried about—the first-generation pocket book. Manutius set to work printing translations of the Greek classics and is responsible for the development of what has come to be known as the *italic* typeface. This typeface was originally designed with graceful, slanting letters to mimic handwritten characters.

Another Venetian printer, Nicolas Jenson, began working around 1470. Jenson was an artist by profession, and is responsible for perfecting the basic form and beauty of the Roman typeface. Roman typefaces are those used in the majority of textbooks and other text-intensive applications. The style of Jenson's letters are essentially those used today in the design and appearance of modern Roman typefaces.

Early type casting was an integrated activity in early print shops. A French printer and typographer, Claude Garamond, was the first person to elevate type design and type casting as a separate undertaking. Garamond began work as a printer, but eventually focused all of his attention to the design and production of typefaces for other printers—the first type foundry. The development of the type foundry as a separate entity from the print shop freed printers from the chore of designing and casting their own type. With this separation they could now concentrate more on the process of printing and page design.

William Caxton was a merchant and writer who, while visiting Belgium, was introduced to the then new art of printing. While in the city of Bruges, Caxton produced the first book printed in the English language. Caxton later returned to England, bringing his printing presses with him. Shortly after setting up shop in London, he produced the first dated book printed in England in 1477.

Through the end of the seventeenth and into the eighteenth century, English printers were forced to rely primarily on imported type from the Netherlands because there were no type foundries in England. Then, in the early eighteenth century, William Caslon, utilizing his background as an engraver, set up the first type foundry in London. Caslon printed a type specimen sheet in 1734 that included typeface designs that still bear his name. His work began an industry that eliminated the need for imported typefaces in England.

John Baskerville, a contemporary of Caslon, was a writing master who later became a type designer and printer. Baskerville's contributions to typeface and typographic design were impressive. His accomplishments included the development of newer, rich-toned printing inks and glossy-surfaced papers. As official printer to Cambridge University, Baskerville printed the bible in 1763, a book which is thought of as one of the finest examples of eighteenth-century printing.

■ COPYRIGHT PROTECTION

In 1709, British Parliament passed the Statute of Anne, which extended the right of copyright protection to all citizens. This statute established for the first time, that intellectual property is, in effect, the property of its creator. The foundations of United States copyright laws are based on this statute. The main purpose of copyright protection is to encourage the creation and dissemination of information while protecting the rights of the creator of the book, photograph, or product along with the right to earn money from his or her creation.

The need for copyright protection was recognized shortly after the invention of the printing press. European governments, fearing that the wide dissemination of printed information could undermine their authority, began to enter into individual copyright agreements with the printers of the time. In these early arrangements, governments would allow printers to publish and sell their materials only if they adhered to and followed government censorship rules.

It is essential that all those working within the graphic design and associated technical industries be familiar with the basic concepts of copyright law. Current U.S. and world-wide copyright law allows the creator of an intellectual property (books, films, photographs, etc.) to control and distribute the creation, earn income from it, as well as prevent others from using it without permission. Copyright protection is a critical issue for those in the graphic design and communication technology areas because questions can often arise as to what property rights exist for materials whose origins are unknown.

As barriers between people and countries continued to break down with increasing computerization and globalization of economies and societies, issues of copyright protection as they apply to the creation of images, image manipulation, and digitization in general have become increasingly complicated, necessitating frequent revisions and updating of the copyright statutes. Although the graphic design and communication technologist needs to become familiar with copyright law, a good rule of thumb on these issues for the beginner is known as "the man on the street rule." This rule states that if someone with no graphic arts or technical training feels that two images bear a striking resemblance to one another, it is reasonable to assume that a copyright infringement has probably taken place. In other words, if you didn't create the image yourself, you can assume that you are using another person's materials. Unless you have permission to use the material, you are likely in violation of the law.

■ THE DEVELOPMENT OF PRINTING IN NORTH AMERICA

The printing industry in North America began in 1638. Stephen Daye, a locksmith from Cambridge, England contracted with a New England minister, Jesse Glover. Glover, interested in promoting an understanding of the bible in the British Colonies, felt the best way to do this was to set up a print shop and spread the word of the bible. On the way back from England with Daye, Glover died before the shop was established. Glover's wife took over the responsibility of setting up the shop, and Stephen Daye fulfilled his contract. In 1640, Daye published, *The Book of Psalmes*, the first book printed in British North America. Taking almost a year to complete, only 11 copies of the 300-page book remain. After the death of Glover's widow (who had eventually remarried a Harvard University president), the press was moved to Harvard. This marked the beginning of what is now the oldest continuously operated press in the United States, the Harvard University Press.

Perhaps the most famous of all American printers was Benjamin Franklin, (Fig. 2.5).

Franklin wore many hats including that of printer, political leader and statesman, inventor, and philosopher. One of 13 children, Franklin began his career in his father's trade as a mechanic and candlemaker. However, he soon began to work as an apprentice for his brother, James, who published the *New England Courant*. Franklin was a prolific reader as well as author

FIGURE 2.5:
Benjamin Franklin: statesman, politician, inventor, printer, and graphic designer
(Courtesy The Smithsonian Institution)

and essayist. He soon began writing articles for the *Courant,* which satirized everything from religion to authoritarianism. Franklin moved from his brother's employ to Philadelphia, where he established the *Pennsylvania Gazette.* Franklin began printing *Poor Richard's Almanac* in 1732, expanding both his business and influence at the same time. Students of American history are familiar with Franklin's other accomplishments including his careers as diplomat, abolitionist, and, of course, one of the designers of the Constitution.

The nineteenth century brought about significant changes in communication technology. Alois Senefelder, a Bavarian musician, was experimenting with lithographic images on limestone rock that would lay the foundations for the offset printing industry. In America, printing press design and construction featured easily disassembled printing presses fabricated from wood and metal. These construction features were adaptable to westward expansion in America. Robert Hoe, working with his furniture manufacturer brothers-in-law bought the patents to several press designs of the time, modified them, and began to build what was known as the Washington Press in the 1830s. Hoe's contemporaries, Isaac and Seth Adams, designed one of the first printing presses to run on steam power in 1830, (Fig. 2.6).

FIGURE 2.6:
Adams steam-powered printing press
(Courtesy The Smithsonian Institution)

The Adams press featured a steam engine to power the movement of the printing press. This adaptation proved to be much faster than the typical hand-powered printing presses of the time. Press technology continued to move along rapidly with the development of the rotary press by Hoe and Company in 1844 and the use of stereotype plates (rather than original type forms) on cylinder presses in the 1860s. Stereotype plates enable printers to run the same job on different printing presses at the same time. The plates were cast replicas from the original type forms, fitted to run on presses with the same cylinder curvatures.

The first steam-driven lithography press was developed in the 1860s. Steam power was used to operate the moving parts on the presses on which lithographic stones were prepared for the image transfer. On March 4, 1880, the first halftone picture to be printed appeared in the *New York Daily Graphic.* The halftone picture process enabled photographs to be broken up into dot patterns so the image could be printed (see Chapter 8 for a complete description of the halftone process). The Washington press, developed earlier, became the standard machine for high-volume printing operations and remained viable into the 1930s at which time higher volume sheet- and web-fed printing presses came into widespread use.

■ PHOTOGRAPHY AND ELECTROSTATIC PRINTING

The introduction of the Kodak® camera in 1888 forever changed the way in which people communicate. Photography has played a key role in communication technology, both as an art form as well as a foundation process used in all of the major printing and graphic reproduction processes.

Hundreds of years prior to the development of the Kodak camera, artists and photographers were using a device called a *camera obscura*. The camera obscura was basically a dark room with a pinhole opening in one of the outside walls. Light from an object that was illuminated outside of the camera obscura passed through this small pinhole opening and was projected upside down on the opposite wall of the room. This process is illustrated in Fig. 2.7.

Experimentation brought about the replacement of the darkened room with a smaller, portable light-tight box. The opening in the wall was replaced by a simple focusing lens, which enabled the image to be projected so that it was right side up. By adding film to the back of a light-tight box to capture the projected image, the modern camera was born.

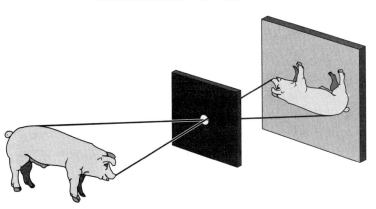

FIGURE 2.7:
Principle of the modern camera from the camera obscura

The first commercial camera in widespread use was developed by a Frenchman named Louis Daguerre. In a process named after its inventor called Daguerreotype, a glass photographic plate, coated with a light-sensitive chemical emulsion, was placed inside the light-tight box. A long exposure was made, after which the plate was processed to hold and fix the image. Daguerreotype was a wet-plate process. The relatively low sensitivity of the chemical emulsions required the long exposure times necessary to produce the pictures. Once again, the stage was set for a technological development that would expedite the photographic process—a flexible film base using dry process chemistry housed within the framework of a portable light-tight box—the Kodak® camera.

The original Kodak® camera came prepackaged from the factory with a 100-exposure roll of film. After taking the pictures, the camera was sent back to the factory where the film was processed. The camera was then reloaded with a new roll of film and returned to the customer. Continuous improvements in film and camera technology, coupled with electronic circuit miniaturization eventually led to the fully automatic point-and-shoot, professional, and digital cameras with which we are familiar.

One-step photography, pioneered by Edwin Land, was developed by Land's Polaroid Corporation in 1947. Land began his pioneering work with polarized light, and then applied this technology to automotive headlights, reduced-glare filters, glasses, and three-dimensional motion picture photography. The single-step Polaroid® camera was introduced to the public in 1947. A color version of the camera became commercially available in 1963.

About the same time that Land was experimenting with polarized light, another American inventor, Chester Carlson, was developing the foundations for what would eventually become electrostatic printing, later to become known as Xerography®. Carlson sold the rights of his process to the Xerox Corporation in 1938.

■ HOT TYPE COMPOSITION

The ancestry of computerized imaging can be traced back to the development of the first typewriter by Christopher Sholes during the post-Civil War era. Sholes's typewriter introduced the now-familiar "QWERTY" layout on the keyboard. Although many patents were issued for mechanical typesetting devices during the latter part of the nineteenth century, mechanized production of the printed word is clearly defined by the invention of the Linotype machine by Ottmar Merganthaler. Merganthaler, a German-born watchmaker, was a skilled constructor of patent models. Financed by a group of publishers, Merganthaler's machine was installed in the New York Tribune building and began producing automatically set type on July 3, 1886. Merganthaler's Linotype machine used molten lead to cast lines of type from brass molds. Separate lines of type could be quickly assembled and made up into complete pages of text by a compositor. The Linotype machine (Fig. 2.8) set the standard in typesetting for the next 60 years.

FIGURE 2.8:
The Merganthaler Linotype machine
(Courtesy The Smithsonian Institution)

A limitation of the Linotype machine was that it could only set standard point sizes of type; it was not capable of setting the larger point sizes of type required for headings and display applications. To fill this gap, a machine was developed by Washington Ludlow in 1913, simply called the "Ludlow machine." The Ludlow machine enabled compositors to set individual lines of display type in a composing stick and, from the composing stick cast the individual handset line of type into a lead slug, similar to the slug produced by the Linotype. Using these two machines, pages containing both text and display type could be quickly created and assembled.

During the next 70 years, both the Linotype and Ludlow machines encountered and successfully fought off competition from a variety of other manufacturers. However, by the late 1960s and early 1970s, the age of hot-metal typesetting was over. First- and second-generation phototypesetters, machines made possible by the transistor and microelectronic circuitry, relegated hot metal typesetting to little more than an art form.

■ THE TRANSISTOR AND MICROELECTRONICS

The invention of the microprocessor stands as a landmark development of the twentieth century, and, along with the development of printing from moveable type, one of the greatest achievements in human history. The transistor set the stage for all future developments in the area of electronic circuit miniaturization and the subsequent computerization of virtually all aspects of modern life.

The transistor was invented in 1948 by three Bell Laboratory physicists, Walter Brattain, John Bardeen, and William Shockley. The transistor is, in effect, an electronic valve. It is able to control large electrical current flow between two areas within a semiconductor crystal using only a small amount of power. The transistor performs the same function as a vacuum tube, acting as either an amplifier or switching mechanism, but is only a fraction of the size of the tube and generates almost no heat and is highly reliable. The operating features of the transistor ushered in the era of smaller and smaller electronic circuits, microelectronics and eventually, the integrated circuit, which is the basis for the heart of all computers—the microprocessor.

FIGURE 2.9:
ENIAC computer
(Courtesy The Smithsonian Institution)

The transistor was invented shortly after the development of the first ENIAC computer. ENIAC, an acronym that stands for electronic numerical integrator and computer, was developed at the Moore School of Engineering at the University of Pennsylvania. Construction started on ENIAC during World War II in order to perform the mathematical calculations necessary for ballistic trajectory tables required by the U. S. Navy. Completed after the War, the ENIAC was a marvel of modern electronic circuitry containing more than 17,000 vacuum tubes and was able to perform 5,000 mathematical calculations per second, an astounding feat for the time. The ENIAC, a section of which is on permanent display at The Smithsonian is pictured in Fig. 2.9.

As an interesting side note on ENIAC, the term *bugs*, referring to modern day computer problems and software glitches, originated from the problems that occurred in ENIAC when insects were often found to get stuck between the contacts of the switching terminals in ENIAC; hence, the present-day meaning of the term. In 1951, John Mauchly and John Eckert, the engineers responsible for building the ENIAC, who were then working for the Remington Rand Corporation, delivered the first UNIVAC (universal automatic computer) to the United States Census Bureau.

The first computers were built using vacuum tubes; however, transistors soon became the dominant electronic features of computer construction by the late 1950s. The introduction of the integrated circuit by Robert Noyce, a physicist working for the Fairchild Semiconductor Corporation in 1959 led to both a reduction in the size and increase in efficiency of the computer. The integrated circuit paved the way for the microprocessor by combining thousands of individual electronic circuit components on one small chip. When the central microprocessor chip was introduced by the Intel Corporation in 1971, the stage was set for the development of powerful personal and business computers. The central microprocessor replaces many integrated circuits, enabling further reduction in size and corresponding increases in both system and circuit efficiency. Figure 2.10 shows a typical computer computer chip. In Fig. 2.11, the cover of the chip has been removed to show the internal layout of the microprocessor.

The first personal computer to gain any degree of public acceptance was the Altair 8800. The Altair, based on an Intel microprocessor, was offered to computer and electronic hobbyists only as a do-it-yourself kit. Other companies, such as Apple and Kaypro then entered the home computer market, producing machines like the Apple 2 series. The infant personal computer market received its biggest boost, however, with the introduction of the IBM personal computer (PC) in 1981. An almost unbelievable explosion in advances in digital technology has taken place since that time. In fact, a viable market has developed for antique computers. First- and second-generation machines such as the Apple 1 series and original IBM PCs have become valuable commodities in a market that defines fifteen-year old technology as "antique."

FIGURE 2.10:
Computer chip
(Courtesy The Smithsonian Institution)

The introduction of the Apple Macintosh computer in 1984 is especially noteworthy. The Macintosh showed that through its graphical user interface (GUI), icon-based intuitive computing is an elegant alternative to arcane command strings that strain both the memory and patience. The effectiveness of the GUI was borne out several years later when Microsoft introduced its Windows® interface. With the introduction of the Power PC® by Apple Computer and other advanced microprocessors, as well as the continued evolution of the Windows® operating environment, the GUI remains an integral part of personal computing.

■ SUMMARY

When we view technological developments in the communication arts from our present-day vantage point, one might wonder why things seemed to move so slowly during the first fifty years of the twentieth century and so quickly since then. For example, the process of offset printing, developed around 1904, today remains similar in its most fundamental aspects since it was first developed. Digital printing presses, however, which didn't exist in 1990, can now electronically print directly from a computer front-end, bypassing all the intermediate steps involved in traditional typesetting, camera work, stripping, platemaking, and makeready time on a printing press. Environmentally friendly, digital printing presses don't rely on any chemicals other than toners—no inks, solvents nor mess. What separates the development of technology and subsequent achievements of the two halves of the twentieth century is the invention of the transistor.

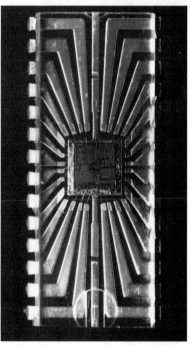

FIGURE 2.11:
Internal microprocessor
(Courtesy The Smithsonian Institution)

However disconnected the rate of development between the first and second halves of the twentieth century might seem, it should be kept in mind that events usually occur in a natural progression, each one building on the other. Also, many devices and technological adaptations often appear years before any practical applications are available for them. For example, the transistor was developed several years before it was used as a component in computers.

It is interesting to note that ancient picture writing, perhaps the earliest form of communication between people, is the format that is increasingly used in modern computers. Icons that represent events or ideas on cave walls are essentially the same form of communication used on computers operating under the Windows® and Macintosh® platforms. The importance of icon-based communication was demonstrated by NASA in 1972, when Pioneer 10 began its journey as the first spacecraft designed to leave our solar system. The illustration on Pioneer's gold plaque is shown in Fig. 2.12.

The illustration highlights a man and a woman and the hydrogen atom and its wavelength. An illustration of our solar system indicates where the spacecraft's journey began and the relationship of Earth to the rest of our solar system. The information on this plaque is simply yet elegantly depicted.

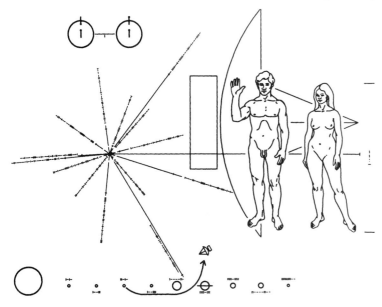

FIGURE 2.12:
Earth announces its existence to the universe via the Pioneer X plaque
(Courtesy National Aeronautics and Space Administration)

In looking at other links to the past, consider that the Roman typeface, developed by the Italian typographer and printer Nicolas Jenson in the latter half of the fifteenth century, is still the type of choice for most text applications.

The practitioner in the graphic arts industry will of necessity be forced to keep a sharp eye out for changing technological patterns and innovations. History will continue to unfold before our eyes. Computers will increasingly become multimedia tools, incorporating all of the standard applications with telephone, audio, and video components and an increasingly interactive mode of operation. The keyboard and mouse will become of secondary importance in making a computer work. Regardless of all of these sophisticated electronic technologies, the historical roots and development of the graphic arts will continue to exert subtle, but nonetheless important, influences on all future developments in how we generate and communicate information and ideas.

■ SUGGESTED STUDENT ACTIVITIES

1. The circumstances surrounding Gutenberg loosing his print shop are misunderstood, and many different stories exist concerning this development. Using the Internet as a research tool, investigate Gutenberg's situation during the time he operated his print shop and try to determine, to the best of your ability, what took place during the time of the publication of the 42-line bible.

2. Construct a time-line of the major printing processes beginning with the development of moveable type by Gutenberg in 1455. The timeline should include all of the major printing processes up to and including the development of the first digital printing press in 1994.

3. Select a period of time and develop a timeline of communication technology innovations.

4. **A.** Select a specific current technological development of interest. Develop a timeline showing the series of significant events that lead up to the specific technology.

   B. Propose a series of technological innovations that could take place in the future, using the chosen specific device or technology as a spring board for future development.

5. Either individually or in small groups, select a particular communication device and, using readily available materials, build a working model of the device.

6. Select one particular aspect of communication technology and prepare an oral presentation to the class. The report will stress the history of the selected topic, its impact(s) on society, and discussion of possible future implications of the technology.

Chapter 3   FUNDAMENTALS OF TYPOGRAPHY

Chapter 3 FUNDAMENTALS OF TYPOGRAPHY

Understand Type Design and Families

Examine Type Printing

Overview of Type Anatomy

Identify Typeface Categories

Develop Methods of Working with Type

■ INTRODUCTION

This chapter introduces the history of type development and printing and discusses the importance of type in graphic design and its use. Because type is one of the most important parts of graphic design, the technical information given in this chapter will help you to better understand how type is categorized, measured, fit, and output. The information found here will give you an understanding of the basic principles of type usage by graphic designers—from early uses of wood and metal type to today's computer-based typesetting.

■ TYPE DESIGN AND FAMILIES

The history of type design dates back to the early stages of printing. Many early type designs were simply wood or metal versions of handlettered type. As printing technology improved, type design allowed for better readability and easier use of type for printers. A large number of early typefaces are still in use today. Typefaces such as Caslon, Baskerville, and Bodoni were designed in the 1700s and their digital versions continue to be popular today.

The heart of printed matter is the text, because written text makes up the majority of most printed communication. Although photographs, illustrations, and other graphic elements support the text, the personality of the printed page is created largely through the choice of typeface and its layout on the page. It is that which conveys the message to the reader. *Typography* is the art of selecting the proper typeface for the job at hand. On a very basic level, type speaks for itself. Consider the typeface examples in Fig. 3.1.

I'm rather Conservative!

I'm very feminine!

I'm tragically Hip!

I'm old-fashioned!

I'm outta my mind!

FIGURE 3.1:
Type speaks for itself

Thousands of type families are available from type foundries and software firms. Given this variety to choose from, a problem arises as to how to make knowledgeable decisions regarding which typeface to use in a given design situation. There are three principles that can help provide a framework for understanding the art of typography:

1. Use a typeface that will properly communicate your message. Some typefaces are elegant, such as those used for wedding invitations. Others reflect a wide variety of emotions, from the informal to even those that are humorous. Type specimen books are available from most type vendors. Look at these specimen books and try some different selections for communicating specific messages.

2. Type size should be related to the importance of your message— the more important the message, the larger the size of type. Headlines and captions should stand out from the body of text in order to highlight the central idea of the page or column. Headlines and captions that are highlighted in this way help the reader to organize information as it is being read—the message gets through more clearly and quickly than when reading undifferentiated captions and headlines.

3. Typefaces throughout a design should be used with consistency. With the great number of typefaces available and resident on a computer, there is a tendency for inexperienced graphic designers to use too many typefaces in one design. This practice results in a graphically confusing page design. In general, headings, subheadings, captions, and text should each be set in the same typeface. In this way, no more than three or four different typefaces are used on any one page. This rule applies to consistency of typeface variety throughout an entire document. It is best to use only a few faces and sizes for text in one design piece.

Following these three principles will help to give a document a distinct personality and identity within the boundaries of type usage in any given design project. Later in this chapter we will discuss various ways of working with type, but first let's get acquainted with the history of how type has been created and printed over the years.

Hot Type

For almost five hundred years following the invention of moveable type by Johann Gutenberg, the printed page was produced in basically the same way. Individual pieces (letters) of type were cast in metal at a type foundry and assembled by hand into words, lines, and pages. Foundry type is stored in wooden cases. In the United States the type case came to be called the California job case (Fig. 3.2).

The California job case was designed to hold thousands of individual pieces of type, stored in individual compartments by letter, number, and symbol. Each type case holds a specific point size and style of a family of type, referred to as a type *font*. For example, the type case in Fig. 3.2 stores 10 point Caslon Italic type; 12 point Caslon Italic type would be stored in a separate case; 14 point Caslon Bold would be stored in a third case, and so on. An interesting side note is that at these early print shops, capital letters were stored in cases on the upper racks of a storage cabinet and small letters on the lower rack. Thus, the terms *uppercase* for capitals and *lowercase* for small letters were derived.

As cumbersome as the procedure of using individual letter forms was, it dominated the printing industries until the invention of the Linotype typecasting machine invented by Ottmar Mergenthaler in the United States in 1886. This machine allowed a typositor (the operator of the machine) to type at a keyboard and have lines of type (hence the name "Linotype") cast immediately. These lines could be more easily assembled for printing than individual letters.

FIGURE 3.2:
A California job case

Later methods of producing type include phototypesetting. First- and second-generation phototypesetting machines used separate film fonts. Light was projected through individual letters in the film font onto a sheet of photographic paper, one letter at a time. As cumbersome as this might seem, production capacity via the phototypesetters was a great improvement over the most sophisticated hot-type-casting machines.

Early computer typesetting machines were complex and involved a programmer's knowledge to operate, as the terminals did not show the actual type being set, but worked by typing in a series of computer commands. The typeset design was not visible until it was printed.

The computer display of type fonts in the early stages of digital technology resulted in characters that were made up of a matrix of bits written into the memory of the computer. On the screen, these characters appeared as dots that corresponded to the memory bits. In this type of system, the character display hardware of the computer determines what you see on the screen. The idea of "what you see is what you get," referred to as WYSIWYG, was waiting in the wings. It was this feature—actually being able to see and control the position of letter forms on a page—that lead us to the development of the personal computer as the primary machine for typesetting. This development also took the job of setting type out of the hands of trained professional typositors and into those of graphic designers.

■ COMPUTERIZED TYPEFACES

Once the setting of type evolved to the point where graphic designers could set it themselves, ways to produce professional quality output of type were needed. First- and second-generation computerized printing attempted to mimic the action of the mechanical typewriter. Dot matrix and daisy wheel printers were the first devices in widespread use to interpret computer input to produce text and graphic images. Although the type images generated by daisy wheel and dot matrix printers are not digitally reproduced, as is the case with laser printers and digital typesetters, they do interpret digitally stored text information, and serve as an introduction to digital output.

Daisy Wheel and Dot Matrix Printers

Daisy wheel printers were the first devices to gain widespread popularity for printing text applications from personal computers. These devices did not have much of an impact on the graphic design profession, but made basic typesetting abilities available to those outside of the typesetting industry. The daisy wheel printer uses a separate printing wheel for each type font. Each character in the font is located on a separate character arm. A hammer behind the wheel is activated to strike a particular character when it is called upon to print. The action of the daisy wheel is similar to that of a conventional electric typewriter. Although many typefaces are available for most daisy wheel printers, such printers can print only one font at a time—whichever font wheel is loaded onto the machine. Most daisy wheel printers are noisy due to the mechanical action of the hammer against the print wheel mechanism. Despite their relatively low-page-per-minute output, daisy wheel printers yield letter-quality results because fully formed letters are transferred from the raised letters on the daisy wheel to the paper.

Dot matrix printers generate characters by selectively firing an array of pins or wires to form printed characters (Fig. 3.3). These printers are available with differing numbers of pins in the print head. The most common print heads are made up of either 9 or 24 pins. The greater the number of pins, the greater the clarity of the finished print. The pin configurations of typical 9- and 24-pin print heads are shown in Fig. 3.4.

To print letters with reasonably high quality, a print head with 9 pins will have to make several passes over the letters, whereas a print head with 18 or 24 pins can print high-quality letters with only one pass of the print head. Figure 3.5 shows a single-pass letter from a 9-pin head, a double pass with the same head, and a single-pass letter with a typical 24-pin print head.

Most dot matrix printers can also operate in a graphics mode, in addition to the text mode, to reproduce graphics that are drawn on the computer screen, within the resolution capability of the printer. A specific application program that runs on the computer or is resident in the system folder builds a bit map of the page, which is then output to the dot matrix printer. The dot matrix printer was the first available printer for the Macintosh computer, and

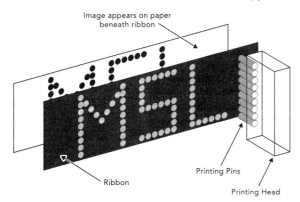

FIGURE 3.3:
How a dot matrix printer works

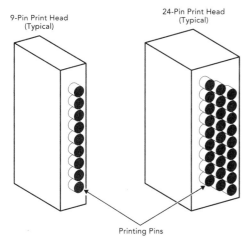

FIGURE 3.4:
Configuration of 9- and 24-pin dot matrix printers

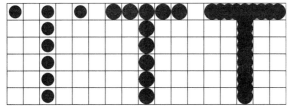

FIGURE 3.5:
Single and multiple pass printing

although it did not replace professional typesetting, it paved the way for designers to combine type and image on the same page. Some early adopters of this technology, such as the designers April Greiman and Rudy Vanderlans in California, created final designs using the dot matrix printer and the first-generation Macintosh computers.

Inkjet Printers

Inkjet printers were introduced around the same time as dot matrix printers. Since then, they have greatly improved and are one of the most popular methods for proofing used today. Their big advantage, even early on, is the ability to print in either full color or black and white. Inkjet printers use liquid inks that are sprayed onto the paper through tiny openings called "jets." There is a separate jet for each color, and, while most inkjet printers use the four printing inks of cyan, magenta, yellow, and black (CMYK), some use a six-color system to create a wider range of color for the printing of photographs. Although the first inkjet printers often had problems with the ink drying and clogging the jets, developments in ink, paper, and design of the jets themselves have greatly increased reliability today. As inkjet printers have become more popular, the prices have also dropped and are affordable to most designers and design students.

Laser Printers (including Imagesetters)

Laser printers brought typesetting into the hands of professional graphic designers because the type produced on them is of reproducible quality and the printers allow for the printing of both type and graphics on the same page. Laser printers work by using a laser to create a static charge on a metal drum. Powdered toner is attracted to the charged areas on the drum. The toner is transferred to a sheet of paper, which then moves through a high-heat "fuser," which fuses the toner to the paper and completes the printing process. Early laser printers were able to print 300 dpi, which is acceptable for low-end print jobs. With advancements in laser printer technology, printers can now print from 600 to 1200 dpi, which is of high enough quality to use for professional work.

Soon after the laser printer for paper was introduced, the laser printing process was also adapted for use in high-end imagesetters. Here, rather than printing on paper with toner, the imagesetter uses the laser to expose type and image areas on either photographic paper or film. The resolution for imagesetters is much higher than for standard laser printers, between 1000–3387 dpi. The printed photographic paper can be used for final mechanical artwork to be sent to the printer, and film can be used for the creation of printing plates. Recently, the laser printing process has also been adapted for use in directly making printing plates. This drastically reduces the steps needed to go from computer to press.

■ DIGITAL TYPE FONTS

Digital type fonts are defined as typefaces that are represented and stored as digitized electronic data. Refinements in technology enabled typesetting to move away from the phototypesetter, where the full-featured letter was photographically transferred from the film font to photographic proofing paper, to type fonts stored as digital information residing within a computer. With the development of Macintosh computers, the generation and display of characters by the computer changed forever. Digital typefaces are currently provided in several different formats.

Bit-Mapped Typefaces

This is the original type format created for the computer. Bit-mapped typefaces use the screen resolution of 72 dpi to display on the computer screen. Figure 3.6 shows an enlargement of how a bit-mapped face is constructed. To display correctly on screen, the computer requires a bit-map of each point size of the typeface that will be used; otherwise, the computer will just enlarge the pixels, leaving a jagged screen image of the type.

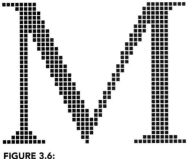

FIGURE 3.6:
A bit-mapped typeface (enlarged)

PostScript Typefaces

PostScript type fonts use both the bit-mapped font and a special PostScript file containing information that describes the outlines and fills of the typefaces. The PostScript file works together with the bit-mapped file, and both are necessary for proper on-screen display and printing.

Programs such as Adobe® Type Manager® (ATM®) interpret the PostScript information for display on the computer screen at any point size. With ATM®, only one size of the bit-map is required, and ATM® and the PostScript file will do the rest.

TrueType® Faces

TrueType® was developed by Apple Computer for use with Macintosh computers and Apple LaserWriters. TrueType® files work with the Macintosh system to create any size type on the computer screen and for printing. It is recommended that TrueType® files and PostScript files for the same font not be used together, as the system will default to the TrueType® font even though the PostScript file and ATM® will display a more accurate representation of the font on screen. TrueType® fonts may also result in printing errors with some PostScript printers, and are generally not used for professional design projects.

Outline Type Fonts

Increased flexibility for more typefaces, point sizes, and rotational qualities is gained from the use of outline type fonts. An outline font generates characters from mathematical descriptions of the letters and symbols in the font. Because outlines can be scaled up or down or rotated in virtually any direction, only one outline is needed to represent a specific character in any size or style of type.

Most printers print type in a bit-map format, so a large amount of processing power is required to change the outline font description to a bit-map format. This processing slows down the overall speed of most printers when working with outline fonts.

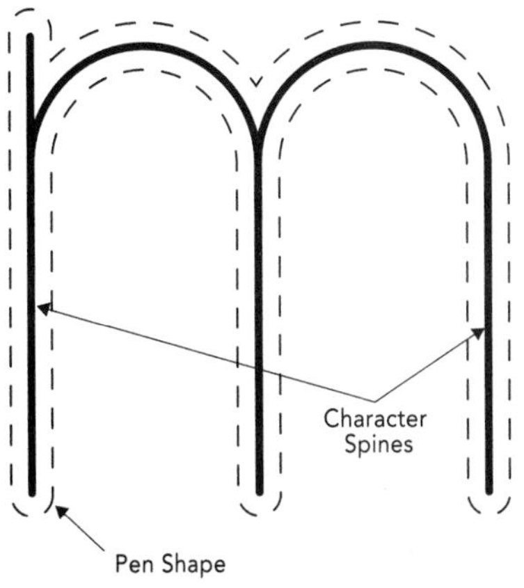

Character Spines

Pen Shape

FIGURE 3.7:
Construction of a stroke font

Stroke Fonts

Stroke fonts are sometimes referred to as *vector* fonts. *Character vectors* are the paths that a pen would follow along the spine of a character to generate a specific letter or symbol (Fig. 3.7). Stroke fonts are similar to outline fonts in that they can be proportionally sized and rotated.

The memory storage requirements of stroke fonts are the smallest of the three types of digital fonts. One major drawback to stroke fonts is that very few typefaces, out of the tens of thousands currently available, can be drawn with just even stroke weights and plain round or square ends.

■ THE NATURE OF TYPE

To understand the nature of type, it is important to know the basic principles behind its design. A typeface consists of more than just the twenty-six letters of the Roman alphabet. It includes upper and lowercase letters, numbers, punctuation, and accent characters, along with ligatures and special characters. Figure 3.8 shows a complete typeface with all of its characters.

Type is designed so that each of the individual characters in the font will work with one another. The weight, shape, and size of each character is carefully proportioned to balance and complement all the other characters in that font so they will fit together well when set.

In addition to the typeface itself, type designers often expand a face to create a type "family." In a family, various weights and styles, such as bold and italic, are created from the original face. In creating a family, the type designer is concerned with having the entire family of typefaces complement one another.

Times Roman

ABCDEFGHIJKLMNOPQRSTUVWXYZ
abcdefghijklmnopqrstuvwxyz
1234567890
!@#$%^&*()_-+=[]{}:;"'’'<>,.?/
œ∑´®†¥¨ˆøπ""«åß∂ƒ©˙∆˚¬…æΩ≈ç√∫˜µ≤≥÷
`/‹›fifl‡°·‚±Œ„'‰ˇÁ¨ˆØ∏"'»
ÅÍÎÏ˝ÓÔÒÚÆ¸˛Ç◊ı˜Â¯˘¿

FIGURE 3.8:
A complete typeface

Traditionally, a type designer would draw each character for a typeface by hand. These drawings would then be converted to type molds in a type foundry. Type foundries still exist, but the term "foundry" no longer applies in the traditional sense of casting type in a metal alloy. Most typefaces today are designed on computers using programs such as Macromedia Fontographer®. Typefaces are then distributed digitally via computer disk, CD-ROM, or as downloads from the Internet.

Many type manufacturers now make their faces accessible via the Internet. A graphic designer simply goes to the distributor's web site and charges the cost of the typeface to a credit card or business account. The font may then be downloaded to the designer's computer.

There are also many typefaces available for free or for small "shareware" fees over the Internet and through services such as America Online® and CompuServe®. It should be noted that "not all typefaces are created equal." Free or inexpensive typefaces do not have the precise detail and attention paid to accurate character rendering, setting and kerning—the spatial relationship between one letter and another—that are integral parts of professionally designed fonts.

Type Anatomy

The anatomy of letterforms, illustrated in Fig. 3.9, is the foundation upon which all rules of typographic design are based. Whether the type is set by hand or machine, type nomenclature defines many of the parameters of the typographer,

FIGURE 3.9:
Anatomy of letterforms
(Times Roman typeface)

graphic artist, and designer. Look closely at various parts of a letter to see how it is put together. Notice how all of the individual elements of the letterform come together in the individual character and also relate to the other characters in the typeface.

Type Categories
• Serif and Sans Serif Type Faces

Basic type categorization begins with serif and sans serif faces. A *serif* is the finishing stroke at the end of each letter. It is speculated that the concept of serif fonts grew out of one of the following methods: In Roman times, when type was carved onto building facades, it would first be painted on by letterers and then chiseled by stone carvers. The first theory is that because it is hard to make a perfect end to a stroke with a brush, the letterers would lift the brush at the end of a stroke, thus creating the serif. Since it was visible when the carvers cut the letters into stone, they would follow the guide they were given. The second theory says that, in order to keep the deep cuts of the primary strokes of the letter from cracking at the ends over time, the Roman carvers would cut shallower paths into the stone at the ends of the letters, thereby creating the serifs. Although either theory may or may not be true, the concept of the serif is still with us today.

A sans serif typeface (*sans*, from the French word meaning without) has no finishing stroke. Sans serif typefaces are thought to have their origins from moveable type being created in wood. As the wood was more brittle than metal, serifs could easily break off, so the people that created the wooden letters would simply leave them off. Although most type was created from metal, the style of these wooden letters eventually became popular for metal type, too. The sans serif style did not become popular on a worldwide scale until the 1920s, when an innovative influential design school, the Bauhaus in Germany, promoted a theory of mechanical simplicity in design.

Typography   Serif face–Goudy

Typography   Sans-serif face–Futura book

FIGURE 3.10:
Serif and sans serif typefaces

Note the comparison between serif and sans serif typefaces in Fig. 3.10.

Serif typefaces, such as the typeface used in the text of this book, are in general used as text typefaces. Serif typefaces, by virtue of their finishing strokes, break up the uniformity of the page and increase its readability. Sans serif typefaces, in contrast, can give the page too much uniformity, making these typefaces more difficult to read in a textbook format. Sans serif faces are generally used for display and advertising purposes, where their relative simplicity of design is an asset and attention grabber. They can also work well when used for smaller amounts of text copy, as in a catalog or brochure. Over the years, as people have become more used to reading sans serif faces, their use for text has increased. Although some designers believe that large amounts of text should never be set in a sans serif face, there are instances when a sans serif face will function as well as a serif face for text.

Other Categories of Type

Although serif and sans serif typefaces make up the majority of fonts, there are other styles that do not fit into either category, or may fall slightly outside the pure definitions of serif and sans serif. These include slab serif, script and handlettered, blackletter, glyphic, handtooled, display, monospaced, and dingbats. Following is a brief description of each of these categories.

- **Slab serif** fonts have square or slightly rounded bold finishing strokes.
- **Script and handlettered** fonts are based on handwriting.
- **Blackletter** fonts are based on early manuscript lettering. They are also often referred to as Gothic or Old English fonts. Although they were once used for text, they are now primarily used for headlines.
- **Glyphic** fonts are based on carved or chiseled letters, or those created with a pen or brush.
- **Handtooled** fonts also give the illusion of carved letters, but with the use of outline to show dimension. They do not print well at small sizes and are generally used for headlines.
- **Display** fonts have been created for use only as headlines or in large sizes. They do not work well as text faces or at small sizes due to their unique characteristics.
- **Monospaced** fonts were originally created for typewriters. Each letter is equally spaced from the next.
- **Dingbat** fonts are picture-based, and are used for symbols and ornaments. Because they are not real letters, they cannot be used for text or display, but are instead used as pictograms or design elements to complement the type in a design.

■ WORKING WITH TYPE

Several typographic principles are used for determining the proper positioning of type, as well as the adjustment of the space between individual characters, words, and lines of type. The typographer must be aware of all of the basic design parameters to ensure maximum readability and legibility of the printed page. These principles cover word and letterspacing as well as the arrangement of text on the page.

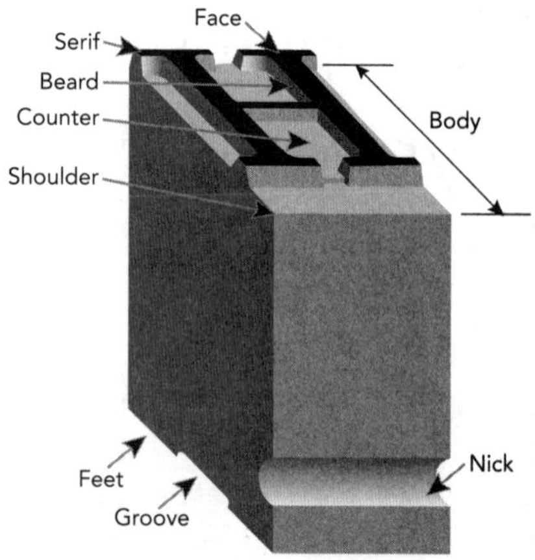

Type Nomenclature and Design
• The Point System of Measurement

Type is measured using the point system. The basic unit of this system is the *point*, which measures 1/72 of an inch. Type measurement is based on the size of the *body* of the type, which is a term carried over from the time that type was cast in metal slugs. The body is the measurement from the top of a typeface's ascender to the bottom of its descender, plus a small amount for the edge (or shoulder) of the metal slug, since the type needed to sit on the slug's surface (Fig. 3.11). What does all this mean today, when almost all type is set on computers? Because the point sys-

FIGURE 3.11:
Cast metal type slug

tem has been carried over from metal typesetting to computer typesetting, it means that you cannot measure type based on how high the letter is in points. For example, although 72 point equals one inch, a 72-point capital letter is not 1 inch high, but about 3/4 of an inch. With use, you will gain experience in choosing the right size type for your designs.

FIGURE 3.12:
Elements of type measurement

60 pt. Futura regular   60 pt. Viking

FIGURE 3.13:
The same-size character varies when set in different fonts

The second basic unit of measure, the *pica*, is used for measuring line length and column size. A pica consists of 12 points. Graphic designers use the point system because it is more precise in measuring small distances, such as the space between letters and lines, than the inch or metric system. However, the use of the computer has had an impact on the use of the pica system of measurement, and many designers and design students now use inches rather than picas while working on computer files.

• Font Measurement (Type Size)

Many different elements make up a typeface. Figure 3.12 illustrates these elements of type measurement. As explained previously, the size of type is not based on its actual size but on the size of its body. Because of this, two typefaces may look to be different sizes even though they measure to be the same size. Figure 3.13 illustrates this principle.

• Text Alignment

The horizontal alignment of text, along with paragraph alignment is as follows:

A line of type set *flush left*   A line of type set *flush right*

A line of type that is *centered*

A paragraph is said to be set *flush left, ragged right* when the left-hand margin is even and the right margin is ragged in appearance. Having a ragged right margin makes the paragraph less uniform, but also adds to its readability, because uniform word spacing is used throughout the paragraph.

Paragraphs are set *flush right, ragged left* when the right-hand margin is uniform and the left-hand margin is ragged. This paragraph arrangement is often used when alignment along the right-hand edge is critical, as in setting up formats used in restaurant menus or advertisements, for example. It doesn't work well for books or for large amounts of copy, because it is difficult to follow the ragged left margin when reading.

A paragraph is *justified* when the type is set evenly between the right and left margins. Justified type gives a very even and balanced appearance to the text. In narrow-width paragraphs, justified type may result in large spaces between the words. This is the result of the computer inserting enough space between the words to make the lines even on both ends. This effect is noticeable in many newspapers that use narrow column widths and justified columns. The wider the paragraph, the less noticeable the justified space between letters will be.

A paragraph is *centered* when each of the lines is equally spaced from a center point of the column. Centered type is the most difficult to read because both margins are ragged. Centered type is usually only used when the paragraph is short in length, such as for captions.

A paragraph can be *shaped* when using a computer program that allows for aligning text in a given shape. This can add a special effect to a page layout or advertisement. It should be kept in mind, however, that readability is always a main concern when working with type, and shaped paragraphs should not be used frivolously.

• Line Length

Proper line length is an important element in typesetting. Too short a line will result in choppy readability. Too long a line will make it difficult for the reader to achieve the continuity to easily follow to the next line. Although some graphic designers have proposed an optimum line length to follow, both of these problems are readily apparent to the eye (Fig. 3.14).

"Increasingly, meanings and attitudes are transmitted and made memorable by aural association–the jingles, the oohs and ahs of m o d e r n advertisement–and by the pictorial means of billboard and television. The read sentence is in retreat before the photograph, the television shot, the picture alphabets of comic books and training manuals. More and more, the average man reads captions into various genres of graphic material. The word is mere servant to the sensory shock."

George Steiner, Literature and Post-History

"Increasingly, meanings and attitudes are transmitted and made memorable by aural association–the jingles, the oohs and ahs of modern advertisement–and by the pictorial means of billboard and television. The read sentence is in retreat before the photograph, the television shot, the picture alphabets of comic books and training manuals. More and more, the average man reads captions into various genres of graphic material. The word is mere servant to the sensory shock."

George Steiner, Literature and Post-History

FIGURE 3.14:
Overly short and long line lengths

• Leading

Leading is the space between lines of type. The term leading comes from the thin strips of lead that were used by typositors to separate lines of foundry type when type was set by hand. Although most type is now set by computer, this term has carried over to the new technology.

Leading is measured in *points*. The process works as follows: The amount of leading is measured by adding the point size of the type to the number of points of added "lead." If you are specifying this to someone else, it is written as a fraction, with the point size on top and the leading below. For example the leading for this book is 10/13 (ten on thirteen). In theory, leading of "0" (zero) means that the descenders of one line will touch the ascenders of another. Once again, because of the system of measurement being carried over from metal typesetting, this is not true. There is a small amount of space left from the shoulder measurement that will keep the lines from touching, With computers, leading can even be set slightly into the negative without totally compromising the appearance of the page. Although this sounds like it might not look correct, the chances of ascenders and descenders touching is rare unless the negative setting is less than -2. Figure 3.15 shows a paragraph of text set with a negative leading of -2. While you would probably agree that the paragraph in Fig. 3.15 is not easy to read, the paragraph does maintain its readability.

As a general rule, minimum leading should be the same as the point size of the type used. When the leading equals the point size of the type, the job is said to be set solid. One rule of thumb for determining the leading is to use one-third of the point size of the type on the current line, plus two-thirds of the point size of type on the next line. Thus, if the copy being set is all 12-point text, the minimum leading is 12 points, measured from baseline to baseline. However, in a line of 12-point type followed by a line of 24-point type, the leading is calculated as follows:

1/3 (12-pt. type) + 2/3 (24-pt. type) = 4 + 16 = 20 points leading

• Kerning and Letterspacing

Before the invention of moveable type, books were handcopied by scribes, one at a time. The correct spacing between letters was done manually, as each line was handlettered. By the time moveable type was being cast, it was recognized that the space between certain pairs of characters needed to be balanced to achieve a proper, legible appearance. The adjustment of spacing between certain pairs of letters is called *kerning*. Most word processing, page composition, and professional typesetting programs contain information within the software to adjust these spaces automatically. Figure 3.16 illustrates some of the kerning pairs of letters.

Kerning is most important when setting a word in a large point size. Here, the type should fit together so that the characters and the white space between them are well balanced. Although computer typefaces have built-in kerning pairs, this feature does not work well with standard setting of large

"If we seek to communicate a situation or event, our problem is not to capture the *reality* of that situation, but to record or create stimuli that will affect the home listener in a manner similar to a listener's or viewer's experience in the real situation. What counts is not reality, as a scientist might measure it, but the ability to communicate the situation in a believable, human way."

Tony Schwartz–*The Responsive Chord*

FIGURE 3.15:
Leading of -2

sizes: hence, the designer often has to manually kern the letterspacing in headlines or logos. In body copy, kerning is not needed because the letterspaces do not look as uneven when using smaller type sizes.

- **Word Spacing**

The amount of space between letters and words affects the appearance of the printed page as well as its readability. If the space between words is too great, then each line of type tends to break down into individual elements rather than maintaining a single line of type where one word flows into the other. In paragraphs where the spacing between words is greater than the spacing between lines, reading becomes difficult because the eye tends to move from the top of the page to the bottom rather than from left to right. Word spacing can be set either manually or automatically. To fit copy into a smaller space, or to fill a larger space, word space can either be condensed or expanded.

When text is aligned as justified, the word spacing will be adjusted automatically to either condense or expand the word spacing for each line. Notice in Fig. 3.17 how each line has slightly different word spacing to allow the copy to be justified. It is important to not set a narrow column of type to be justified because the words will be forced to space themselves too far apart in some lines and too close together in others and gaps will be left in the column (Fig. 3.18).

- **Paragraph Color**

Paragraph color has nothing to do with what hue the type is printed in; rather, it refers to the shade of gray created by the block of text on the page. Different typefaces and different settings of alignment, leading, letterspacing, and word spacing can be used to lighten or darken a paragraph's color and to give a variety of appearances to a page. When working with a specific writing, it is important for the designer to use the color of the page to enhance the meaning of the text as written by the author. Although many typefaces are similar in color and may not change the character of the page all that much, choosing a specific typeface for its color may add an additional level of meaning to a design when used appropriately.

AT AY AV AW Ay Av Aw A' FA F. F, f' ff TO TA Ta Te To Ti Tu Ty Tw Ts Tc T. T, T: T; T- LT LY LV LW L' PA P. P, VA Va Ve Vo Vi Vr Vu VY V. V, V: V; V- RT RV RW RY Ry W. W, W: W; W- YA Ya Ye Yo Yi Yp Yu Yv Y, Y, Y. Y: Y- '' 's 't '' re ro rg rc rq rd r. r, y. y, v. v, w. w,

FIGURE 3.16:
Character kerning pairs

"If we seek to communicate a situation or event, our problem is not to capture the *reality* of that situation, but to record or create stimuli that will affect the home listener in a manner similar to a listener's or viewer's experience in the real situation. What counts is not reality, as a scientist might measure it, but the ability to communicate the situation in a believable, human way."

Tony Schwartz–The Responsive Chord

FIGURE 3.17:
Properly justified text

"If we seek to communicate a situation or event, our problem is not to capture the *reality* of that situation, but to record or create stimuli that will affect the home listener in a manner similar to a listener's or viewer's experience in the real situation. What counts is not reality, as a scientist might measure it, but the ability to communicate the situation in a believable, human way."

Tony Schwartz–The Responsive Chord

FIGURE 3.18:
Poorly justified text

Times Roman 10/11

"Increasingly, meanings and attitudes are transmitted and made memorable by aural association–the jingles, the oohs and ahs of modern advertisement–and by the pictorial means of billboard and television. The read sentence is in retreat before the photograph, the television shot, the picture alphabets of comic books and training manuals. More and more, the average man reads captions into various genres of graphic material. The word is mere servant to the sensory shock."

George Steiner, Literature and Post-History

FIGURE 3.19:
The same amount and size of type set in thee different typefaces

Helvetica Regular 10/11

"Increasingly, meanings and attitudes are transmitted and made memorable by aural association–the jingles, the oohs and ahs of modern advertisement–and by the pictorial means of billboard and television. The read sentence is in retreat before the photograph, the television shot, the picture alphabets of comic books and training manuals. More and more, the average man reads captions into various genres of graphic material. The word is mere servant to the sensory shock."

George Steiner, Literature and Post-History

Avant Garde Book 10/11

"Increasingly, meanings and attitudes are transmitted and made memorable by aural association–the jingles, the oohs and ahs of modern advertisement–and by the pictorial means of billboard and television. The read sentence is in retreat before the photograph, the television shot, the picture alphabets of comic books and training manuals. More and more, the average man reads captions into various genres of graphic material. The word is mere servant to the sensory shock."

George Steiner, Literature and Post-History

Copyfitting Techniques

Copyfitting is the process of determining how much text of a chosen typeface will fit into a given amount of space. The amount of space needed for a given amount of text varies from typeface to typeface (Fig. 3.19).

When setting the type for a book, for instance, choosing one typeface over another based solely on the font's appearance may add several pages to the length of the book. As length is usually predetermined prior to typesetting, it becomes important that the designer chooses type that will fit into the correct limits.

Before computers were available, designers used a system of calculating type character sizes, line counts, and column widths to determine how much copy would fit in any given space. This information would then be sent to the typesetter along with the final typewritten copy. After the type was set, the designer would check to make sure it was set correctly and manually paste it into the design.

With computers in the hands of designers, this process has changed dramatically. Most graphic designers today have retired their type gauges and are now able to try a variety of copyfitting options while they work on the design. This gives the designer more control over how the text will look. It also allows the designer to make fine adjustments in leading, size, kerning, and tracking to make the type fit as needed in the final design.

The E Gauge

One of the tools previously used in calculating copy is still very handy for the graphic designer. This tool is referred to as an *E gauge* (Fig. 3.20). It is simply a clear piece of plastic printed with a capital "E" in various point sizes, along with scales marked with different leading amounts. The E gauge is most useful when the designer must reproduce an existing printed piece, such as an ad or page layout. Rather than guessing at the point size, leading, and column width, the E gauge can be placed over the existing copy to determine these measurements. It is then an easy task to reproduce the design, either manually or on a computer.

E gauges are available in varying qualities of manufacture. Inexpensive ones are less accurate than expensive ones, but work well for basic measurements. High-quality gauges are printed with fine, accurate dimensions on a special thin mylar. They will not shrink or expand with temperature changes and are also flexible enough to measure curved surfaces. New E gauges that include various computer-specific annotations such as pixel measurement and inch-to-decimal conversion have recently been introduced.

Notations and Proofreading Symbols

All copy needs to be proofed and often changed during the design process. To aid communication among writers, editors, and designers, a standard system of proofreader's marks is used. This saves each person time by being able to quickly "mark up" text changes so that they may be understood by everyone working with the text.

In marking up text, two sets of marks are used. One is the actual correction, which is placed in the margin area where it can be seen easily. Each correction should be placed next to the line to be corrected. The second mark (a caret—^) is placed at the point of correction. The chart shown in Fig. 3.21 shows a full range of both sets of proofreader's marks.

■ SUMMARY

In this chapter, we discussed the developments in typesetting and the fundamental principles used in working with type. The ability to create exceptional graphic design works with type is a learned art. Through an understanding of the basic principles of type use, the beginning designer has a foundation from which to build on. As you work with type in your designs, you will begin to see how the many facets of its design and use can be manipulated to create original, exciting graphic communication.

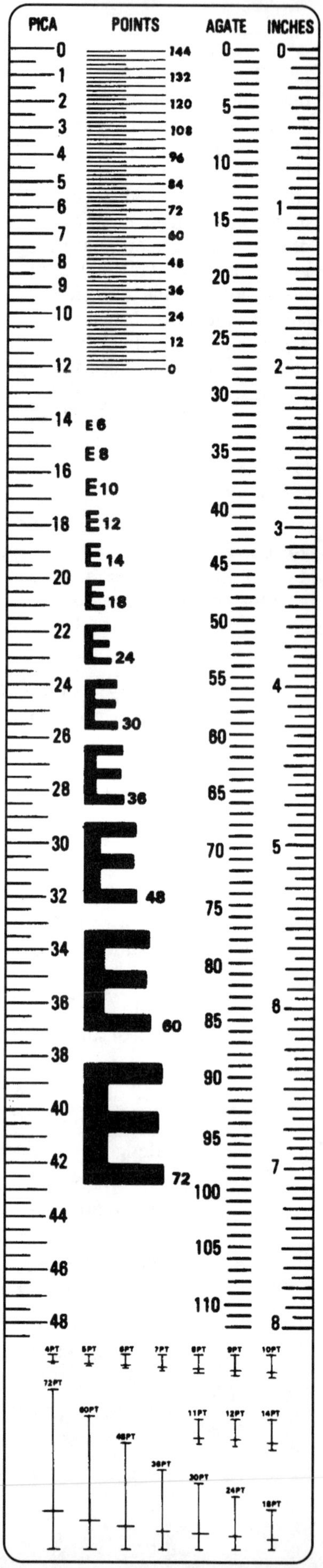

FIGURE 3.20:
An E gauge (actual size)

Correction needed	Mark in margin	Mark in text
Period	⊙	∧
Comma	⌃	∧
Apostrophe	⌄	∧
Open quotes	⌄⌄	∧
Close quotes	⌄⌄	∧
Semicolon	;/	∧
Colon	⊙	∧
Hyphen	=/	∧
Dash	N̄	∧
Parentheses	( )	∧
Brackets	[ ]	∧
Delete text	ℓ	/ or ✐ or ___ through text
Insert omitted text	out	∧
Disregard correction	stet	dot under character
Make new paragraph	⌗	∧
Indent	☐	⊐
Remove paragraph, run text together	run in	⌇
Move right	⊐	⊐
Move left	⊏	⊏
Raise	⊓	⊓
Lower	⊔	⊔
Center	ctr	⌐ ¬
Flush left	fl L	⊏
Flush right	fl R	⊐
Align horizontally	=	lines at correction
Align vertically	‖	lines at correction
Transpose	tr	⎍
Insert space	#	∧
Equalize space	eq sp	∧∧∧
Close up space	◡	◡
Wrong font	wf	circle
Lower case	lc	/ through character
Capitals	cap	≡
Small caps	sc	=
Roman text	rom	circle
Italic text	ital	—
Bold text	bf	∿
Superior character	∨3	∧
Inferior character	∧3	∧
Broken type	×	circle
Invert type	↺	circle
Move type down	⊥	circle
Spell out name	sp	circle
Question for author	who?	∧ or circle

FIGURE 3.21:
Proofreader's marks

■ SUGGESTED STUDENT ACTIVITIES

1. Pick three different emotions and choose a typeface to represent each.

2. Handletter your first and last name in a serif typeface at a large size (200 points). Pay attention to the kerning of each letter as it relates to the next character. Look for consistency of stroke weight and detail of each letter in the typeface chosen. Repeat the process with a sans serif typeface and compare the two.

3. Choose three different typefaces that you feel would work well together in a page layout. Discuss what makes them work together and how each would be used on the page.

4. Set a paragraph of copy in three different typefaces at the same point size, leading, and paragraph alignment. Note the differences among each in length, character, and color.

5. Experiment with creating a hierarchy of type on a page using three words in different typefaces and sizes. Note how changing the parameters of one word affects the other words on the page.

Chapter 4 THE DESIGN PROCESS

Chapter 4 THE DESIGN PROCESS

■ INTRODUCTION

This chapter discusses the basic problem-solving techniques applicable to a graphic design project. At the end of this chapter, six graphic communication design problems will be explored. We will also explain how to approach these projects using the problem-solving model presented in this chapter, from initial design concept to execution of the final printed piece.

■ THE GRAPHIC DESIGN PROBLEM-SOLVING MODEL

The problem-solving model explained here is a method that graphic designers use to provide the best possible solution to a given graphic design problem. It highlights the decisions faced by a designer in creating a typical design job. Following this model will assist you in creating better designed projects in a timely fashion.

Figure 4.1 shows a graphic representation of the graphic design problem-solving model.

Defining the Problem

The most important step in creating an effective graphic communication is to properly define the problem at hand. Although this may appear easy, decisions made at this stage will affect later phases of the project and will relate directly to the success or failure of the job.

All clients have a basic idea of what they are looking for when they hire a graphic designer. For example, the designer may be asked to design a specific item such as a logo or brochure. Or, the job may be more general, such as creating graphics for an upcoming event, where the choice of what form those graphics take is up to the designer. In any case, this is the time for the designer to ask specific questions to determine the client's exact expectations for the project.

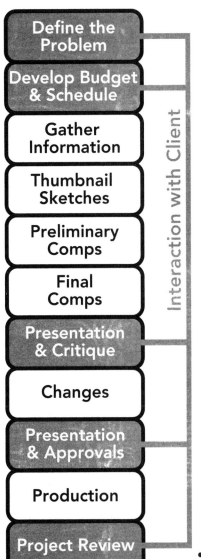

Interaction with Client

- Define the Problem
- Develop Budget & Schedule
- Gather Information
- Thumbnail Sketches
- Preliminary Comps
- Final Comps
- Presentation & Critique
- Changes
- Presentation & Approvals
- Production
- Project Review

FIGURE 4.1:
The graphic design problem-solving model

This part of the design process can be confusing if the client is vague in his or her expectation and simply states, "I want a new logo." In this case, the graphic designer needs to find out what the client feels a new logo will accomplish and assist in deciding if that is the best form of communication for the client's business. For example, the client may want the new logo to reflect a change in his or her business, which will bring in new clients.

When designing the logo, you also would need to know how the new design would be implemented. Will it be used only on business cards? If so, how many cards has the client given out in the past? If only a few have been used previously, the designer might want to recommend other ways of implementing the logo so that a greater number of potential customers will be exposed to it. For a small business, this might mean taking out ads in the local newspapers or sending out flyers. For a larger business, it might mean national television spots and billboards for more extensive coverage.

Properly defining the problem means first finding out what the design should accomplish, and then determining the best form for the design to take to accomplish those ends. As a graphic designer, clients will look to you to assist them in choosing the best way to communicate their messages. Professional expertise in handling the job will build a good designer–client relationship.

Developing Budgets and Schedules

After determining the parameters of the job, a budget and schedule must be developed to successfully complete the project within cost and on time. These two areas have a major effect on the project's outcome and they should be considered carefully at the start of every job.

• Budget

A project budget is developed in consultation with the client. After the initial meeting to determine what services will be provided, the designer develops a preliminary budget. Charges for time, costs for other people who work on the project (such as production help, illustrators, photographers, and programmers), and costs for materials and production of the final design piece all need to be taken into consideration.

Cost-Estimating Techniques

Many references are available to assist graphic designers in estimating costs. These range from consultation with other designers about their fees to books and periodicals published by the design industry, such as the Graphic Artists Guild *Guide to Pricing and Ethical Guidelines*. Large design firms have set rates for charges; if you work for such a firm, you will not have to be involved in the process except to estimate your time for the job. When self-employed, however, there are steps to aid you in determining what you should charge.

A simple way to figure what you need to charge for a job is to first determine what you need each month to run your office or studio. The costs for rental of space, equipment, insurance, and general monthly office supplies should be included in this figure. This amount is divided by the number of hours you plan on working each month. The results in your hourly rate needed to make ends meet. Of course, this will not be enough to make a profit! Therefore, you will need to increase that amount to make a fair profit. Most designers add 20–50% to the rate for profit.

Another cost-estimating technique is to charge on a per-project, flat-rate fee. To do this, you will have to do some research into what project charges currently are in your geographical area. Local design organizations may have discussion groups or printed information available to help in this process. It is important to remember that design fees will vary from state to state and from job to job. For example, a large corporation should pay more for a logo than a local business because the corporation's logo will be used more extensively.

When figuring out your personal design fees, do not undervalue your own work. If you charge too little, you will not get satisfaction out of the job, and you will not gain the client's respect. Graphic design is a business, and treating it as one will increase your chances of success in the field.

Charges for subcontractors, such as illustrators, photographers, other designers, and/or computer programmers involved in the design process, must be included in your bid. Therefore, you will need to get a firm estimate from these persons. It will be your responsibility to pay these subcontractors, so it is not uncommon to add a reasonable additional charge to their bids to cover your costs.

Costs for paper, printing, and other production materials for the final production run round out the final cost estimates. These costs can be listed as a lump sum on the bid or itemized if requested by the client. Most design studios add a 10 to 25% surcharge to all supplies they buy for the client. In effect, they are making a loan to the client by purchasing the materials. By doing so, they are justified in charging an interest fee for this loan. If the client wants to pay for the printing charges directly, you can quote the actual cost; however, be sure to specify on the bid that it is the client's responsibility to have the work printed. It is also a good idea to describe on the bid how changes to the design will be handled. Most designers will cover the first round of changes at no additional charge, but some clients may demand more than a few initial changes. Because of this possibility, you should specify on the bid the billing rate for additional changes.

When the bid is presented to the client, go over it item by item to ensure that the client understands all the charges involved. It is important to have the client sign off on the bid. Signed copies should be made for each of you to minimize any future misunderstandings of costs at a later date.

It is good business practice to get from 15 to 50% of the costs of the job from the client after the bid agreement is signed. For the designer, it indicates that the client is comfortable with the price of the job. Also be aware that a client who is unwilling to pay any money at this stage may also be reluctant to pay later!

The bid process is both challenging and constraining. Not only does it lock the client into the amount to be paid, but it also locks the designer into the same figure. If you underestimate the job, the money comes out of your pocket! In time, however, you will find that the bidding process becomes a normal part of the design practice.

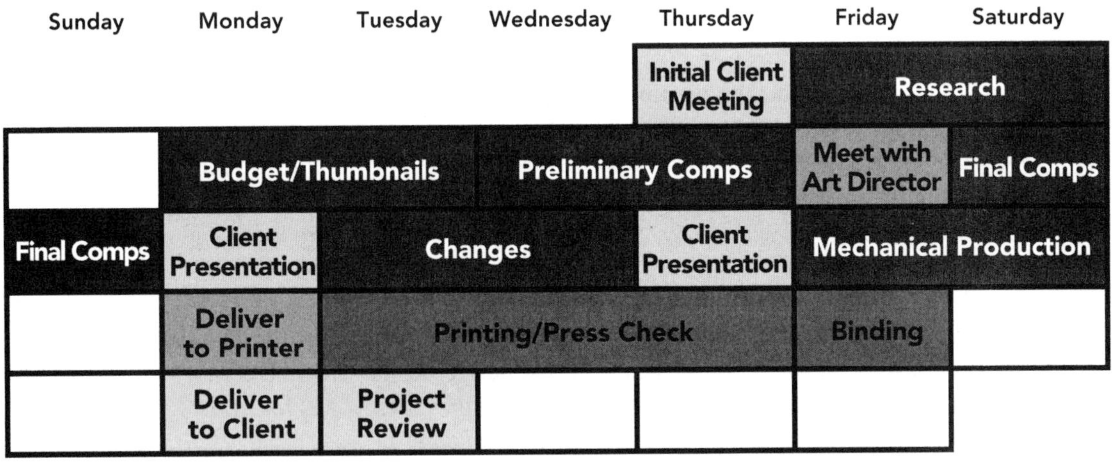

Sunday	Monday	Tuesday	Wednesday	Thursday	Friday	Saturday
				Initial Client Meeting	Research	
	Budget/Thumbnails		Preliminary Comps		Meet with Art Director	Final Comps
Final Comps	Client Presentation	Changes		Client Presentation	Mechanical Production	
	Deliver to Printer	Printing/Press Check			Binding	
	Deliver to Client	Project Review				

FIGURE 4.2:
Sample project schedule

• Developing a Schedule

A project schedule helps keep the project on track and assists the designer in juggling more than one project at a time. In most design offices, schedulers take a graphic approach to creating a weekly or monthly chart, which is then posted where it can be referred to easily. Figure 4.2 shows a sample schedule for a job.

When developing a schedule, it is best to work in reverse, starting with the delivery date of the job to the client. From there, it can be determined how much time is needed to finish each phase of the project. Here are two very important tips when working with schedules:

• Do not assume that any subcontractors you hire will be able to adapt to your schedule. Call all the other parties involved in the project (illustrator, photographer, paper supplier, printer, etc.) and get a commitment for the dates required. Certain items, such as paper, may have to be specially ordered, and the time needed for such special orders should be factored into the schedule. Most printing firms reserve time on the press for each job. Be sure you get your job to them on time, or you may have to pay for time the press is sitting idle.

• Do not procrastinate. You may be able to design a job overnight, but as stated previously, you are rarely the only one involved. It is important to remember that each phase of the project takes time to get finished, and missing one deadline can cause the entire project to suffer!

Gathering Information

Information gathering is an integral part of the design process and is a process that continues through all phases of a project. This research can take many forms, from talking to the client to hiring a professional research firm. The amount of research needed largely depends on the size of the job, the budget, and the timeframe allowed for the project.

• Why Research?

The answer to this question is easy. Research helps you to better understand the project, to see variations that others have done in similar areas of design, and to see what options are available. With the proper research, a mediocre project can become an outstanding one.

• What to Research

Although the exact kinds of information that needs to be gathered will vary for each project, some basic things must be done for each project. These include looking into what has been done before, seeing what the competition is currently using, and determining what the potential is for your job—let's call these three categories *past, present,* and *future.*

Past

Design has a rich history. Many design books are available, with excellent photographs of items created for all types of needs. For example, if you are designing a logo, you could easily find thousands of examples of logo designs printed in books. Looking at these examples can give you a sense of how logos have been used for many different and various-sized companies from around the world.

When doing historical research, it is important to remember that you are looking for inspiration—not the answer to your problem. Plagiarism in design, as in any field, is illegal and unethical, and can end up getting you in trouble if your client or the originator of the copied design happens to see a design similar to theirs elsewhere. There are many cases where a student or professional designer, short on time and with a deadline rapidly approaching, fell to the temptation of taking someone else's design and "changing it a bit" to get something done on time. For professional designers, this can land them in court for copyright infringement.

Present

Competition is everywhere. You want to make sure your design stands out from the competition, but not so much that it looks like something entirely different in context. For example, you would not want a liquor bottle label to look like a liquid soap bottle label! The best way to see how your ideas fit in is to find out what other companies that sell the same or similar products are using in their designs. Go to libraries, supermarkets, and stores where the competition's products can be found. Many design publications feature good examples of contemporary design. It is a good idea to subscribe to a few of them.

Future

This category is important of the three because well-executed research here will affect the final outcome of your design. Research of the future is essentially research of the present, with a focus on finding the best available materials for your design in progress. It may mean calling paper merchants for the latest samples, talking to an architect or industrial designer to find out about innovations in materials in their respective industries, visiting trade shows, or even looking at common materials from a different perspective. By doing this, you can create a design that will stand out above the competition. Think about how your design will be used after it is completed. Consider its longevity, ability to be recycled, and impact on the environment if it cannot be recycled.

• Where to Research

Gathering information can take a great deal of time, so it is a good idea to build a listing of local contacts that can assist you in the process. Some large design studios have full-time research assistants. If you are working alone, make a list of telephone numbers and contacts at local public and college libraries, design studios, paper merchants, and printers. These sources can be helpful in answering particular questions that may arise during your workday.

In addition to using local college and community libraries, you should build your own library of reference materials. Along with books and magazines, create files on different subject matters that you would like to see yourself working with in the future. Files of photos and illustrations can also come in handy when you have to prepare a quick sketch and need a visual reference.

The Internet can also provide a good source of information but it can also be problematic. Whereas books and magazines have large staffs of writers, proofreaders, and editors to check that information is correct and consistent, the Internet is literally open for anyone who wishes to post a Web page. This means that information may be out of date, inaccurate, or even "made up." Be careful to check any information you find on the Internet against other reliable sources before using it. Also, be careful to avoid the temptation to copy information off the Internet to use as your own. This is plagiarism, and most instructors can find the sites as easily as you did if they have concerns about your work. Do not rely on the Internet as a source for images to include in a design. Most work is copyrighted and it is illegal to use an image created by another artist without written permission. Also, images taken from the Internet are usually 72 dpi images and the resolution is too low for proper printing.

Although the idea of networking; that is, "talking to strangers" is a frightening one for some people, making an effort to introduce yourself to others at social and professional functions can pay off later. You never know when you will meet someone who may be able to assist you with a problem at a later date! Because the design profession works in an interdisciplinary manner and deals in communications, almost anyone can be a valuable ally when you need specialized information. It's a good idea to join local or national design organizations while still a student; they often provide benefits that can assist you in finding information.

■ STARTING A DESIGN PROJECT
Thumbnail Sketches

Initial sketches, referred to as *thumbnail sketches* or simply *thumbnails,* are the first step in any design project. Thumbnails allow you to explore ideas visually, without trying to find any "definite" solution to the design problem at hand. They are a method for visual thinking. Always explore a variety of ideas for every project. When doing thumbnails, don't rush to find the "right" solution to the design problem. Instead, use this process to play with many different ways of thinking about the problem.

The creation of thumbnails can start at any time—even at the first meeting with the client—but primarily are done during and after the research phase. These sketches are the main part of the conceptual process. In creating thumbnails, remember that you are generating ideas and approaches to solving the problem, not just looking for "the answer." Therefore, thumbnail sketches are often small, lack specific detail, and are quickly executed, as shown in Fig. 4.3.

Thumbnails can be created anywhere and on almost anything. Many designers say that their best ideas have been developed on napkins at restaurants. Because no special materials are needed to produce them, thumbnails

FIGURE 4.3:
Thumbnails

are often the part of the process graphic designers enjoy the most. Thumbnails help the designer to think visually about the problem at hand and are the first step to a creative solution.

It is best to avoid using the computer to try to create thumbnail ideas. The computer doesn't allow for the process necessary to create a variety of ideas quickly. Most people, when exploring conceptual ideas on a computer, have a tendency to spend too much time refining a single idea. The purpose of creating thumbnails is to create a wide variety of simple ideas in a short amount of time. They can be refined later.

Preliminary Comps

Taking one or more of the thumbnail ideas, a designer develops a *preliminary composite* (commonly known as a comp and sometimes referred to as a rough comp or a "rough"). This is first used to see how a thumbnail idea will work at actual size and is more detailed than the thumbnail sketch. Type is rendered more accurately, color is introduced, and decisions about photography or illustrations are implied in the preliminary comps. These comps may be created on a computer or by hand. The designer should always remember, however, that although the computer can produce a finished-looking work, this is still a rough idea, not yet fully developed at this stage of the process.

FIGURE 4.4:
Preliminary comp

Depending on how detailed a preliminary comp is, it may be used for presentations, either to superiors in a design firm or to the client. It is important to present preliminary comps to the client as beginning *ideas*, and although they may look finished (especially if executed by computer), the client should be encouraged to suggest changes as needed. These are not finished designs at this stage! Figure 4.4 shows an example of a preliminary comp done by hand.

Final Comps

Final comps are the closest example of how the final job will look. These are most often done with the use of a computer, using the actual typefaces and colors of

the final design with all the required elements in place. In effect, you are trying to produce a comp that is the closest it can be to the actual finished product without paying for production and printing or manufacturing (see Fig. 4.5). Final comps of several of the best concepts are prepared for presentation to the client.

In summary, notice how the design changes with each phase of the project. Ideas created at the thumbnail stage are evaluated, refined, and developed into final comps, with many changes along the way. Rarely, if ever, does a thumbnail idea make it through to a final design without significant changes and input from many various people. The problem-solving model assists the designer in developing the best ideas to the final stages, allowing time for evaluation during the design process.

FIGURE 4.5:
Final comp

■ PRESENTATIONS

The First Presentation

The initial presentation to the client is very important. It is your opportunity to show the client how your design solutions address his or her concerns and at the same time get feedback for any changes. The presentation should be approached professionally. All work should be mounted to same-sized boards protected with overlays of tissue or paper.

Usually, several of the best design ideas are presented to the client. Sometimes, a few others are prepared in reserve in case the client responds negatively to the initial ideas. Most designers try to pick three or four good ideas that will show a variety of approaches to the problem, rather than variations of only one idea. This way they can get feedback on the entire process instead of risking it all on a single concept. How many are chosen to be presented often depends on time, budget, and client requests.

The success of the first presentation depends on the designer's ability to answer any questions the client has about the designs. It is a good idea to prepare a short verbal introduction of the work to be presented, briefly going over your development process and stressing how your solutions best meet the client's needs. Do not assume the client remembers everything he or she said at the initial meeting. The client has most likely been involved in many other issues while you have been focusing on this one. Be sure to review the project from the beginning and repeat any points on which you have received positive feedback during previous meetings with co-workers or the client. Design jobs are often won by a well-thought-out verbal presentation that complements the visual one.

After the presentation, the client should initial any approvals or minor changes to be made. If the client does not approve any of the designs, it is important to discuss the project further before proceeding. Generally, most designers will meet with the client for a second presentation at no extra charge. More than one round of changes often requires that the client pay an additional fee. Charges to clients for changes should be spelled out carefully in your budget proposal.

Some clients may be more involved in the design process than others and will want to see rough ideas as well. A word of caution: Be careful not to show the client too many initial ideas. This may weaken the effect of your best ones. Also, never present anything to your client that you are not happy with yourself. The client just might pick the idea you don't like, and there is no point in designing something that you would not be proud to include in your portfolio.

Critique

At the presentation, the client will have the opportunity to critique your work. This can often be a nervous time for you as a designer, even if you are confident that you have done what is best for the client. Critique of your work should never be seen as a negative event, but one to allow for the exchange and refinement of your ideas with the client. Be open to the comments given and do not be afraid to explain your concepts when necessary. During the critique, make notes and changes to the work on an overlay so that you will remember what should be altered when you get back to the office. Be careful not to become defensive or let your feelings be visibly hurt by the client during the meeting. You will find that some clients are easier to deal with than others, but you should always keep in mind that you are working together on the project to achieve the best outcome for everyone involved.

Changes and Correction

When you are asked to make changes or corrections in your design, be careful to make only those changes requested by the client. It is easy to be tempted to further refine the design after the presentation. If the client does not like changes you initiated, however, you will be required to change it back on your own time. If you feel it is necessary to make changes other than those specified by the client, go back for approval before proceeding or present your new ideas on a separate comp to be discussed with the client.

Final Presentation

A final review is necessary if many changes were required by the client, approvals were not given at the first presentation, or if the client requests it. Depending on the client, this presentation may have to be even more polished than the first one. For example, in a package design job, you might have shown mounted renderings at the first meeting and actual models of the packages for the final presentation. If the client signs off on the project after this presentation, it is time to go into production.

■ PRODUCTION

Production techniques vary from one project to another (this is discussed further in Chapter 11). What is most important is that the chosen production method best fulfills both your and your client's expectations of what the final production design should be. As a professional designer, you will always be looking for the best quality at the lowest price. Making sure the production mechanicals are executed professionally and accurately will ensure that the final project is completed correctly. Be sure to check with the printer or fabricator to make sure any computer files are in the correct format for their use. Always make back-up copies of final computer files for yourself in case they are needed at another time.

■ FINAL PROJECT REVIEW

After the job has been produced, it is important that you give it one last look before moving on. The client may be involved in this critique, or it may be done with a design team or by you alone. This is an opportunity to review how well the project met its intended goals. Also look for problems that should be kept in mind for the next job, and evaluate your involvement and the involvement of others in the design process. It is valuable to make notes of the problems and successes of each project so that you can learn what steps will aid you in the future. In printed work, the first evaluation is done as the item comes off the press by checking that the visual elements (color, registration, print and paper quality) have turned out correctly. Evaluation of how well the design met its intended function is done after the piece has been distributed to its intended audience. In projects such as signage, you may want to check the project after a few months or years to see how well the specified materials held up in the location in which it was installed.

■ APPLICATIONS OF THE GRAPHIC DESIGN PROBLEM-SOLVING MODEL

Following are several examples of the problem-solving model as it is applied in graphic design. Each step of the process is explained in terms of how it applies to the particular piece of design.

Your Résumé

A résumé (Fig. 4.6) is a simple piece of graphic design and one that every design student will eventually need. As you are both client and designer in this case, many of the steps are handled informally. Although this is not a true graphic design project in terms of the designer–client relationship, it is a good exercise to get you started thinking about applying the design process.

Defining the problem is important. The purpose of a résumé is clear—to get you a job. What you need to think about is what the résumé will say about you in its design and how this is reflected in the style of the résumé. To whom will the résumé be sent? What would they be interested in? Does it need to be faxed? Can it be provided on disk? Is a scanable copy necessary?

Budget and schedule are easy in this application. How much can you afford? Can you afford to have it printed, or should it be photocopied? When do you need to send it out? All these questions will determine your budget and schedule.

FIGURE 4.6:
Sample résumé

Some points to consider: Although a printed résumé will often look better, it is more expensive and does not readily allow for changes. Also, the printing process may take up to a few weeks to complete. Some designers print the masthead, which they can also use for cover letter and invoices, then run the printed letterhead through a laser or ink jet printer to print the résumé information. Whether the résumé is printed or photocopied, what kind of paper should it be on? If the paper is special order, how much of it will you need? How long will it take to get it? This list could go on, but you can see that there are quite a few decisions to be made for even a simple project.

Regarding the research aspect of the job, you may want to look at résumés of other people in the same field. This is not always an option, but if you have friends looking for similar positions, ask to see theirs. You can also check with employment services for assistance in résumé preparation for different jobs.

In the design process, you should do a few quick thumbnail sketches of various layout ideas. Also, look at several typefaces and try them together in a sample layout.

For feedback in the presentation phase of the job, show the rough design to friends and your instructor. Ask them if they find it clear and easy to understand—the most important part of résumé design. Carefully examine the résumé for spelling and consistency errors. All phone numbers and state names should be listed the same way throughout the résumé. For example, a common mistake is to put "Wisconsin" in one place, "W.I." in another, and "WI" in yet another. This inconsistency disrupts the flow of the document. If you know people who own a business similar to the one to which you are applying, be sure to ask them for feedback. Their opinion will be important because they are likely to see many résumés from job applicants. Test faxing a copy to yourself or a friend to see how well it transmits. Make a photocopy of the résumé, too.

After any necessary changes are made, get your resume produced and send it out. In this case, you will know how well you have done by the response you get in your job search!

Business Letterhead

Designing a letterhead may involve designing a logo, or applying a logo that has been supplied to you by the client to stationery. In the following example we use the latter case and discuss the process involved in applying an existing logo.

A letterhead (Fig. 4.7) is a fairly straightforward design. You want it to reflect the style of the business and allow enough room for correspondence. In defining the problem, ask your clients the following questions:

1. What is the average length of the letters they write? This will help you to determine whether to use a full or half sheet, or if they will need a second page.

2. Do they most often write by hand, use a typewriter, or use a word processor? Each has its own format considerations. For a word processor, for example, you could create a file with their logo for them to print at any time.

FIGURE 4.7:
Business letterhead

3. How many sheets do they plan to have printed? This will help you to figure costs. It is cheaper per piece to print a large number of multicolor pieces than to print only a few.

4. What can they afford to spend? Along with the previous question, this will aid you in determining how much you can afford for printing and paper. The client may not always be ready to answer this question immediately, but may want you to price the job several ways and then compare those costs.

In gathering research information, look to design books on letterhead and to letterheads of other businesses dealing in similar goods or services.

Creating thumbnails for a letterhead is like playing with a kit full of parts. You have a few elements: logo, address, phone and fax numbers, perhaps an e-mail address, and Internet URL. You want to put them together in a way that makes the best sense for your client. In your sketches, try various placements to see the visual effects they create, testing symmetry/asymmetry, foreground/background, and so on. After the exploration of thumbnails, create several tighter versions to present to the client.

In your presentation, show each letterhead in context. Place a fictitious letter (or a real one from the client) on the page to show how the stationery will look in use. Mount each design on a separate board so that you can easily eliminate any designs that are not in the running. Listen to the client and note any changes needed. Have the client sign off on the design if it is approved.

After the final design is approved, you only need to create the mechanicals and have the letterhead printed.

In reviewing the final product, make note of the following: Was the design produced accurately to your specifications? Are the colors correct? Is the printing crisp and the type sharp? How does the paper work with the design? How well does the design work in use? Is it easy to use, fold, and mail?

FIGURE 4.8:
Package label

Label Design

When designing a label for a package (Fig. 4.8), the designer must take several more considerations into account than with a resume or letterhead. In the following example, we show how these considerations fit into the design process.

When defining the problem, the designer should find out the pre-existing product specifications, including package size, materials, and copy to appear on the label. Further questions about budget and deadlines should also be asked.

73

A schedule and budget should be developed next. When preparing the budget, the designer needs to speak directly with a package design printer. This is a very specialized printing field and labels for different products have to be printed in different ways. Things to consider here include whether the label is to be printed on a box, attached to a bottle, or applied directly to a surface, such as silk-screening on glass. Each process has special considerations that will affect the design.

In addition to the printing research, the designer also needs to investigate the design of competing brands. Usually, the easiest way to do this is to make a trip to a local store that carries competing products. While at the store, be sure not only to examine the competitor's packages individually, but also to notice how the packages are displayed on the shelf. Packages, when displayed as a group, can create a different visual impression than when viewed individually. You may want to purchase several examples of the competition so you can later test how your design will look alongside them in your studio.

When starting the thumbnails, check the notes you have made thus far. Does your research suggest a more thorough design than the client originally suggested? For instance, you might now feel that the bottle should be redesigned to make it stand out more distinctly from the competition. If so, you should make the client aware of your concerns before going further. If not, be sure to work on an idea that will make your design stand out above the rest, but yet have good shelf presence. Think about how to use color and typography to create a distinctive package.

Again, based on the client's needs, review your thumbnails to determine which designs should be worked up to a rough stage. In the rough, you will be able to see which of your designs will work best at actual size, with color and typography treated more accurately.

At the first presentation, you will be showing several of your best concepts. For packaging at this stage, you will probably be showing only a rendering of the front of the package. The objective here is to give the client an impression of the overall look of the package, not to show every side of the package in detail. If the client chooses one or more of the designs for you to take further, you will bring the completed designs to the final presentation meeting. In the packaging business, this phase of the project may also involve the use of marketing professionals and focus groups— groups of people from a specific social and economic range that the client is targeting for the product. Often the designer is not involved in this phase except to create a variety of comps to be presented.

When changes or corrections are made in a label, it is time for you to get to the specifics of the final label. There are many rules for applying nutritional information and requirements for the Universal Product Code (UPC or bar code). These guidelines must be followed precisely. The final design is often mocked up to resemble the package in three-dimensional form, either constructed as a foamboard box or applied to a bottle to present to the client.

Once the client approves the final design, mechanicals must be made to send to the printer. These are most often done on the computer; wherein the design is given to the printer as an electronic file to create the color separations.

In conducting a final project review, go back to the store and see how the product looks on the shelf. Does it stand out from the competition? Does it meet the client's expectations? Is the printing of high quality? If you designed the package

MEMBERSHIP APPLICATION

1959 Vespa 400 Convertible

FIGURE 4.9:
Brochure

FIGURE 4.10:
Thumbnail sketches

itself, check the fit and finish of its construction. Take notes on your observations for reference when doing similar projects in the future.

Brochure

Here we trace an actual job and present a case study for a tri-fold brochure created for a car club (Fig. 4.9). The brochure used in this example includes textual information, a membership application form, photographs, and illustrations. The steps reflect how these elements came together to create the final brochure.

In the initial client meeting in this case study, the basic needs of the client were discussed: What will the piece be used for? What will it communicate? How many pieces are to be printed? What is the budget for the piece? With this information, printing estimates from several printers were requested to determine the best way to produce the brochure.

In the case study, the designer found that the client had a limited budget, so the design was created to follow these specifications: standard tri-fold brochure, 8.5 x 11-inch paper; one color ink; printed two-sided. The budget did allow for special paper, so different stocks and weights were investigated.

As mentioned, the client in this example was an international car club for small cars, "The Microcar & Minicar Club." They already had a logo and gave the designer a variety of images from their archives to use in the brochure. Additional research for imagery was unnecessary in this case because the designer had more than enough images from which to choose. The designer did, however, talk extensively with representatives from the club to determine which cars were the most popular and should be featured in the brochure. As this brochure was to be used as a membership application, some additional research into form design was done at the local library.

Thumbnail sketches were done, exploring different placements of the logo, photos, and text (Fig. 4.10).

From the thumbnails, three initial ideas were worked up to size on the computer. The designer, referring back to notes made at the initial client meeting and to specifications given to him by the printer, determined that two of the comps best met the client's needs. These were completed as final comps to show to the client. For the final comps, the designer laser-printed the designs on several types of paper and folded them to give the client some different perspectives on how the design could look.

The client decided to go with an uncoated paper that had a light blue fiber woven into it. To complement this, the designer suggested using a dark blue ink rather than black. This was approved by the client (a Pantone®

75

color ink guide was brought to the meeting to show the client different ink choices. You can read more about the Pantone® color system in Chapter 5. The client signed off on the final design and the piece went into production.

In reviewing the final printed piece, the designer checked ink quality, how well the paper folded, ink coverage across the folded areas, and alignment of the paper when folded (one photograph was placed to cross over a folded section as shown in Fig. 4.11). Feedback from the club was very positive. The brochure was easy to mail, and the professional look of the piece helped to increase the membership!

■ SUMMARY

This chapter has shown how the graphic design problem-solving model can be applied to various design jobs. You will find that using this process in your own design jobs will help you to be better organized. It will also help you to create more appropriate solutions for your clients and assure that your solutions meet the expectations of both you and your clients.

FIGURE 4.11:
Detail of folding design

■ SUGGESTED STUDENT ACTIVITIES

1. Choose a decade since 1890 and research the styles of graphic design found within that decade. How did the design styles reflect the culture of the time? How do the designs from the past look compared with the designs from today? What similarities do they share, if any?

2. For a given design project, try to create as many thumbnail sketches as you can within a half hour. After completion, look carefully at your ideas for the following:

    (a). The total number you were able to accomplish.

    (b). A wide variety of ideas (try not to do variations on a single idea).

    (c). Varied use of composition and emphasis.

    (d). Your overall use of typographic and image elements. Compare your ideas to others in your class (assuming they do the exercise, too).

3. Prepare a presentation about a particular process (for example, changing a tire). Make the initial presentation verbally or in written form. Then create the same presentation using only images (drawings, photographs, or symbols). Take note of how many images you need to explain the process clearly with images alone.

4. Create three different design ideas for a book cover in comp form. For one, create the comp entirely with found images and type (from cut-up magazines). For another, create the comp using only hand skills (colored pencil, marker, paint). For the third, create the comp on the computer. Notice how the materials affect your design ideas and note the strengths and weaknesses of each process.

5. Find two pieces of graphic design: one that you feel works well and one that you feel is not working. In a group critique in class, with other students doing the same exercise, present the good work and explain why you feel it works. Do the same with the bad piece. Have each person in the critique respond with their viewpoints and vote on each piece at the end as to whether it belongs in the "working" or "not working" category. When everyone is finished, discuss what elements the work in each category share.

Chapter 5   ELEMENTS OF CREATIVE GRAPHIC DESIGN

Chapter 5   ELEMENTS OF CREATIVE GRAPHIC DESIGN

Understand the Elements of Type and Image

Examine Style in Design

Understand Graphic Elements

Develop and Understanding of Type Selection

Investigate Methods of Page Layout

Understand Color Usage in Graphic Design

Understand Paper Selection

■ INTRODUCTION

Good communication is primarily simple and direct. Just as it is hard to pick out one voice in a crowd it is equally as difficult to see the message in an overly complex piece of graphic design. Yet, most inexperienced designers often try to put too much into their work, as in Fig. 5.1. This leaves the viewer trying to figure out what is being communicated and results in quickly losing the viewer's attention.

Achieving clear communication in graphic design is not always easy, however. Clients sometimes want the graphic designer to fit a large amount of information into the given space, which can be a challenge. This chapter helps you find some ways to organize space and shows you how to combine type and imagery on a page to create good designs with clear communication.

■ TYPE AND IMAGE

Type and image are the two major elements with which every designer works. Type communicates written information; image supports the text and adds to the visual interest of the piece. It is important to understand how each of these elements works both individually and with each another.

Type is a part of virtually every piece of graphic design. It is the element that directly informs the viewer of your message. It is the most challenging of the two elements, and the most easily

FIGURE 5.1:

An overly complex design

overlooked by beginning designers. Working creatively with type is a learned art; therefore, it is important that you never think of type as something that you are forced to "deal with," but rather as the most important design element.

Image, unlike type, can rarely stand on its own and still communicate a complete idea. Except in the case of pictograms, such as road signs, visual images work hand in hand with the written information, first to attract the viewer's attention and then to supplement the text. A good designer chooses images that work with the text to create well-communicated ideas and messages.

Two categories of images are used in graphic design: photography and illustration. The designer chooses which category will work best with the design he or she is creating. This decision is made during the initial stages of the project—generally when making thumbnails and more specifically when creating preliminary comps. In designs where accurate representation is needed, a photographic image is usually the choice. Where more freedom is available, or when a concept that would be difficult to photograph is required, illustration can add extra punch to a design. Sometimes the designer uses an illustration to provide additional information in the form of a diagram or overlay to supplement a photograph.

There are no fixed rules when it comes to choosing photography or illustration in a piece of graphic design, as there are many different styles of both. With the expanding use of computer imaging, the line between the two categories can sometimes blur.

Although it is the designer who chooses and lays out the typeface and photographic or illustration elements, most of these elements usually come from outside sources. For example, typefaces are available for computer typesetting from many vendors. Most design studios have libraries of books showing examples of the work of photographers and illustrators. When an illustrator is required for a project, these books allow access to professionals who can be hired when their style is appropriate. Several Web sites also feature illustrators' portfolios.

FIGURE 5.2:
Type and image working in support of one another

◼ STYLE

In well-designed pieces, type and image work closely together. For example, in an article on Victorian interiors featuring antique photographs of rooms, you would try to pick a typeface that has the character of the Victorian age for the headline (see Fig. 5.2). The correct typeface ties the text and imagery together, creating a personality for the layout. This personality is called *style*.

In the selection of both type and image, style plays an important role. The variety of styles for type and imagery is virtually endless. With the dominant role of computers in today's graphic design profession, more type styles become available each day. Therefore, today's graphic designers must keep abreast of new developments in typeface design, photography, and illustration to know where to find the styles necessary for their work.

When taking a project to the preliminary comp stage, the designer must decide what style an image will take. For example, let's say you drew a thumbnail sketch of a basket full of apples on a poster for an orchard. When you take that sketch to the comp stage, will that basket of apples be represented as a photograph? If so, will it be black and white? Sepia-toned? Color? Handcolored? Or will it be an illustration? In pastel? Oil paint? Gouache? From what angle will the basket be shown? How many apples will be in the basket? As you can see, such a list of options could go on and on. It is the designer's responsibility to choose the best representation of the basket of apples for that particular client.

There are always factors of time and budget to be considered as well, which may help to narrow the choices. Nevertheless, it is up to the designer to produce the best image for the client. Your reputation, as well as the client's, are riding on it!

FIGURE 5.3:
Vertical rules used to define space on a page

■ GRAPHIC ELEMENTS
Rules, Borders, Boxes, and Shading

In addition to the two major elements of type and image, designers also work with another category of elements, which act as accents to type and image. Rules, borders, boxes, and shading can help to organize a design and give it visual weight. Each of these elements has its own particular uses.

Rules may be used to separate information or to provide a base for a page layout. When placed horizontally between lines of text, they can show a break of information. They can be used in the same fashion to create a barrier between text and image. Used vertically, rules provide the same functions, in addition to defining columns on the page (Fig. 5.3).

Rules are measured by weight in points from a *hairline* (the thinnest line that will print evenly on an imagesetter—.25 point) on up. The width you use depends on how well it integrates with the text and imagery in your design (Fig. 5.4).

Borders work as a frame to separate one element from another. If an element, such as a chart or graph, needs special emphasis in a design, placing a border around it can help it to stand on its own. With a photograph, borders can define the edges of the photo as well as separate it from the text. This is especially helpful when the photo does not have a well-defined edge (Fig. 5.5). Borders can range from simple lines, again measured by points, to complex decorative elements (Fig. 5.6).

Boxes are simply borders that are filled in. Often the box will even exist on its own, without a separately defined border. You can fill in a box with a color, or use a tint of color to fill it. Boxes work best with larger type sizes and graphic elements because small type sizes easily get lost against the box's fill. When a box has a dark enough fill, however, type can be reversed out of this fill to compensate for readability problems (Fig. 5.7). Boxes are used for the same purpose as borders: to separate an element within the design.

Shading, or the use of tinted screens that are positioned behind type, is accomplished by using screens with built-in rulings that are graduated in darkness from a light (10%) tint to a dark (90%) tint. These percentages refer to the

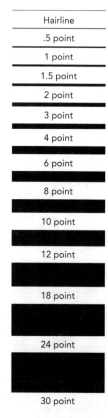

Hairline
.5 point
1 point
1.5 point
2 point
3 point
4 point
6 point
8 point
10 point
12 point
18 point
24 point
30 point

FIGURE 5.4:
Rule weights using a point measuring scale

FIGURE 5.5:
How a border helps to define a photograph's edges

FIGURE 5.6:
Examples of borders

When using a
dark or black box,
bold reversed type
is most legible.

FIGURE 5.7:
Using reversed type in a box

| 10% |
| 20% |
| 30% |
| 40% |
| 50% |
| 60% |
| 70% |
| 80% |

FIGURE 5.8:
10–80% tint screens

Legibility

Legibility

FIGURE 5.9:
Readability of type over a 20% and 80% tint screen

amount of space that the black tint dot occupies within an allocated box, or matrix. For example, a screen or box with a 50% tint means that the black dot occupies 50% of the white space within the matrix area. Increasing the tint screen to 90% means that the dot occupies 90% of the available space. Boxes with tints, or shades, that range from 10 to 80% are shown in Fig. 5.8. Commonly used screen sizes range from 65 to 150 lines per inch. For example, a 133-line screen means that there can be a maximum of 133 dots per linear inch across each inch of the screen area. A 100-line screen is coarser than the 133-line screen, with only 100 dots per inch available for detail or for shading. Screen sizes higher than 150 lines per inch are used in reproductions where high detail and quality, such as in artistic reproduction, are required. For newspapers, where lower quality paper and inks are used, a 65-line screen is the standard.

The designer should keep in mind that type is more difficult to read when placed over a shaded area, because this reduces contrast between the type and the background. If the shade pattern is too dark, the type becomes almost unreadable. Compare the readability of type placed over a 20% tint as opposed to the readability of the same type over an 80% tint (Fig. 5.9).

■ TYPOGRAPHY
Type Selection

Selecting the proper typeface can seem like an arduous task. However, as you learn more about the character of type and how it works, this task becomes easier. In every piece of graphic design, the designer deals with levels of textual information, which make the choice of typefaces very important. Let's look at type choice in context.

In a book, there are chapter titles, section titles, body copy, headings, page numbers, and other text elements that have to be distinguished from one another on each page. A designer needs to make decisions as to how these elements will appear with one another on the page.

Take this book, for example. The chapter titles are set in Avenir Black, the body text in Jaeger Daily News Regular, and the page numbers also in Avenir Black. The designer of the book had to make choices to make the layout work visually. Because this is a textbook, it must be easy to read and study; therefore, the design is more conservative than you might find in a consumer fashion magazine where photographs usually play a larger role. A designer must always be aware of how the piece of graphic design will be used before the typefaces are chosen.

The designer works with a client first to determine the style of the piece, as well as which elements of the text are most important. He or she then prioritizes the different elements of text in the design. By choosing typefaces that work well together, the design should be successful. After a while, you will find those successful choices are not that difficult to make. Although thousands of typefaces are available, following some simple rules can make the decision easier.

One primary rule for selecting typefaces that work well together is to try to use only a few for each design. The right combination of typefaces for the job allows variety without creating visual chaos. When looking at different faces to use with one another, you can either choose faces that work well together because of their similarities (Fig. 5.10), or choose ones that complement each other due to their differences (Fig. 5.11).

When choosing dissimilar typefaces, it is best to set the majority of the text in similar faces, with one different typeface as an accent element. If you use too many different typefaces on one page, you can easily end up with a "ransom note" look that will surely be confusing to the viewer (unless you're designing a ransom note, of course).

Type Styles and Styling

Each typeface is available in different styles. These styles include weight (such as light, medium, bold, extra bold), italics (usually regular and bold), and different cases (for example, all capitals, small capitals). This gives the designer options within each set of typefaces (called a *family*) to create variety. In a family of typefaces, each of the styles created by the typeface designer was designed to work well with one another. Although strong differences may be apparent between a face's regular and italic styles, they still belong to the same family. The designer can even create variety in a design through the use of different styles of the same typeface family. Figure 5.12 shows an example of the type family Futura.

Most computers are equipped with options for styling type (application styling) with shadows, outlines, or underlines. Although the novice designer may be tempted to use these computer-applied styles, they are not as well constructed as the original family; the computer applies the instructions to the typeface rather than the typeface's designer in creating the style. These styles also do not print correctly when sent to an imagesetter and are the cause of many production problems and nightmares for printers. You should always find a type family that offers you these options rather than using applied styles. Figure 5.13 shows a few typefaces that are designed to have special styles.

Futura extra bold
Gill Sans light

FIGURE 5.10:
Typefaces that complement one another due to similarities

Univers 75 Black
Times Roman

FIGURE 5.11:
Typefaces that complement one another due to differences

Futura Condensed Light
Futura Condensed Light Oblique
Futura Condensed
Futura Condensed Oblique
Futura Condensed Bold
Futura Condensed Bold Oblique
Futura Condensed Extra Bold
Futura Condensed Extra Bold Oblique
Futura Light
Futura Light Oblique
Futura Book
Futura Book Oblique
Futura Regular
Futura Oblique
Futura Bold
Futura Bold Oblique
Futura Heavy
Futura Heavy Oblique
Futura Extra Bold
Futura Extra Bold Oblique

FIGURE 5.12:
A portion of the Futura type family

CASTELLAR MT

Goudy Hantooled BT

Industria Inline

Monotype Oldstyle MT

Dotfont

Garamond Condensed

Univers Extended

FIGURE 5.13:
Typefaces designed with
special styling

FIGURE 5.14:
Example of how scaling
distorts a letter

FIGURE 5.15:
Varying column lengths

• **Scaling Fonts**

Almost every computer program has the capability to scale fonts by compressing or extending the characters in either direction. Scaling fonts can be used to fit more type into a smaller space or to extend type to fill a larger one. Scaling should be done very carefully because a typeface will become distorted if it is scaled too much, as shown in Fig. 5.14. As you can see by comparing the original type on the left to the type scaled to a width of 200% on the right, certain parts of the type become too thick while others thin out. Beginning computer users often use scaling too often. Type scaling should be used sparingly because it can easily destroy the proportions of the letterform. A good rule of thumb is to not extend or condense a typeface more than 10% in either direction.

■ **PAGE LAYOUT**
Columns

All type fits into a column of some sort. A *column* is the width and height of the block of text. When a graphic designer determines how the type will be worked into the design, a grid is set up that shows a column number and width. When dealing with large amounts of type, the type will normally be broken into several columns on the page. The designer has several decisions to make when working with column formats.

First, a decision must be made as to how many columns will be used. This can often be a simple matter of measuring the width of the page and considering the size of the type. The design objective is to make the length of each line of type easily readable, so that the lines will be neither short and choppy nor too long. If a line of type is too long, it is difficult for readers to find their place when moving from the right end of the column back to the left, as discussed in Chapter 3.

Columns are generally of equal width on the page so that a consistency of reading is established. The designer wants the reader to be able to follow the text smoothly and effortlessly without having the design get in the way of readability.

Second, the designer deals with the height of columns on a page. Most often, an upper- and lower-column boundary is set for a design; however, columns can also vary in height to allow for variety and image placement on a page, as shown in Fig. 5.15.

When designing the page, text can easily be made to wrap around an image. This changes the width of the column and can also add variety to the design. However, the designer must ensure that the type does not become too compressed nor expanded as it wraps around an image. Figure 5.16 shows improper and proper use of text wrap.

Grids

To create a strong design that ties all of the graphic elements together visually, the designer uses a system of grids. In a one-page design, such as a poster, grids are not always necessary. For any design with repeating pages (for example, magazines, catalogs, and brochures), a grid is an extremely valuable aid to the designer.

When text wraps around an image, it is important that enough space is left on either side of the image. Otherwise the text breaks into uneven spacing that is difficult to read. This example shows improper use of text wrap around an image. See how the words are left hanging at either side of the image.

When text wraps around an image, it is important that enough space is left on either side of the image. Otherwise the text breaks into uneven spacing that is difficult to read. This example shows proper use of text wrap around an image. Notice that there are no single words or uneven spaces left around the image.

FIGURE 5.16:
Improper and proper use of text wrap around an image

A grid (Fig. 5.17) creates a framework within which the the designer will lay out the page. The grid shows basic information such as the left and right margins, top and bottom margins, and column layout. It can also show where the page number, titles, and subtitles are to be placed. It can even show where images will be placed. With a well-thought-out grid design, a magazine or catalog can be laid out quickly and efficiently. The grid as the design foundation ties the pages together and helps to create the publication's personality.

It may sound as if the grid is a very limiting device, which causes every page to look alike, but this is not the case. A well-designed grid allows great flexibility, and many different layouts can be made from a single grid (Fig. 5.18).

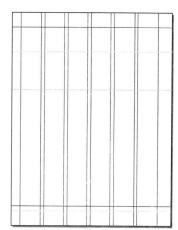

FIGURE 5.17:
A grid design for a magazine

FIGURE 5.18:
Examples of three layouts designed from the grid shown in Figure 5.17

Image Placement

At the beginning of this chapter we discussed decisions that have to be made in the selection of images. When dealing with the layout, the placement of images comes into play. Depending on the grid structure of the design, a logical placement for images may or may not be obvious. Remember, the main issue for the graphic designer is the balance between the placement of text and graphics.

The balance between type and image is an important one, and varies with the intent of the individual piece. The designer must determine which of the elements is most important and adjust the visual balance accordingly.

White Space

White space is the negative area of the page—the areas without text or image. This white space acts as a visual "rest stop" for our eyes. White space around the edges of the page acts as a frame, holding the design together and separating it from its surroundings.

Imagine one poster placed among many others on a wall. White space around the edges can help to make that one poster stand out from the others by separating it from the visual clutter of the wall.

On a magazine or book page, white space allows the reader room to hold the edges of the page while reading an article. In this way, white space not only visually separates graphic elements, but also serves a functional purpose as well.

White space should be thought about from the beginning of any project and evaluated with each step. This is especially important during the design of the page grid.

Although there are no set rules as to how much white space is needed in a piece of graphic design, it is important to understand how this negative space works in a design and how it assists the viewer in understanding the message. A page design from *ILFORD Photo Instructor* magazine is shown in Fig. 5.19. In this layout, a large amount of white space has been used in the design. Notice how the white space is used to draw attention to the various elements on the page.

FIGURE 5.19:
Use of white space in a magazine page layout

■ COLOR

Color can play a central role in graphic design. The designer creates with various combinations of color, from a simple black-and-white project to multicolored pieces. Most often, work falls into one of the following categories.

1/Color. A one-color piece does not necessarily mean black and white, although it can. It means that only one ink color will be applied to the paper. This can be any color of the designer's choosing.

2/Color. The next step up from a single-color piece, a second color can often be used for emphasis without costing much more. Often, "two colors" refers to black ink plus one additional color ink, but this need not always be the case. Any two colors may be used.

3/Color. Not used as frequently as one or two color designs, it allows the placement of any three colors on the piece.

4/Color. Four-color process is how most color photography and full color design work is printed. Technically, it means that four separate inks are printed. Cyan, magenta, yellow, and black inks make up the four process colors that are used to reproduce full color images (see Chapter 10 for more details on four-color process printing). It can also mean that four separate colors are chosen by the designer.

More Than Four Colors. Sometimes the designer may want to print full color along with special colors, metallic inks, or varnishes. To do this, a press capable of printing more than four colors is required, or the piece will need to be run through the press more than one time. Many large offset print shops have six- to eight-color printing presses available for this type of work. An alternate method, if you are printing sheetfed work, is to run the job a second time through a smaller press to add more colors. This process is a bit harder to deal with because the registration of colors from one pass to another is more difficult to control than on a single-pass press printing more than four colors.

Choosing Color

Color should always be tied to the concept of the piece and not chosen because of the personal preference of either the designer or the client. The designer should also try to stay away from picking a color just because it is currently fashionable or because it was used in a similar piece. Every once in a while it is helpful for a graphic designer to lay out all of his or her recent work to observe how he or she has used color. Is there variety or do you rely only on a certain range? By doing this periodically you will become more aware of your use of color.

Color choice can be challenging. In addition to selecting the colors for an initial comp, you must also be aware of how they will be affected by the medium in which they will be finally put to use. This is where color systems come into play.

Color Systems

Graphic designers use various systems of color depending on the medium they are working in. Here are some of the primary systems you will become familiar with when working in graphic design. (Refer to the inside front and back covers of this book for examples of some of these color systems. Not all of them could be printed due to the unique processes required for each.) Although most of you are familiar with the subtractive primary colors of red, yellow, and blue, these primaries are not used in the process of graphic design production. While not part of production, that does not mean, however, that you cannot use red, yellow, and blue in your designs.

• Pantone® Color System

The Pantone® system of color management is one of the most common ways for graphic designers in the United States to specify color. The

Pantone® system consists of numbered colors that can be used by a designer and later mixed by the printer to match the same number. Pantone® color can be specified for ink, paint, and even fabric. It is important to use the Pantone® *Library of Color* books when specifying colors. These books are printed with the actual mixed inks for each color. Choosing the Pantone® color from a computer monitor or inkjet print will not be an accurate color match. Pantone® solid colors are used in one-, two- or three-color print jobs—they are not used to print color photographs.

Pantone® also makes a *Solid to Process Guide*, which compares the mixed-ink color to the closest color match if printed in CMYK color. This is a handy guidebook for students and professional designers and it is well worth the somewhat expensive investment.

• CMYK

As discussed previously, CMYK color uses four separate primary color inks, Cyan, Magenta, Yellow, and blacK to combine and represent all other colors. It is used for printing color photographs and other images in full color. The CMYK process (also referred to as *Process Color* or *Four-Color Process*) uses a system of printing small dots of the four process primaries in varying sizes. These dots mix optically to create a wide spectrum of color. You can see this by looking at any color-printed piece through a magnifying glass or a loupe. You will see a series of small dots of cyan, magenta, yellow, and black on the paper. How small these dots are depends on the quality of the paper and printing. Uncoated papers, such as newsprint, absorb ink and need to be printed with larger dots than coated papers.

Prior to printing, full-color images to be printed in CMYK need to be "color separated" into the four process colors. Today, this is usually done on a computer, making four separate images, each with only the dots needed for that color. The dots on each color separation need to be printed at slightly different angles so that when they are printed together they will not line up on the page and create a moiré—an unwanted pattern of visible dots. The CMYK process is the most common printing method used for color printing worldwide.

• Hexachrome®

Hexachrome® is a six-color printing process developed by Pantone®, Inc. The colors used are specially developed and enhanced versions of cyan, magenta, yellow, and black, plus two additional colors, vivid orange and green. With the process colors broken down to six primaries rather than four, the Hexachrome® process provides a wider color range than four-color process printing. In addition to reproducing more brilliant color images, the Hexachrome® process is capable of accurately simulating over 90% of solid Pantone® colors—close to twice the number that can be simulated using CMYK printing. Due to the additional two ink colors, the process is more expensive than CMYK printing, but does provide high-quality results when accurate color is important in the design.

- **RGB**

  RGB stands for Red, Green, and Blue, the three colors of projected (or additive) light. This system is used in computer monitors and TVs, and is important for use in Web, television, and multimedia design. If you are designing for any of these platforms, RGB colors can be mixed on-screen by choosing the RGB color model available in most computer programs. Keep in mind that there is color variation within all monitors, therefore RGB color cannot be guaranteed accurate from one monitor or TV to another.

- **Web-Safe Colors**

  Web-safe colors are part of the RGB spectrum. Although a computer monitor can display many more colors than the 216 colors of the Web-safe model, this system was created so that monitors set at a resolution of 256 colors, on either a Macintosh or PC platform, could see the range of Web-safe colors without dithering (the breaking of a solid color into pixels of different colors). The reason there are only 216 Web-safe colors when monitors are set at 256 colors is because the 256 colors of the Macintosh platform are not the same 256 colors of the PC platform; hence, only 216 colors match across both platforms.

■ CHOOSING PAPER

For printed work, paper is another very important factor. The right paper can add depth to a piece of graphic design. Conversely, the wrong choice can ruin a good design concept. When creating a design for print, graphic designers rely on special paper merchants that carry a wide range of papers especially made for printing. These paper suppliers offer samples of all the various papers they carry. It is a good idea to build your own library of these samples for use in determining which paper will be right for a particular job. Look through any graphic design magazine and you will see many advertisements for different kinds of paper. Many of these companies offer free booklets with samples of the papers they make.

Paper has both a visual side and a textural one as well. If you are designing a piece that will be held, think about how the paper will feel in the viewer's hands. A paper that works for one project may not work well for another. For example, if you are designing a brochure for a nature conservancy, you may want to pick a more textured, recycled paper rather than a slick, glossy sheet. In this way, the actual feel of the piece aids in communicating your concept.

When choosing paper, the designer needs to check several parameters. Probably the first thing you would think of is color, but there's much more to choosing paper than that. Paper is made by a variety of manufacturers and comes in various sizes and weights. Not all colors are available in all sizes or weights. With a paper sample book, available at no charge from the paper distributor or the peper manufacturer, the designer can check to see whether the paper he or she wants to use is available in the needed color, size, and weight. Many paper distributors will also provide free larger sample sheets for use in making comps.

Because paper is one of the most expensive parts of a print job, it is important to design so that there is little or no waste from the sheet being printed. Waste cannot always be avoided, however. If you are printing a design that bleeds (when the ink goes right to the edge of the paper on the final design) the paper needs to be larger than the design. This allows the paper to run through the press correctly (the press grippers need a small amount of unprinted paper to grab on to while the paper feeds through the press). The paper is then trimmed down to size after it is printed. The excess (also known as *trim*) is either thrown away or, hopefully, recycled.

The designer also needs to determine what quality of image he or she wants on the printed page. Uncoated papers allow the ink to soak into the page and on rougher papers this can make an image blurry. The dot screen for printing on uncoated papers needs to be larger also, and this, too, makes the image of lower resolution. Coated papers have a thin layer of clay skimmed over the surface during the paper-making process. This allows ink to sit on the surface rather than being absorbed, which creates a sharper image and more vibrant colors.

Other decisions about paper include how the piece will be printed and how many pieces will be needed. High volume magazines and books are printed from a continuous roll of paper (referred to as web printing). The choices of paper stock are not as great for web printing as they are for sheetfed printing. How long the piece is intended to last also affects paper choice. Paper made with a high percentage of wood fiber will not last as long as paper made with cotton fiber.

As you can see, the decisions about paper are many and need to be planned early on in the design project to ensure that the amount you need is available when you need it.

■ SUMMARY

Understanding the basic elements of graphic design gives you a "kit of tools" to use when constructing strong layouts. Good graphic design composition comes with use of the elements discussed in this chapter: white space, proper typeface and image choices, design and application of grids, supplemental elements of rules, borders, boxes, and shading, along with color and paper choices. With practice and evaluation of your work (by yourself and others), you can develop your own methods of refining these basic principles to create effective communication with these graphic design tools.

1. Find a photograph in a magazine or book. Try to find a particular typeface that works best with the character of the photograph. Describe why you feel the type and image work well together.

2. Draw an object in five different ways using five different styles. Don't rely on media alone to differentiate each style but also on how a medium is used in the illustration (for example, colored pencil could be used as a solid fill or as pencil lines creating a pattern).

3. Create a grid design for a magazine on a piece of paper. Create columns, margins, and gutters as part of the grid. Then use the grid to create a variety of different designs. Notice that the more complex the grid is, the more flexibility the designer has.

4. Create a design and change the colors of the elements to create several more designs. Discuss how the color changes affect the readability and style of the design.

5. Buy a copy of a design magazine (*How, Step-by-Step,* and *Print* are good choices) and look through it for paper samples and suppliers. Discuss in class the differences between the papers found and decide how each could be best put to use in a printed design.

Chapter 6 FUNDAMENTALS OF COMPUTER GRAPHICS AND ELECTRONIC PAGE COMPOSITION

Chapter 6 FUNDAMENTALS OF COMPUTER GRAPHICS AND ELECTRONIC PAGE COMPOSITION

Understand Computer Graphic Design

Examine the Use of Drawing Programs

Examine the Use of Painting Programs

Examine the Use of Page Layout Programs

Understand Fundamentals of the Electronic Page

Investigate Combining Programs

Understand File Formats

Examine Computer Type Usage

■ INTRODUCTION

The computer has become an indispensable tool for graphic designers. It speeds the production process, allows for easy changes in typography and layout, and gives the designer more control over work than previously possible. Entry-level design jobs now demand computer skills as part of the production process. Hand skills are still important and looked for in a beginning designer, but most employers also want designers to be comfortable working at the computer.

The most popular computers for graphic design are the Macintosh and IBM-compatible (Windows®) machines. Most companies that produce software for graphic design production now make their software for either computer platform. Which one to choose is a matter of personal and professional preference. If you are trying to decide which platform you should learn or buy, call local design studios and find out what most of them are using. Also look through the help wanted sections under "graphic design" to see which platform most employers are requesting applicants to know. Although both platforms are moving closer together, it is still important for you to be trained on the one most popular in your area to increase your marketability. Many young designers now learn to work on either platform, which can be a benefit when looking for a job, especially in the fields of Web design and multimedia.

This chapter discusses the types of computer programs designers work with and explains the unique characteristics of each. The chapter is not geared toward any one platform or specific programs, instead it discusses the general use of various computer design programs.

COMPUTER GRAPHIC DESIGN

Although computers have been in use for many decades, their impact in the graphic design profession was not felt until the mid-1980s. At that time, the personal computer, together with the availability of specialized graphics software, reached the point of being useful in a professional setting. Early computer programs such as Aldus PageMaker® (now owned by Adobe) made it easy to produce page layouts combining both type and graphics. From the mid-1980s to the early 1990s, advances in hardware, software, and printing technologies quickly increased the quality standards of the industry. By the early 1990s, most graphic design firms had made the switch from traditional typesetting and hand preparation of mechanicals to computerized graphic design.

Because of the relative ease of use of the computer and the low cost of equipment, the term *desktop publishers* was coined to describe a new group of low-budget computer graphic designers. Although most design firms shy away from use of the term, the concept of desktop publishing has opened the graphic design field to many people who would have never been involved in the traditional sense. Although some say this has lessened the professional quality of graphic design, it has also brought in new influences and competition and made traditional designers rethink the ways in which we communicate—making graphic design even better.

TYPES OF DESIGN PROGRAMS AVAILABLE

Computer programs used in graphic design can be divided into three major categories: drawing, painting, and page layout programs. Although this list by no means describes every type of program available for the computer, it highlights the program types most frequently used by graphic designers. In the following sections, each type is discussed and examples of each program are given.

Drawing Programs

Drawing programs are used primarily for creating hard-edged graphics. In a drawing program, you create lines using connected points (Fig. 6.1). The elements you create in a drawing program are referred to as *object-oriented*, meaning that the computer sees them as complete and separate objects that may be moved around on the page.

FIGURE 6.1:
Connected points create a line

FIGURE 6.2:
Bezier curve

Curves are made through use of the Bezier process. Each curve has an "anchor" point and two "control" points, as illustrated in Fig. 6.2. The control points can be selected individually and changing their position relative to the anchor point changes the arc of the curve. Neither the anchor point nor the control points are visible in the final print.

Shapes are created by connecting a series of points to create a single closed shape as shown in Fig. 6.3.

In any design job, planning the page in advance is the most important step. As discussed in Chapter 4, the design process involves working closely with the client to develop ideas to meet the requirements of the job. In production, it also involves choosing the computer program that will best create the kind of images you want to produce. Popular drawing programs include Adobe Illustrator®, Macromedia Freehand®, Corel Draw®, and Deneba Canvas®.

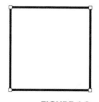

Advanced drawing programs give the ability to create three-dimensional shapes and to render these shapes with lighting, shading, and reflection. The basic principles of these programs are the same as the drawing programs mentioned previously, but their sophisticated controls require much more memory to render the created objects. Strata's Vision 3D®, Adobe Dimensions®, auto•des•systems' Form•Z®, Alias Sketch®, MetaCreations' Bryce®, Discreet 3D Studio Max®, MetaCreations' Carrara®, and Ray Dream Designer® are some of the 3-D drawing programs currently available. Figure 6.4 shows an example from a 3-D drawing program.

Drawing programs handle type well, but not in large amounts. Currently, these programs cannot create multiple pages of linked text. In dealing with text, however, drawing programs have the ability to convert type to outlines, making type into a graphic format. This is handy when designing logos because type can be altered to have its own unique look, and type converted to outline will not require the typeface's individual PostScript® files for printing.

Because of their strengths in creating hard-edged graphics, drawing programs are used for producing package designs, logos, charts and graphs, posters, hard-edge illustrations and other "single-item" designs. Finished drawings can easily be saved as PostScript files and imported into other programs to combine them with other elements (see the section on page layout programs). It is important, when saving a PostScript file to be imported into another program, that the designer either convert all the fonts to outlines or make note of which fonts were used and include them with the file. Otherwise, the fonts will not print correctly when sent to an imagesetter.

Painting Programs

Painting programs allow the user more freedom than drawing programs in creating softer surfaces and a wide range of textures. They also function quite differently from drawing programs. Painting programs use a bit-map process for display and printing. Items are not individual elements, as in a drawing program, but are composed of individual pixels, or bits, making up the whole image. In a black-and-white image, pixels are turned either on or off to create black or white. Color programs use pixel depth, changing the color of each pixel on the screen, to create illustrations with a wider use of color, texture, and focus than possible with a drawing program. A computer screen, for example, has a resolution of 72 pixels per inch, but painting programs allow for much higher resolutions. Painting programs are most often used for photo retouching, illustration, and Web design (Fig. 6.5).

In a painting program, the tools used by the designer on the computer mimic the ones with which traditional artists and designers are familiar. Brushes, pens, and airbrushes have been converted to a digital format. The results are familiar to the tra-

FIGURE 6.5:
An illustration created in
a painting program
©Jason Alders

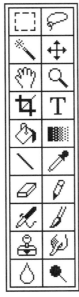

FIGURE 6.6:
Specialized tools in
a painting program

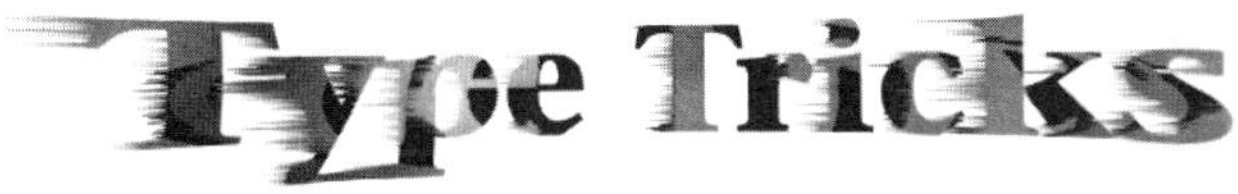

FIGURE 6.7:
Special effects for typography
created in a painting program

ditional artist, yet the process is electronic. No mess to clean up when you're finished, either! There are also many tools available that photographers will recognize: special filters, focus (often called sharpness in a computer program), dodge, and burn tools, to name a few.

Many of the more interesting computerized tools are completely new to the designer, and are time savers. There are tools that allow you to quickly change the color in a given area, to apply textures, or to layer images and blend them together. Figure 6.6 shows some of the specialized tools that painting programs offer.

Although painting programs have the capability to create type (Fig. 6.7), it is best used in small amounts (such as for headlines, headings, and other one-word or short-phrase uses). It is not as easy to create large amounts of text as it is in either drawing programs or page layout programs. It is also difficult to edit the type once a file from a painting program is placed in a page layout program (the only way to do it is to go back to the original painting file, edit it, resave it in the correct format and update it). Popular painting programs include Adobe Photoshop® and MetaCreations' Painter®.

Some painting programs allow the designer to open a drawing program file. This feature enables you to create an item, such as a logo or label, using the strengths of the drawing program and then to bring these elements in for placement on a scanned-in photograph (Fig. 6.8). If you do this, however, be sure to convert the image to the right resolution for your final output: for inkjet comps, 150–200 dpi; for most final output, 300 dpi; for the Web, 72 dpi. All images should be converted to the actual size that they will appear in your design.

Page Layout Programs

Page layout programs, which feature great flexibility, are available to assist the designer in creating computerized mechanicals. In a page layout program, you can quickly bring together text and images to create layouts for magazines, books, brochures, flyers, or posters. The most popular page layout programs are QuarkXPress®, Adobe InDesign™, and Adobe PageMaker®.

The backbone of a page layout program is its ability to set up grids for many different kind of page layouts. As discussed in Chapter 5, grids make up the skeleton

FIGURE 6.8:
A drawing file placed within
a painting program

of the page and allow the designer to work faster while keeping consistency in the design. A good page layout program allows you to create several different grid layouts as "master pages," which can then be applied to the document's pages. These grid lines show up as light lines across the page on screen although they do not print on the document (Fig. 6.9).

Page layout programs contain specialized text tools, which offer a wide degree of flexibility in setting type. Provisions for fine adjustments in kerning, tracking, and leading are standard in most page layout programs. Together with controls for typeface, type size, and justification, these tools give the designer control over the typography in the final layout. These freedoms, which traditionally would have been communicated to a typesetter, also demand more of the designer's time for production. Therefore, many studios hire specific computer production people to handle the "typesetting" portion of the design job. Often, entry-level positions start the beginning graphic designer out in computer production before moving up to a designer level.

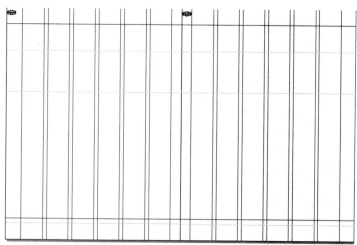

FIGURE 6.9:
A grid design created in a page layout program

Although spell-checking features exist in most word processing and page layout programs, the designer must take care also to check for grammatical and punctuation errors, which were once the typesetter's responsibility. Therefore, it is still important for a designer to be a good proofreader.

Page layout programs offer only basic drawing tools. It is expected that complex illustrations will be done in either a drawing or painting program and then imported into the page layout. Because of this, page layout programs are set up to allow the designer to easily place graphics created in different file types.

Page layout programs often contain many different kinds of placed images and many typefaces. To ensure all the various files that the printer will need are on the final disk, page layout programs give the designer the ability to collect all of the files together for output. By doing this, copies of the layout file, plus copies of all images used—wherever they may be in the disk, are placed in a single folder, along with a report which lists all the typefaces and images used in the layout. This double-check comes in handy when the files must be sent out for film or paper output.

Because page layout programs form the core of so many operations within the area of computer graphics, let us examine some of the techniques associated with electronic page composition in greater detail.

■ FUNDAMENTALS OF THE ELECTRONIC PAGE

Designing a page electronically allows quick design and production changes, which can be of great benefit to the graphic designer. It does, however, pose problems as well. This section discusses the process of page design on the computer.

Initial sketches may be done by hand or on the computer. A drawback to using the computer for thumbnail sketches is the temptation to spend too much time refining an idea, when your time could be better spent developing many quick ideas to explore a variety of possibilities. Another problem can be that the designer, when using the computer in the initial sketch phase, will use "design formulas"—common layout ideas—rather than trying to develop specific concepts for a particular project.

The main points to consider when planning the layout are page size, type use, image use, and how the piece will be printed. These factors should be narrowed down before going to the computer. It will be helpful to make up a few "dummy" pages to assist in making typeface, type size, column width, and margin decisions. These elements do not have to be finalized at this stage, as they often change during the course of the design. It is important, however, to have a good idea of what general style the publication will use from the beginning.

■ DESIGN CONSIDERATIONS

Once initial concepts have been completed, the design can be started using the computer. Using a page layout program, the designer can create the basic structure for the layout.

Grid and Column Sizes

Grid design is the first phase of the project in a page layout program. A well-designed grid allows flexibility in placement of both text and graphics and it can be used for successive issues of the publication.

In a page layout program, the grid should be set up on the master pages. These master pages allow you to set up guides for the grid in one place and then apply them to all of the pages automatically. Repeating elements, such as page numbers, volume and issue numbers, dates, and rules, should be set on the master pages. Take the time to read the manual that came with the page layout program you use. You will even find ways to make the pages self-number in the correct order!

Page layout programs enable the designer to set up several different master pages. This is handy when using different grids or element layouts for different sections within the same publication. Empty text boxes can also be made on the master pages. These boxes will be later filled when text is imported onto the pages.

Repeating Elements

• Graphics and Artwork

Elements such as titles or logos may become a permanent part of the layout. These items may be placed on special master pages or on the publication's regular pages. It is important that their placement be part of the initial layout so they do not have to be squeezed in later.

• Other Repeating Elements

In most publications, several elements tend to be repeated in each issue. These include the masthead and the statement of publication, which should be included in the initial layout.

■ DESIGN CRITERIA APPLIED TO THE JOB

As in any graphic design job, it is important to review and evaluate the work as it progresses. This may be done by the designer independently, or by a group consisting of the designer, client(s), and production people. In a publication design, evaluation is a crucial part of the process because the design will be in use over a longer time period than most other types of graphic design. Principles such as readability, flexibility, and cost should be examined carefully.

Once the design has been approved by the client, creation of the actual publication can begin.

Designing Templates

If the layout will be used for a regularly issued publication such as a monthly magazine, it may be desirable to create a *template* for the design. A template is a stripped-down version of the publication that can be used each time the magazine is produced. The template contains all the repeating elements that are featured in each issue of the publication.

In a page layout program, the design can be saved as a specific template file. When saving a design in this format the program will open the template as an untitled file, forcing the user to save it under a new name and protecting the template as a master file for future use.

Importing Text

Most of the text in publications is prepared using a word processing program and then imported into a page layout program. Often, the design studio receives all of the copy for a publication as computer text files, proofed and ready for use in the layout. This is the preferable way of working, as it leaves the responsibility for typographic errors with the client. Receiving the text files electronically does have its drawbacks, however. Sometimes the client may not deliver the latest version of the file, thus shifting the proofreading responsibilities on to the designer.

Page layout programs have special features called *filters,* which allow text to be imported from a variety of word processing programs. This makes for easy placement of text from different sources. For example, the Macintosh computer also reads PC files with a special program called "PC Exchange." Thus, although the text was created on a different computer platform, it can still be imported into the Mac, while leaving the disk in its original PC format.

Importing Graphics

Graphic images can also be imported from a variety of sources. The most important part of importing graphics is whether files will be used for final output or simply "for position only" (FPO). FPO graphics will later be replaced with high-quality images at the printer or prepress house. High-resolution color photographs are the most common graphics replaced with FPO images in a layout. This is because the technology for scanning high quality color photographs is generally too expensive for most design studios, and the files created by them may be too large to be used on the average designer's computer.

FPO images are scanned into the computer at a resolution of 72 dpi (screen pixel resolution) so that they will display well on screen while keeping the file size

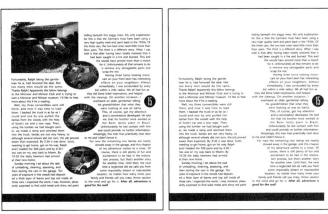

FIGURE 6.10:
Onscreen and printed views of photos tagged "not to print"

small. Color images may even be scanned in grayscale to hold down the file size.

Hint: When working with a combination of images to be used for printing (logos, line art, specially created type files) and FPO images, it is a good idea to assign an unused color to all of the FPO images, just to keep track of them.

Some page layout programs enable the marking of image files so they will not print while text set to wrap around them will print. This is a handy feature, which most designers take advantage of often when using FPO images. A printed file with images marked not to print is shown in Fig. 6.10.

Reworking Text and Graphics

Text and graphics often have to be altered for use in a layout. This section discusses some of the many and various ways each can be changed for use in a design.

• Text Changes

After importing, the text is changed by the designer into the typeface and format of the final publication. To aid in this process, page layout programs have the ability to create style sheets (which will discussed in more detail later in this chapter in the Initial Layout section). By creating style sheets for each of the different type elements in a layout, text can be easily changed. This is very important because the type imported from the word processing program rarely, if ever, matches that of the publication. Many design students, however, do not want to spend the time setting up a series of style sheets. They would rather start working on the design right away. However, you will quickly learn that the time you spent on creating style sheets at the beginning of a project will be well worth it later!

Other text changes may be necessary during the course of the publication layout. These changes may include editing for length or content or last-minute replacements for stories. (Unfortunately, writers are as busy as designers and can rarely provide completed copy when it is needed.) Although these changes are not always welcomed by the designer, page layout programs have built-in aids to assist the designer in making last-minute changes.

A *search-and-replace feature* helps when a name or word has to be changed throughout the publication. For example, if a name was misspelled in the original file it will have to be replaced in every occurrence throughout the document.

A *linking feature* can link the placed text to an original word processing file so that if any changes are made to the word processing file the page layout program will automatically make the necessary changes within the text.

Using the special features of a page layout program can make text changes much easier to deal with. With practice and knowledge of the page layout program, the designer can make any necessary changes without it becoming a time-consuming task.

- **Graphics Changes**

Changes in graphic images may come from two sources. In the first instance, an original graphic file may have to be changed or replaced because of alterations in material content. In the second instance, the designer may decide to make changes to the graphic within the program to enhance the visual appearance of the layout.

If changes are made to the original graphic file, the process is the same as the text changes mentioned earlier. The file can simply be updated by placing the new file onto the page, or the page layout program can be configured to automatically update graphic file changes.

The designer is also able to make some changes to a graphic file after it has been placed in the page layout program. Changes such as size and color are fairly simple to make. Certain graphics files may have a wide variety of changes made to them within the page layout program, including size, color, contrast, and brightness. Using these features within a page layout program, the designer can screen an image into the background or convert it to a high-contrast image for special graphic effects (Fig. 6.11). It should be noted, however, that changes made to graphics within the page layout program require a longer time to print than if the same changes were made in an image editing program. To speed up printing time, changes made in the page lay-

FIGURE 6.11:
A TIFF image altered from within a page layout program (Original on left; right screened and made high-contrast)

out stage should be done sparingly, or simply to explore an alternate design idea. If you like the change, go back to your image editing program, make the same change, and update the image file in the page layout program.

■ COMBINING COMPUTER DESIGN PROGRAMS

A designer's familiarity with all of the programs and their features aids in making decisions as to which program best fits the requirements of the job. Most often, the designer uses a combination of two to four programs in producing a job so it is important to know how the programs work together. There is nothing more frustrating than trying to get a program to do something it was not designed to do! Although you may be able to create a drawing in a page layout program, it is easier

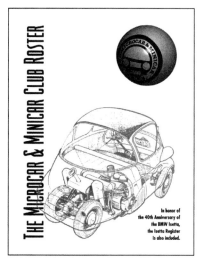

FIGURE 6.12:
A design combining several computer programs

and requires less time to do it in a drawing program and then import the drawing into the layout.

Let us take a sample design job and trace the uses of the computer in its production. To produce the cover shown in Fig. 6.12, a drawing program was first used to produce the logo. The logo was then wrapped onto the sphere in a 3-D drawing program. The image of the car was scanned in and cleaned up in a painting program. The two illustrations were then brought into a page layout program where the type was created. Using these four programs, the designer was able to achieve the desired results in a timely fashion.

■ FILE FORMATS

To create and save various kinds of files, many different file formats were created for the computer. Some of the major formats used in electronic page composition are described here.

Macintosh File Formats

EPS (encapsulated PostScript®). EPS files are actually two files in one. One file contains the PostScript® information as text that the file needs for printing, the other the QuickDraw information (a picture, or PICT image) that the computer uses for display of images on the screen. *Important note:* When working between a PostScript® drawing program or painting program and a page layout program, do not simply drag an image from an open window into the page layout program. This will only give you the PICT image and not the PostScript® information. You must save the file and place it into the page layout program for it to print correctly.

TIFF or TIF (tagged image file format). This format is a good way to save scanned images. The TIFF format allows for changes in contrast, density, and color to be made easily. A TIFF file is saved in bit-mapped format, but unlike the standard 72-dpi bitmap, the TIFF file can be any resolution you choose. The main drawback to saving a file in TIFF format is that, because of the large amount of information saved, the file size may be quite large.

PICT (PICT is not an acronym; it is short for picture). PICT files are common on the Macintosh computer and contain QuickDraw information that the Mac converts into an image. A PICT file may contain bit-mapped or object-oriented elements. PICT files are not recommended for files being sent to an imagesetter because they do not process and print well.

GIF (graphics interchange format). The GIF format was developed by CompuServe, Inc., an information service. It is a standard file format that works on all computer platforms. GIF images are also used for display on the Internet.

JPEG (joint photographic experts group, the name of the committee that created the format). JPEG is not actually a file format; rather, it is a method of file compression that creates small files sizes to reduce download and printing times. It is the primary means of saving photographic images for use on the Internet. This format also works on all computer platforms.

PC File Formats

EPS, TIFF, GIF, and JPEG. These are the same as those on the Macintosh

PCX. The PCX format is used for saving files produced in the program Paintbrush. PCX works with all Windows® drawings created in Paintbrush as well as those created in many non-Windows® applications.

Monochrome Bitmap. This is the format of choice for illustrations done in black and white and when a monochrome monitor is used on the computer.

16- and 256-color Bitmap. These are the color choices to be made depending on the type of graphics monitor and video card installed on any specific PC. The 256-color format is used on most current PCs.

TGA, SunRaster, and SGI. These formats were developed by manufacturers for their high-end workstations such as Targa, Sun, and Silicon Graphics.

VIFF. The visual image file format, or VIFF, is the image file format for the Khoros Imaging package used for scientific research and imaging projects.

■ BASIC SKILLS USED IN COMPUTER GRAPHIC PROGRAMS

Next we examine some of the primary skills a designer uses when working with computer programs.

Initial Layout

The first step toward working with any computer program is to plan the design. This is done using your thumbnails and rough sketches as guides, which will save a great deal of time in producing the job.

The initial layout requires, at a minimum, choosing the size of the page and the method of measurement (inches, picas/points, agates, or millimeters). The designer must also select guidelines to help in aligning elements or for creating a grid in a page layout program. (Refer to Chapter 5 for further information on grid design.)

Multipage documents may also require the creation of *style sheets* for typesetting. Once created within the program, style sheets allow the designer to easily and quickly apply a typeface, point size, leading, and other type characteristics to a paragraph or word. A big benefit of this is that once the basic style sheets have been created, the designer can go back and change elements of the style sheet. All of the text that was defined by that original style sheet will then change to match the new style sheet definition. This feature is very handy when working on multi-page documents such as catalogs, books, or magazines.

Rules, Lines, and Shapes

Rules are one of the most common elements a designer uses. In a computer program, making a rule is as simple as making a beginning point and an endpoint. Rule thickness can be set or changed quickly and the rule can be duplicated easily.

Lines in a computer program can be made using the same technique used for making rules, or can be curved by using multiple points along the line. The common way to do this is through the Bezier method, as discussed previously in this chapter.

Many programs offer the ability to add geometric shapes by using specific shape tools. These shapes usually include squares, rectangles, circles, and ellipses as minimum choices. Other choices may include pentagons, hexagons, octagons, or shapes with any number of sides. Some programs even include the ability to make special shapes such as stars.

Free-form shapes are simply a series of curved or straight lines made into a solid shape by connecting the last point to the first and making it a solid.

Shades and Fills

• Shades

Most shapes created in a program can be either shaded or filled. By specifying a color and shade, a shape will take on greater definition. Although the designer can create any shade from 1% to 100% in increments of one, it is best to use shades in 10% increments. (It's almost impossible to see a real difference between a 10% and 11% shade in most printing.) Wider shading increments help to separate various elements on the page.

When working with shades, it is a good idea to do a test of a sample shade scale on the printer that will be used for final output. Computers and printers are not perfect in their shading controls, and what is specified to be a particular shade in a computer program may end up being either lighter or darker when actually printed.

• Fills

Fills may be a color, a pattern, or an image. All programs allow color to be set as a fill. Many programs also allow patterns or images to be used as fills and usually offer a choice of fills. Some programs allow the operator to create custom fill patterns.

When using an image as a fill, a shape is first created using the method described earlier. An image is then placed into that shape (although the method of doing this varies from program to program). The result of this process is shown in Fig. 6.13.

• Airbrushing Techniques

Airbrushing is a technique available only in painting programs, although drawing programs can sometimes mimic the effect. The method is very similar to the traditional way of using an airbrush to apply paint. However, because this is a computer, the tool is infinitely more versatile than the real thing! An airbrush on the computer can be used to erase, dodge or burn, tint, lighten or darken, or even reveal parts of an underlying image.

■ THE RIGHT TYPE FOR THE JOB

There are thousands of typefaces available for the computer, and each design studio will own different faces. The designer should not always only depend on the typefaces available on one computer; fonts can easily be ordered and are not very expensive. A good designer will determine which type is best for the job and obtain that typeface instead of relying on only those readily available. When doing a large job, the price of the typeface can often be charged to the client. It is a good idea to keep up to date on new font releases, and, many type companies will put you on their mailing lists once you buy from them.

Inexpensive CD-ROMs are available with "hundreds of fonts" for a low price, but these are not often well constructed, and may not set well for professional use. They may, however, be a good starting point for a design student. If you do buy these, or any other fonts, be sure to purchase and use only PostScript® fonts. Many inexpensive fonts are available only in TrueType® format and will be a problem in imagesetting. If both TrueType® and PostScript® versions are included, install only the PostScript® format for best results when printing.

■ COMBINING TYPE AND IMAGE

As discussed in Chapter 5, type and image are the mainstays of graphic design. The computer gives the designer a great deal of flexibility on how these two elements can be combined. Some of those options are discussed in the following sections.

Separating

Separating the text from the image is easy to do on the computer. Figure 6.14 shows a simple example of separated text and image. One advantage to placing an image on the computer is that you can set the text to automatically break over and below the image. In this way, text editing is easier and does not have to be reset if text changes are made.

Wrapping

Wrapping text around an image, also referred to as *runaround*, is also easy to do in a page layout program. There are settings for method of wrap (around the image box or around the image perimeter, see Fig. 6.15) and for the distance the text will wrap around the image. The designer should be careful not to wrap the text too close to the image because this makes the type less readable.

Superimposing

Placing the text on the image, or *superimposing*, is another design method (Fig. 6.16). It is important that the image be light enough, or of a contrasting color, so that the type will stand out from the image and be easy to read.

FIGURE 6.13:
An image placed inside of a shape

The BMW Isetta

The BMW Isetta was built from 1955 through 1962. It was powered by a one-cylinder BMW motorcyle engine capable of speeds up to 60 mph. The Isetta sat two adults, with entrance to the car through a front-hinged door. Unusual in its design and appearance, the Isetta sold well in Europe as a city car for people who preferred an economical all-weather car over the purchase of a motorcycle. Although they were sold in the United States, they were not very popular, and were sometimes even given away with larger automobile purchases.

FIGURE 6.14:
Separated text and image
image ©Lynda Hong

The BMW Isetta was built from 1955 through 1962. It was powered by a one-cylinder BMW motorcyle engine capable of speeds up to 60 mph. The Isetta sat two adults, with entrance to the car through a front-hinged door. Unusual in its design and appearance, the Isetta sold well in Europe as a city car for people who preferred an economical all-weather car over the purchase of a motorcycle. Although they were sold in the United States, they were not very popular, and were sometimes even given away with larger automobile purchases.

FIGURE 6.15:
Text wrapped around an image
image ©Lynda Hong

FIGURE 6.16:
Type superimposed on an image

FIGURE 6.17:
Type knocked out of an image

FIGURE 6.18:
Type ghosted over an image

Knocking Out

Knocking out the type from the image is readily accomplished on the computer by setting the type color the same as the background (Fig. 6.17). Again, readability should be the main criterion, and the designer must be sure the type is of sufficient size so that it will not close up during printing.

Ghosting

A popular computer manipulation of type is to *ghost* the type over the image. This can only be done when the type is large enough to read easily, and involves using a painting program to construct a word as a graphic with the image as its fill. The type image is then darkened or lightened and matched to the original image as shown in Fig. 6.18.

■ SUMMARY

This chapter provided insights into the basic operations of computer graphic design and page layout tools. These principles lay a foundation for your future design work.

The computer has changed the way graphic designers work and will continue to do so as new technologies and applications are developed. The development of electronic page composition has opened up the design, printing, and publication field, which was once restricted to the world of the printer and traditional graphic designer. It has also created new areas for designers to work in—Web design, multimedia, and animation. The graphic designer of the future may be working across broad disciplines, and it is important to remember that constant changes in technology requires that a designer needs to adapt and learn the new technologies while not losing sight of his or her talents as a visual communicator.

1. Use a drawing program to create a logo design. Enlarge and reduce the design several times on the page. On a printout, observe how the image outlines remain crisp and clear at any size. Create the same logo in a painting program. Enlarge and reduce it and observe how the image changes each time.

2. In a painting program, save the same image in various formats (RGB, CMYK, grayscale, bitmap). Keep the resolution for all images at 600 dpi. Compare the file sizes for each. Save copies of the same images at 300 dpi. Compare the new file sizes to the original ones.

3. Set up a ten-page book design in a page layout program. Define style sheets for the various text elements (titles, subheads, body text, pull quotes, page numbers). Edit the style sheets and notice how all the styled elements change throughout the document. Observe any changes in the length of the book as changes are made to point size, typeface, tracking, and leading.

4. Select several advertisements from popular magazines:

   A. Try to determine what kind of computer program was necessary to create each of the elements (photographs, illustrations, headlines, body copy, graphic elements) in the ad.

   B. Try to re-create the ad using the computer programs you determined the original was created in.

Chapter 7 DIGITIZING DATA

Chapter 7 DIGITIZING DATA

Understand the Nature of Digital Data

Provide an Overview of the Requirements of Desktop Scanning, Storage, and Data Transfer Systems

Identify Major Components of Scanner Technology Including Digital Photographic Techniques

Examine the Variety of Available Storage Devices

Develop an Understanding of CD-ROM Technology

■ INTRODUCTION

Any type of information, whether text or illustration, must be in a digital format to be processed by a computer. This chapter highlights some of the ways in which text and illustrations are changed from their original analog format into the digital format required by the computer.

One way to prepare digital information is to do so directly with the computer. This is done by using word processing, illustration, or photo manipulation programs. Using these software packages will result in files that are ready for either storage or printing.

Existing printed materials such as text, illustrations, and photographs must be digitized during an input process. Most data input devices rely on some form of optical scanning to accomplish digitization. Scanners read and interpret the intensity of light reflecting from either the text or illustration and change this varying light intensity into digital format. Once digitized, the copy can be manipulated, modified, and enhanced to meet the objectives of the job: gray cloudy skies become blue skies with scattered clouds at the click of a mouse button. Before looking at some digitizing options, we'll examine what the term "digital" really means.

■ WHAT ARE DIGITAL DATA?

The world that surrounds us is largely "analog" shades of grays rather than black and whites and absolutes. The familiar speedometer in an automobile, which uses a needle that moves along a circular path to show the vehicle's speed, is an analog instrument. However, if the speedometer displays vehicle speed as a number rather than a moving needle, the readout is digital instead of analog. Because natural phenomenon are analog rather than digital (different colors in a photograph or shades of gray in a black and white picture), the analog information must be converted into a digital format in order to be understood and processed by computers.

Character	Binary Equivalent
0	0011 0000
1	0011 0001
2	0011 0010
3	0011 0011
4	0011 0100
5	0011 0101
6	0011 0110
7	0011 0111
8	0011 1000
9	0011 1001
A	0100 0001
B	0100 0010
C	0100 0011
D	0100 0100
E	0100 0101
F	0100 0110
G	0100 0111
H	0100 1000
I	0100 1001
J	0100 1010
K	0100 1011
L	0100 1100
M	0100 1101
N	0100 1110
O	0100 1111
P	0101 0000
Q	0101 0001
R	0101 0010
S	0101 0011
T	0101 0100
U	0101 0101
V	0101 0110
W	0101 0111
X	0101 1000
Y	0101 1001
Z	0101 1010

FIGURE 7.1:
Binary numbering system

FIGURE 7.2:
Weighted positions of a binary number

The Binary Numbering System

Almost all natural and manmade phenomenon can be digitized: colors, shades of gray, letters of the alphabet, and numbers. Digital circuitry relies on a system known as the *binary* numbering system in order to operate. In the binary system, all numbers are composed of either zeroes and ones. Figure 7.1 shows the binary equivalents of the numbers 0 through 9 and the 26 letters of the alphabet.

The key to understanding the binary numbering system is the idea of weighted number positions. In the decimal system, the value of a number depends on how many places to the left of the decimal point the number is. For example, the number 5.0 = five ones; 70.0 = 7 tens; 600.0 = 6 hundreds; and so on. Each move to the left of the decimal point multiplies the value of the number by 10.

The binary systems also uses weighted symbol positions, starting to the left of the binary point. The binary point is the equivalent of the decimal point, but uses multiples of 2 rather than 10. Thus, 1 = one 1 (0001); the number 10 = one 2 (0010); the number 100 = one 4 (0100); and so on. The weighted positions of an eight-figure binary number are shown in Fig. 7.2.

The number illustrated in Fig. 7.2 equals 76: one 4, one 8, and one 64, which added together equals 76.

For a computer to process any binary number, it turns electrical circuits on and off based on the number: A binary "0" is represented with 0 volts and the binary "1" is represented with 5 volts. In this way, circuits are turned on and off, sounds are generated, and video is displayed in color. The longer the binary, or digital code, the more information is represented and the greater the clarity of the sounds, resolution of the picture, or color depth displayed on the monitor.

■ HOW ORIGINAL DATA ARE DIGITIZED

Most methods of digitizing any type of data rely on scanning technology. Scanning technology works by shining a high-intensity light on an original text, black-and-white illustration, or color illustration. As the scanner moves across the surface of the copy, the amount of light reflected from the original is analyzed and assigned a binary number, in effect giving the reflected light a digital value. The copy is thus "digitized." The more information gathered and analyzed by the scanner in each packet, or bit of data, the more complete and accurate the scan will be.

Figure 7.3 summarizes the methods used to digitize a variety of original materials. Note that although a number of different devices are available for inputting originals, output options are less selective.

Almost all copy is output to either imagesetters, laser printers, digital copiers, or direct-to-plate or direct-to-press systems. Different scanning techniques are used to scan black-and-white copy as opposed to color originals. Although adaptations are incorporated into the scanning process to ensure color accuracy, outputting a color file to a laser printer or imagesetter is the same as outputting a file that contains only a black-and-white, pen-and-ink drawing to the same device.

We'll examine the input process more closely, beginning with a look at the various options available in the scanning process.

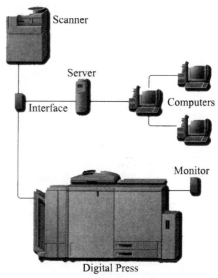

FIGURE 7.3:
Methods of digitizing copy

■ REQUIREMENTS OF A DESKTOP SCANNING SYSTEM

Differences of opinion always surface regarding the ideal combination of system components and processing power for a complete scanning system. Generalizations in this area are made more difficult because of "backwards compatibility," the ability of new pieces of hardware to work efficiently with older computer systems and components.

In this regard, some information technology (IT) specialists rely on minimum system requirements recommended in what is known as the "MPC" (for multimedia personal computer) level of specifications. These specifications detail the computer hardware configurations necessary to deliver base-level performance characteristics for most software, game, and entertainment titles. Keeping in mind that system requirements will change with advances in associated technologies, we can make some generalizations on a component-by-component basis.

Computer Requirements

Computers on the Windows®/Intel® (Wintel) platform are currently available with processors operating at 600 megahertz (MHz) and above. Macintosh® Power PCs (PPCs) with G3 and G4 chips are currently available with processing speeds over 500 MHz. For most scanning and related tasks, Wintel PCs above 300 MHz and Macintosh PPCs above 333 MHz should be considered minimum processor speeds for satisfactory performance. Even if a computer will not be used to play multimedia and entertainment titles, the information appetite of a modern 36-bit scanner is enormous, especially when scanning and processing full-page color illustrations and photographs. In this regard, speed is definitely your friend!

■ DATA TRANSFER OPTIONS

Methods of moving information between computers, and from computers to peripherals, are varied and continue to evolve. The current options are listed below.

Universal Serial Bus

Coupled with processor speed are interface options for external hardware that is incorporated into most computer hardware. Both Macintosh® and Wintel PCs are currently equipped with "universal serial bus" (USB) transfer capabilities. USB is a high-speed data port, operating at 12 megabits-per-second (Mbps), for connecting external scanners, drives, video cameras, and a variety of other peripheral devices to the computer. (USB II proposals are in the works.)

Small Computer Systems Interface (SCSI) Options

High-speed "small computer systems interface" (or SCSI, pronounced Scuzzy) terminals were standard equipment for many years on all Macintosh computers. The original SCSI-1 specification was developed in 1986. The protocol was revised in 1992 and referred to as SCSI-2; it can transfer data at speeds up to 10 megabytes (MB) under most conditions. Some manufacturers use what is referred to as Ultra SCSI which allows data transfer rates up to 40 MB using 16-bit SCSI cables. A faster, SCSI-3 interface is also available with drives and peripherals that operate up to 100 MB at "burst rate," with sustained data transfer rates of 50 MB. In many computer models, SCSI connections are no longer standard and require the installation of a SCSI board into one of the computer system's expansion slots to provide the SCSI interface option. Up to seven devices can be connected in a conventional SCSI chain (special hardware and software adaptations are available that allow more than seven devices to be connected). Each SCSI device in the chain is assigned its own number, which enables the computer to differentiate one device from the other.

Firewire®

Firewire® is Apple Computer's name for a high-speed data transfer port that is similar in ease of use to USB but operates about 30 times faster, at speeds of up to 400 Mbps. Firewire® is an ideal data port for directly connecting video camcorders to either a Macintosh or PC and requires neither a peripheral identification number, or termination device. Firewire® is continuing the take over the data transfer chores formerly handled by conventional SCSI ports.

General-Purpose Interface Board

General-purpose interface boards (GPIBs) are usually purchased separately from a scanner or other peripheral device. The GPIB is installed into one of the expansion slots on a PC motherboard, and the scanner is then connected to the board.

TWAIN Software Protocol

To help ensure the compatibility between the largest number of hardware and software combinations found in scanners produced by a variety of manufacturers, manufacturers began to adopt what is known as the TWAIN protocol in 1992. TWAIN is a software protocol, or instructional package, that enables a user to scan a wide variety of material directly while in a software application program. This feature eliminates the need for special software drivers for each type of hardware platform. For example, a TWAIN-compliant spreadsheet program would allow the user to scan a full-page color bar graph from a printed report directly into a spreadsheet program without the need to edit or convert the bar graph. Large numbers of word processors, spreadsheet, database and desktop publishing packages support the TWAIN compatibility standard, which makes a variety of scanning tasks easy and productive.

CD-ROM and DVD Drives

CD-ROM drives are currently available in rotational speeds above 50 "X." The "X" stands for the base-line, first-generation, single-speed CD-ROM drive. Therefore, a 50X drive operates at a rotational speed that is 50 times faster than an original first general CD drive. Drives of less than 20X should be avoided, not because they won't work but because they can't access large amounts of information quickly enough to deliver satisfactory performance. "Digital versatile disk," or DVD, drives, capable of reading audio and standard CD-ROMs and information in the DVD format will eventually replace the conventional CD drive on most computers. DVD drives are a good choice if only one CD drive will be installed in the computer. DVDs are discussed later in this chapter.

Memory and Storage Options

Memory requirements for desktop computer systems expand at ever-increasing rates. Presently, desktop systems should be equipped with a minimum of 128 MB of system RAM for best all-around performance. Although a computer with 64 MB of random access memory (RAM) will process many scans and serve most multimedia requirements, the ability of the computer to generate and redisplay artwork edited both on the scanner and in photoediting software programs can be slow. When assessing system RAM requirements, video RAM should be considered as well. Four MB of dedicated video RAM for general display requirements should be considered minimum. If the computer system will be displaying multimedia and 3-D video games, minimum video RAM should be increased to 8–12 MB.

Internal hard drives of less than 6.0 gigabytes (GB) of capacity are inadequate for storing current programs and data—double-digit GB storage capacity is preferable. Only a few short years ago, hard drives that were designed for audio and video playback were designated as "AV" drives. Modern hard drives incorporate data access times of less than 9.0 milliseconds and are capable of processing virtually any type of data quickly and efficiently. Keep in mind that large color photographs, whether scanned or downloaded from digital cameras, take up huge amounts of disk space when stored as high resolution images. When working with large scans or downloaded data, hard drive storage capacity can never be too large.

External storage systems, such as removable disks (Zip® drives), external hard drives, and recordable and nonrecordable CD-ROMs increase system flexibility and offer the user virtually unlimited storage capacity. Removable media such as Zip® Disks, currently at 250 MB of capacity, as well as multi-gigabyte removable optical media are inexpensive and standardized, allowing for their interchangeability. Files can be easily mailed between customer and client and from one user to another. Generating information and then burning a CD-ROM offers unrivaled flexibility and storage capacity. Again, there is no such thing as too much storage space.

■ DISPLAY REQUIREMENTS

For intensive scanning and graphics editing, monitors with less than 17-inch displays should be avoided; 19-inch and 21-inch monitors are preferable. Color balance and accuracy are a prerequisite for all computer monitors. Monitors should have a maximum dot pitch of .28 mm (the dot pitch is the space between the dot structures on the computer screen). A dot pitch greater than .28 is basically a television screen enclosed in a computer display case and should be avoided. The monitor should be noninterlaced (an interlaced monitor refreshes, or redisplays, only half of the lines on the screen during each refresh cycle, which limits overall resolution and image quality). Also, current monitors should be equipped with color calibration and screen adjustment hardware and software incorporated into the display.

■ SCANNER TECHNOLOGY

Few devices in the graphic design and prepress area offer as much flexibility, or enable the designer to achieve as much productivity, as scanners. Although the majority of scanners have evolved into a desktop technology, the variety of scanners available that both fit on a desktop, as well as larger floor model counterparts, offer design and production personnel a wealth of features and price ranges from which to choose. Scanning technology evolved from electronic devices known as "scanner/recorders" that produced color separations from original transparent or reflective copy. These machines relied on well-trained, skilled operators to manually adjust the scanner/recorder to produce accurate color separations. Current scanners, coupled with sophisticated software packages, offer machines that are far more sophisticated, less expensive, and much easier to operate than their earlier counterparts. Scanners are now designed more for people with a general knowledge of the technology than for highly trained scanning professionals. Scanners can be divided into low-, medium-, and high-end systems. Low-end systems, typical of the inexpensive desktop scanners, are available for under $500, with some units costing under $100. Prices for medium-range scanners start at about $1,000 and can go up as high as $10,000. High-end color and black-and-white scanners generally run from $20,000 to almost $100,000. Newer scanners incorporate network capability; however, the majority are not networkable devices. They are connected and dedicated to one computer.

The choice of which type of scanner to purchase was once a complicated decision. When desktop scanners first became available in the mid 1980s, purchasing choices were based on the majority of the work to be performed by the unit. Archiving and scanning black-and-white data required only a black-and-white scanner. The additional money necessary to purchase a color scanner was usually not justifiable if the scanner would only be performing black-and-white operations. Advances in scanner technology have resulted in scanners capable of recognizing and reproducing more than 16 million individual colors, 256 shades of gray at greater than 48 bits of color information per picture element (pixel), resolutions greater than 5,000 lines per inch, and price levels that most individuals can afford.

During the scanning process, the amount of red, green, and blue light reflecting from the original copy is measured, digitized, and stored in the scanned file. The process of color scanning is depicted in Fig. 7.4.

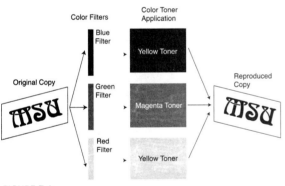

FIGURE 7.4:
The process of color scanning

Cold and Hot Scan Technologies

Two types of light sources are currently used in scanners. These light sources are referred to as either "hot" or "cold." Hot scanners use a fluorescent or xenon light source that is coupled with a cooling fan to regulate the temperature of the light. Cold scanners typically use xenon cold cathode bulbs that limit light deterioration when working with color originals. Cold scanning also eliminates the need for cooling fans because the bulbs, which are sealed in dust-free enclosures, generate very little heat. Hot scanners are less expensive than their cold scan counterparts.

Single- and Three-Pass Scanners

Single-pass scanners capture all of the color information from the original copy during one pass of the scanner head. Three-pass scanners require three passes of the scanner head and take three separate exposures of the original to capture color information. Most desktop scanners currently produced for the general consumer market are of the single-pass type.

Flatbed Scanners

Flatbed scanners continue to become increasingly sophisticated and affordable and currently rival the high quality standards that have typically been associated with drum scanners (discussed later). Flatbed scanners resemble traditional photocopy machines in appearance. The original copy is placed on a flat glass bed and is scanned from beneath by a moving beam of light. Light strikes the copy and is reflected off a mirror and then through a focusing lens. The lens focuses this light onto a light sensor converter, which then changes the light into electrical impulses that are assigned binary numbers, thereby digitizing the signal and scanning the copy line by line (This linear array scanning technique is also used in digital cameras.) Figure 7.5 shows a typical flatbed scanner, equipped with a transparency adapter that enables scanning both reflective and transparent copy.

The light sensor converter in the scanner is referred to as a "charge-couple-device," or CCD. CCDs have undergone major technological improvements over the past several years. This has resulted in flatbed scanners that can rival drum scanners in capturing both resolution and dynamic range or the overall contrast range that can be captured by the scanning head. Software that comes bundled with the flatbed scanner has also undergone major revisions and improvement. The quality of the scanning software applications is important because the software is required to improve the quality of a raw, scanned image. Interpolating and retouching original scans, such as smoothing color gradations to eliminate banding marks, can often take up significant amounts of time. Not long ago, scanning software could be used only to control the scanning process and to change the contrast, size, and resolution of the scanned image. Currently, some programs allow scanner operators to make image corrections and modifications, even from prescanned images. The development of high-end scanner software can significantly affect the delivered price of the scanner; therefore, these features should be carefully evaluated before making any purchasing decisions.

FIGURE 7.5:
Flatbed scanner

Drum Scanners

Drum scanners incorporate cylindrical rotating drums on which the original copy is mounted. As the drum rotates, a light source moves across the surface of the copy, capturing the image, pixel by pixel. Some drum scanners have fixed rotating drums; others use removable drums that simplify the mounting of different types of originals such as transparencies, color negatives, photographs, and other types of line and illustration copy. Originals are mounted to the surface of the drum using either adhesion oils or tape. Two light sources are available, based on the type of copy to be scanned. Reflective copy uses a light source that moves over the coy on the outside of the drum; transparent copy uses an internal light source that shines through the drum and the mounted copy onto the light sensors.

Drum scanners use photomultiplier tubes (PMTs) to sense light from the original copy and digitize the scan. PMTs have traditionally yielded higher density ranges than their CCD counterparts although this quality gap has narrowed significantly in the past several years. High-end drum scanners use four PMTs: one for each of the primary colors (red, green, and blue) and a fourth for unsharp masking, a process that places an unseen outline around objects thereby creating a greater sense of detail by lightening the light areas and darkening the dark areas in transition areas of the original. Drum scanners incorporate high optical/mechanical resolutions in their designs by imaging the original copy pixel by pixel, which results in high quality imaging capabilities. Optical resolutions of 5,000 lines per inch and greater are typical of these machines. Figure 7.6 shows original copy being loaded onto the pick-up side of the drum scanner.

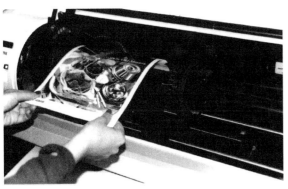

FIGURE 7.6:
Drum scanner

Slide Scanners

Although drum and flatbed scanners offer transparency adapters as either standard equipment or an optional accessory, dedicated slide scanners are used where a high volume of either negatives or transparencies must be digitized. Slide scanners incorporate flatbed technology to move either the transparency holder or light source across the film. The software interfaces and operating characteristics of slide scanners are similar in most other respects to their conventional flatbed counterparts (Fig. 7.7).

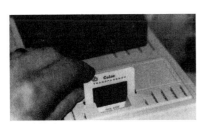

FIGURE 7.7:
Slide scanner

■ LINE ART AND GRAYSCALE SCANNING

The printed color revolution notwithstanding, the majority of printed materials is still reproduced in only one color. Line art and grayscale images make up the majority of monochrome scanning requirements. When scanning line art, the scanner senses each pixel as either black or white, regardless of the shading characteristics of the original. In the grayscale operating mode, the scanner is usually capable of detecting up to 256 shades of gray in the original copy.

Most scanners have a prescan feature that allows the operator to first scan the original at low resolution and then adjust size, cropping, positioning, highlighting, and contrasting. Advanced scanning software also allows the operator to make color and other precision adjustments from the prescanned image. Enhanced prescanning features save time that would otherwise have to be spent on the completed raw-scanned image.

Scanning Line Art

When scanning line art, the computer needs only one piece of information for each picture element, or pixel: whether the pixel is black or white. Black and white digitally translates into zeros and ones or on and off electrical signals. To help make this determination when scanning, a density threshold is set by the scanner operator. If the density as sensed by the CCD or PMT is above the threshold level, the computer assigns that pixel as black; if below the threshold, the density is assigned as white. Proper density thresholds are important in order to eliminate unwanted blemishes and other stray marks that may be on the original or when scanning copy that is either faded or discolored due to aging or damage.

The computer pixel then requires only one computer bit of information: whether the electrical signal is on or off. Because line art is defined primarily by its edges and outlines, the resolution for scanned line copy must be higher than for halftone pictures and grayscale art work. The minimum acceptable resolution for most line art is 400 lines per inch. Halftone and gray-scale illustrations should be scanned at a minimum of 300 lines per inch, suitable for printing the halftone illustration with a screen ruling of 133–150 lines per inch (see the formula for determining screen rulings later in this section).

Scanning Grayscale Copy

When scanning grayscale copy, the scanner is sensitive to the overall density of each pixel. Some color scanners have dedicated grayscale sensors and filters; others use all three sensors (red, green, and blue) to scan the image and then average the densities detected by each of the sensors to produce the correct shade of gray. In some systems, one of the sensors, either red, green, or blue, is used for the grayscale scan. Color images are turned into grayscale pictures by first scanning the picture in color and then changing to grayscale with post-processing or scanning application software.

Quality grayscale scans require a minimum 8-bit scanner capable of capturing 256 levels of gray. The important factor in grayscale scanning is the level of gray each gray area is. In this instance, each pixel is assigned 8 bits (which is equivalent to one byte) of computer memory allocation. This enables the computer to display 256 shades of gray. There are advantages to capturing more than 8 bits of information when scanning grayscale images: The more information captured, the greater the quality and detail of the scanned images. Current scanning technology allows 48-bit scanning; however, the evolution of scanning technology continues to increase scanner resolution and sensitivity with an accompanying decline in price for both drum and flatbed scanners.

Scanning Text

A major use of scanners has always been for archiving information. In this process, original copy is scanned and then saved on removable optical hard disks and CD-ROMs. When scanning text, optical character recognition (OCR) software enables the computer to compare the letters of the scanned text to predefined patterns for the letters of the alphabet stored in the OCR software program. After scanning, the document can either be stored immediately or brought into a word processing program for reformatting, if necessary. Figure 7.8 illustrates scanned text copy using typical OCR software.

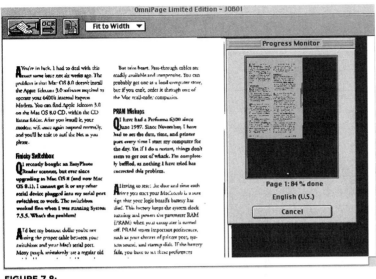

FIGURE 7.8:
OCR text scan

Although OCR software is highly accurate (more than 95% accuracy is typical), this figure still represents more than one error in every fifteen words. Therefore, all scanned text should be run through a spell-check program to ensure the accuracy of the scanned document prior to storage or printout. Even with accurate spell-check programs, final proofreading of all scans is still required (refer to Chapter 3 for detailed information on proofreading and proofreading symbols).

Scanning Color Originals

High-quality color scanners currently offer 16 bits of information per color (for a total of 48-bit scanning depth) at high resolution. Optical resolutions in excess of 4,500 lines per inch are required for scans to be considered photographic quality. These resolutions are available from high-end drum scanners; however, only a handful of high-end flatbed units offer them. Although most scanner software packages offer high interpolated resolutions, it should be kept in mind that the interpolation software is, in effect, guessing as to what colors fill in the gaps based on the algorithm, or design, of the software. Therefore, utilizing optical or built-in scanner resolution is always preferable for achieving high-quality color scans (see the section on optical and interpolated resolution later in this section).

To ensure both accurate color rendition and consistent color values from a scanner, service bureaus that specialize in high-volume color scanning implement some type of color management system on the host computer. Although the goal of color management is often referred to as "better color," the true value of color management is to minimize wasted time and deliver consistently accurate color renditions. Color management involves a considerable investment in equipment, training, and time. A complete system incorporates the use of profiling tools for scanner and monitor calibration, measuring instruments such as colorimeters and densitometers, workflow tools to facilitate color proofing and production, and training and consulting services.

Most scanners are currently set up as plug-in applications to photo-editing programs such as Photoshop®. The completed scan opens up in the program making it ready for touch-up and rendering. The quality of the post-processing program used to handle, modify, and finally store the scan cannot be underestimated.

■ PRODUCING HALFTONES ON COMPUTERS

There are several methods available for producing halftone, or continuous tone, images and negatives using computer-based systems. Most often, original photographs and illustrations must first be digitized. After the photograph is digitized, it can be manipulated using any one of several available software programs. During this stage, the density and tonal range, brightness and contrast of the photograph can all be modified. The photograph can then be output directly to either film or paper using conventional computer printers or high-end imagesetters. The use of digital cameras to take pictures eliminates the need to digitize the image through scanning. The camera digitizes the image during the exposure process. The images from digital cameras are then downloaded to the computer using software transfer programs supplied with the camera.

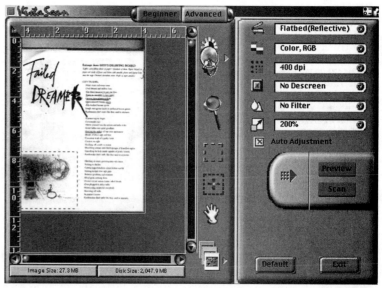

FIGURE 7.9:
Software interface for scanner

Digital cameras aside, the most common method of computerizing continuous-tone originals is through the use of a scanner. Depending on the type of the original and the quality required in the printed image, either a flatbed or drum scanner is used for digitizing the original. High-quality reproductions usually call for originals to be digitized using a drum scanner as illustrated in Fig. 7.6. Drum scanners are capable of delivering higher resolution and greater contrast ranges than their flatbed counterparts. On-going advances in flatbed scanning technology will probably narrow the quality gap between flatbed and drum scanners in the coming years.

The plug-in mode of scanner operation provides a flexible interface for the digitizing and software processing of the scanned image. The scanner uses its own software to capture and digitize the image, then turns the image over, in effect, to the editing program for further changes. Most scanner software incorporates basic image editing and manipulating capabilities to maximize the quality of image capture (Fig. 7.9). Serious image editing, however, should be left to specialized software packages.

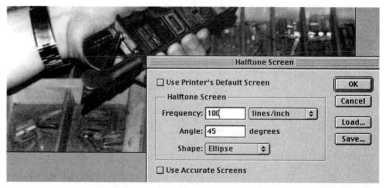

FIGURE 7.10:
Selecting halftone choices from the output menu

When using computers, the conversion of a continuous-tone image to screened copy is done when the digitized illustration is output to film, paper, or plate material. All aspects of the halftone screen are selected on the output menu prior to printing, (Fig. 7.10).

When outputting color separation negatives and positives, the software incorporates screen angle selection for each of the colors to be printed.

In the direct-to-film technique, even though imagesetters take the place of the process camera, all of the parameters that affect photographic film, including proper exposures, processing, and handling must still be carefully considered. For example, settings that control film density in the imagestter are just as important for proper dot formation as are the use of densitometers and correct exposure times when using process cameras. Although imagesetters use automatic film processors, the settings that control processing chemistry temperature and the speed of film travel through the processor must be carefully controlled to maximize image quality. Therefore, even when using computers to generate halftone images, although the process is digitized, quality control cuts across all automated technologies, including computers.

Unsharp Masking

Unsharp masking, referred to as USM, creates an invisible outline around an image. This outline gives the image a greater sense of detail. In high-end scanners, the ability to perform unsharp masking on the fly—that is, during the actual scan—saves considerable operator time by eliminating some postscan processing. In drum scanners, an additional PMT tube is incorporated into the scanner hardware to accomplish on-the-fly masking. With this process, the scanner increases the contrast in transitional areas of the original by lightening light areas and darkening the dark areas of the scan.

Item	Resolution Required
Newspaper Photographs	55–100
Textbook Illustrations	133–150
Standard Halftone Photograph	133–330
Digital Typesetter	1800–2500+
Early Generation Scanners	300
Color Drum Scanners	600–5000

FIGURE 7.11:
DPI requirements for various printed products

Scanning Resolution

The resolution that a scanner is capable of delivering is listed as the number of pixels per inch (ppi), also referred to as dots per inch (dpi). The higher the resolution of the scan, the greater the detail and contrast will be captured. To put scanner resolution into perspective, consider the dpi requirements of the materials listed in Fig. 7.11.

Optical and Interpolated Resolution

Scanners can operate at two different resolution rates known as the *optical* (or hardware) resolution and the *interpolated* (or software-interpreted) resolution. Scanners for the consumer market manufactured from the mid-1980s through the early 1990s were usually limited to resolutions of 300 dpi. Resolution capability has increased considerably since that time.

Optical scanning resolution is the actual, mechanical resolution ability of the scanner, utilizing its built-in optical and hardware power for physically distinguishing the number of lines, or dots per inch. For example, a drum scanner with an optical resolution of 4,000 lpi will move 1/4,000th of an inch across an original each time the drum rotates. Thus, the drum must rotate 4,000 times before the light source moves one inch across the original.

Most scanner manufacturers supply software programs that boost the optical resolution of their scanners. This is called interpolated resolution, and it relies on software that uses a mathematical formula called an algorithm. The algorithm analyzes the original scan and adds pixels to fill in the spaces between the original and final scan requirements. Although software interpolation usually works well, the program is essentially a guess, and not an actual measurement, of what additional colors the pixels should be.

Both optical and interpolated resolutions are given as specifications for a scanner. For example, a scanner may be listed as having an optical resolution of 600 x 1,200 dpi, with an interpolated resolution of 2,400 x 2,400 dpi. The two figures for each specification represent the horizontal and vertical resolutions of the scanner. Since interpolated resolutions are guesses as to how the computer completes the scan, the interpolated resolution is of a lower quality than would be achieved if the scanner had the higher optical resolution figure. When scanning quality is a high priority, optical/hardware resolution, rather than interpolated figures, should influence the purchasing decision.

Calculating Optimum Resolution for Halftones

In almost all instances, the scanning resolution for line art is generally higher than that required for halftone scanning. This is due to the necessity for capturing fine detail in the outlines of objects in line art. When working with continuous-tone originals, if the scanning resolution is too low then the quality of the finished scan will obviously be poor. Conversely, if the scanning resolution is too high, the resulting file will be too large, with little extra benefit in the nature of detail or quality. Large files slow down image manipulation and transmission time between the computer and laser printer or imagesetter. The optimum resolution for most continuous-tone images can be determined easily with the following formulas.

For copy to be scanned at 100% (same size as the original), use the formula:

Scanning resolution = screen size (in lines per inch) x 2

For example, if the screen size of the reproduction will be 150 lines per inch, then the scanning resolution should be:

Scanning resolution = 150 x (2) = 300 lpi

When copy is to be either enlarged or reduced, the enlargement or reduction factor should be entered into the equation:

Scanning resolution = screen size x 2 x enlargement/reduction

Using the same screen size as the previous example, let's assume that we are going to scan our original photograph at 75% or its original size, giving us a reduction factor of .75. Entering this figure into the equation, we get:

Scanning resolution = 150 x 2 x .75 = 225

Note from this example that reductions require lower scanning resolutions than do enlargements.

Always clean the scanner flatbed glass or glass drum before each scan. Drum scanners often have remnants of tape on the drum from previous copy that must be removed before scanning new originals. Also, be sure to use the register marks on the scanner when aligning copy. This minimizes the need for the scanning program to automatically straighten crooked or misaligned images.

Manipulating Scanned Images

The software packages that come bundled with modern scanners make the scanning and editing process relatively simple and uncomplicated. When the scanning software is first opened, a control palette on the screen enables the operator to select specific scan controls and functions (Fig. 7.12).

When beginning the job, the operator has the choice of either prescanning an image or beginning the scanning process immediately. Prescanning is performed at low resolution and allows the operator to crop, position, and make adjustments such as highlighting and contrasting before making a final scan. These preliminary adjustments save editing time later on. A prescanned image in the scan control window is shown in Fig. 7.13.

After the final scan is completed, the image automatically opens up in the imaging program that the scanner software is plugged into and is ready for editing and adjustment as required.

The editing capabilities of most imaging programs are very powerful. Images can be resized, sharpened, rotated, cropped, filtered, contrasted, highlighted, color-adjusted, and skillfully modified so as not to resemble the original. (Refer to Chapters 4, 5, and 6 as well as application software manuals for both general and specific image-editing capabilities.)

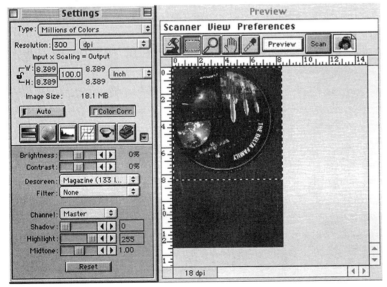

FIGURE 7.12:
Scan control palette

FIGURE 7.13:
Prescanned image in control palette

■ DIGITAL PHOTOGRAPHY

Ever since their introduction in 1991, digital cameras have held the promise of a film-free future. The introduction of Apple's QuickTake® single exposure point-and-shoot camera in the mid 1990s opened up the digital camera market to desktop publishing. Even though, for many traditional photographers, digital cameras will never be quite good enough, the industry seems to be betting on a digital future as evidenced by the introduction of more than 100 different models of digital cameras in 1999 alone. Among the most popular methods for storing pictures are either memory flash cards or conventional floppy diskettes (Fig. 7.14).

FIGURE 7.14:
Digital camera

Presently, there is widespread use and acceptance of digital cameras in the prepress field. Today's camera vendors are putting most of their efforts into developing the general consumer market. Photographic-quality 2-megapixel CCD cameras currently offer instant gratification and photographic quality pictures without the wait and cost of traditional photo-lab processing. New 6-megapixel cameras housed in conventional 35-mm camera bodies, using standard lenses and accessories, have begun to appear on the professional photography scene as well. In most systems, raw image data are compressed and stored in interchangeable data cards placed in the camera. When the images are downloaded onto a computer and opened in a program such as Photoshop®, the compressed data expands to allow for image editing. Additional cards add infinite storage capacity to these cameras.

As with any developing industry, camera technology is changing. Digital cameras act essentially like scanners and use either charged couple devices (CCD) or complimentary metal oxide semiconductors (CMOS) arrays to capture images. The CCD arrays are arranged in a square configuration and scan the subject in one exposure. This scanning procedure differs from flatbed scanners which capture images, line by line rather than in one complete exposure sequence. CCDs, the backbone of flatbed scanners and early-generation digital cameras and camcorders since the early 1980s, have a proven track record in this area. However, CCDs require significant amounts of energy, which causes rapid battery drain in most digital cameras. CMOS arrays are relatively light on power requirements. Recent advances in CMOS hardware and software technology have addressed historical weaknesses in the arrays regarding low light sensitivity and high levels of signal noise that can cause

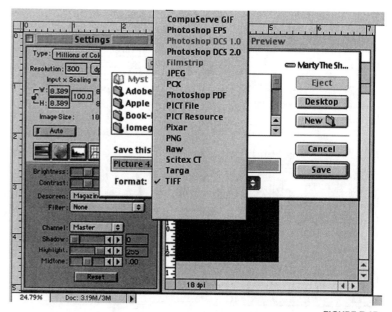

FIGURE 7.15:
Save options dialogue box

distortion in the recorded images. The consumer can expect to see continued changes in technology, features, and pricing as digital photography continues to grow and expand in market penetration.

■ SAVING SCANNED IMAGES

After final editing, the operator has a choice of several file formats in which to save the image. These options appear in the "Save" dialogue box (Fig. 7.15).

The choice of file format is important because the format determines how easy it will be to move or exchange images between different operating systems and hardware platforms. Also, specific page layout and Web-editing software packages only allow for importing specific file formats. (File forms are discussed in greater detail in Chapter 6.)

■ STORAGE DEVICES

Removable magnetic media, hard drives, and tape drives are the most common types of computer storage devices. These devices use magnetic material called *media* for storing information and they each operate in essentially the same way.

Floppy Disk Drives

Although floppy drives are beginning to loose their status as *the* storage device for small files, they are still arguably one of the most widely used information storage systems. Installed as standard equipment on virtually all computers since the early 1980s, new computers are no longer necessarily shipped with floppy drives. Instead, newer high capacity "super drives" are replacing the venerable floppy. The first floppy disks were eight inches in diameter. In the early 1980s, IBM PCs were first available with 5-1/4-inch drives and, later on, with 3-1/2-inch floppy drives. The disks are manufactured from flexible plastic sheet, hence the term "floppy." Original drives were able to store 180 kilobytes (Kb) of information. As the drives became more sophisticated, disk capacity increased to its current 2 MB (uncompressed) capacity.

During drive operation, information is transferred from the computer to the disk through the disk drive head, which records information as small magnetic patches on the disk surface. As the disk rotates in the drive mechanism, the drive head produces circles of information on the disk. These circles are called *tracks*. The tracks are divided into individual sectors. The tracks and sectors can be likened to a file cabinet with individual file folders; the tracks are the drawers of the file cabinet and the sectors are the individual file folders within the drawers.

Hard Disk Drives

Hard disks are so named because, rather than using a thin flexible plastic disk for data storage, a hard platter, coated with a metal oxide, is the actual disk media. Depending on the capacity of the drive, several media platters are mounted inside the drive casing. During operation, the electromagnetic read/write drive heads float on a cushion of air about a millionth of an inch above the drive media and never actually touch the surface of the disk. Hard drive malfunctions can occur during a drive "crash," which occurs if the drive heads come into contact with the drive platter. This type of hardware crash renders the hard drive inoperable and is usually accompanied by partial or complete loss of all data stored on the drive.

The drive heads are located at the end of an actuator arm. The arm moves the heads across the surface to retrieve or write information on different tracks of the disk. Whereas first-generation hard drives were able to store 5 MB of data, current minimum hard drive specifications for most PCs start between 6 to 8 gigabytes (one gigabyte is equal to 1,000 megabytes). A multiple-platter hard disk drive arrangement is shown in Fig. 7.16.

FIGURE 7.16:
Typical hard disk drive configuration

RAID Drives

The purpose of a redundant array of independent (or inexpensive) disks (RAID) system is to increase system speed and performance as well as provide a high degree of data security (data security as used here refers to data that are backed-up, or duplicated, as opposed to security access for registered users only). RAID systems are installed where data-intensive applications such as high-speed video, image processing, and other disk-intensive operations are the primary system operations. The RAID system shown in Fig. 7.17 is used to power an internet server. Each of the servers illustrated can withstand two hard drives crashing simultaneously without affecting the performance of the server. The remaining drives will automatically rebuild the two affected drives. This type of system is capable of handling up to 30,000 connections, or "hits," simultaneously.

There are six different levels of RAID technology, designated as levels 0 through 5, used to write and retrieve data from the drive array. For example, in a level 0 RAID array, segments of data are written to successive hard drives. This process is called *stripping*. In level 1, two hard drives

FIGURE 7.17:
RAID array
(Courtesy SIRS Mandarin)

are used. All data that are written to one drive are automatically duplicated onto the second drive, providing continuous data back-up. This process is called "mirroring." The higher the RAID number, the greater the sophistication in data storage and security. For example, a level 5 RAID array, typical of internet file servers, can experience a failure of two hard drives simultaneously without any loss of data access to customers and simultaneously rebuild the lost data from the other drives in the system.

Magnetic Tape Drives

Magnetic tape drives were the original systems used for storing computer information. Tape drives were dominant features of large, mainframe computers during the 1960s. Currently, the main use for magnetic tape drives is for backing up and archiving, or storing, information. Figure 7.18 shows an external tape back-up drive, which features multiple gigabyte storage capacity. Software that comes bundled with the tape drive enables automatic back-up of the computer hard drive on a daily or weekly basis and is software selectable.

FIGURE 7.18:
Tape drive

FIGURE 7.19:
MO drive

FIGURE 7.20:
Zip® Drive

Magnetic/Optical Drives

Magnetic/optical (MO) drives are available in different removable cartridge sizes for backing up or storing large files. The cartridges resemble thick floppy disks. During the data recording process, a laser heats a magnetic alloy recording layer on the disk to approximately 150 degrees. At this temperature, the alloy can be magnetized. The disks can be either single- or double-sided, depending on disk size. Some MO drives support the CD-ROM recording specification, in which the MO disk is recorded in a manner similar to CD-ROMs. First-generation MO disks were limited to 44 MB of storage capacity; current models can hold several gigabytes.

MO disks are slower in writing and retrieving information than are conventional hard drives. For this reason, MO drives are used primarily for archiving data and storing large files that have to be loaded only once. MO drives are ideal for backing up internal hard drives. Since they feature removable and erasable cartridges, they enable infinite data storage. An MO drive with an optical storage cartridge is shown in Fig. 7.19.

Zip® Drives

Zip® drives began to appear as drive options during the mid-1990s and have become the standard removable media storage system on most computers. The drives utilize a flexible plastic 3-1/2 inch disk housed within a rigid plastic case, and feature both 100 and 250 MB of data storage. Both the drives and disks are easily transportable, making them a favorite with graphic designers and printers for exchanging files. Zip® drives come in both internal and external versions for both Macs and PCs (Fig. 7.20).

■ CD-ROM TECHNOLOGY

The use of CD-ROM technology for a variety of storage and output tasks speaks to the great versatility of the compact disc as a flexible storage medium. The CD-ROM was developed by Phillips and Sony Corporation in 1981 as a medium for playing stereo music recordings. CDs replaced vinyl records and made up for many of the shortcomings of traditional album recordings: CDs had fewer limitations in recreating the full range of sounds, were not easily damaged, and virtually eliminated crosstalk, where loud passages could sometimes be heard on adjacent quiet passage recording tracks. Also, since the laser head never touches the CD, there is virtually no wear on the disc. The "ROM" in CD-ROM means "read-only-memory": once the disc has been produced, it cannot be altered. Even the "ROM" has been replaced by the CD-E format, which stands for CD-erasable discs that can be recorded, erased, and rerecorded.

Conventional CDs can hold up to 680 MB of information, the equivalent of almost 500 standard 1.4 MB floppy disks. Despite the versatility and storage capacity of the CD, all is not well in CD land. The venerable compact disc is under assault, both from the Internet and from a new CD format known as digital versatile disc, or DVD. We'll first examine the standard compact disc in more detail to better understand the technology.

Data Classification

Most CDs contain a variety of data, depending on the use of the disc. The information on a typical CD can be text and still-image graphics, video, graphic animations, as well as audio.

The original CD-audio standard introduced by the Phillips and Sony Corp. is referred to as the *Red Book* standard. All compact discs in music stores today are manufactured according to the *Red Book* standard. Because of this standard, all audio CDs can be played in any conventional CD player, a major factor responsible for the rapid growth of the industry. The *Red Book* standard was modified in 1984 by the Phillips and Sony Corp. with the CD-ROM standard, commonly known as the *Yellow Book* standard. The *Yellow Book* standard added two new types of tracks to the conventional CD audio track. These tracks are known as Mode 1 for computer data, and Mode 2 for compressed audio and vide/picture data. Mode 2 is sometimes also referred to as "XA." The "XA" standard, which allows audio and computer data to share the same data track on the CD, was officially introduced in 1989 by Microsoft, Phillips and the Sony Corp.

Graphic Data File Formats

Some of the file formats used for storing graphic images on CDs are:

Bit-Map Images: Sometimes called "computer raster images," pictures in bitmap are made up of individual dots or pixels. Bitmap images are the type generated by paint programs for which a specific number of bits or memory are required to generate each dot on the computer display. In black-and-white illustrations, one bit is turned either on or off to create white or black on the screen. For shaded images, more bits are required to create the proper shaded characteristics for each dot. File sizes are important in bit-map images because the size of the file required to store the image is dependent on the size of the image, the number of colors in the image, and whether or not the file is compressed when it is generated or stored. To get an idea of how file size changes based on format and color requirements, consult Fig. 7.21.

Object-Oriented/Vector Images: These types of images are generated in computer-aided drafting (CAD) and drawing programs. The image generated on the computer screen is stored as a series of connected lines and shapes. Object-oriented images require less storage space than do bit-map images.

Video Frame Capture Images: Full-motion video is captured at 30 frames per second by the computer and stored in a raster (or object-oriented) format. Capturing full-motion video requires a great deal of computer memory. One frame of video can require about 1 megabyte of computer memory, running the memory requirements to more than 30 MB for a one-second video sequence, depending on the size of the stored picture. Several methods of file compression are used to accommodate these large file sizes. File compression schemes used for video capture are referred to as "codecs." "Codec," which stands for the term compression–decompression, is a mathematical algorithm or formula that fills in the blanks from frame to frame in video pictures. This technique reduces the size of the video files. Some of the popular compression algorithms in use are:

Comparative File Sizes of a 4x5 Color and B&W Picture		
	Color	B & W
TIFF	5.2 MB	1.7 MB
EPS	7.0 MB	1.8 MB
PICT	2.3 MB	1.7 MB
JPEG	194 K	146 K
PSD	5.0 MB	1.7 MB

FIGURE 7.21:
Storage size of different types of files

JPEG: Stands for joint photographic experts group and uses a codec that removes repeated elements between frames. This technique is called "intraframe compression." JPEG compression is also a favorite for World Wide Web graphics.

MPEG: MPEG is an acronym for motion pictures experts group. MPEG uses an algorithm to create one compressed "interframe," and then removes repeated elements from succeeding frames and codes only the differences. MPEG was created for digital video and consists of two standards, one for CD-ROMs and the other for studio-quality video playback. MPEG has undergone three revisions since its first introduction, with level-3 being the most current.

MP3: MP3 is an audio file format compression, an extension of the MPEG file format above. MP3 offers much smaller files (about 1/10th the size) than traditional MPEG files for reproducing CD quality audio.

Cinepak: Compression software developed by SuperMac® Technology.

Indeo: Video software compression developed by Intel®.

QuickTime and QuickTime VR: Software developed by Apple Computer Corporation for playing back both compressed video images on a standard desktop Apple computer and for developing and playing back virtual reality applications.

QuickTime for Windows®: The Windows® version of QuickTime®.

Video for Windows®: The Microsoft version of QuickTime®, it allows compressed video to be played on desktop computers running Microsoft Windows®.

PAL Standard: The phase alteration line (PAL) standard is based on 25-frames-per-second video and is used in most of Europe and South America.

NTSC Standard: NTSC is an acronym for the National Television Systems Committee. This system, based on 30-frame-per-second video, is the color television standard for the United States, Japan, Canada, Mexico, Taiwan, and other countries.

Secam: This is the television standard used in France.

Computer Animation: A variety of animation programs is normally used to move objects from one part of the screen to another. These programs typically run between 5- to 15-frames-per-second (fps). Slide show motion is another type of animation program, in which motion is achieved by displaying successive video frames on the computer screen in rapid succession. These files are normally stored in the application file format in which they were created. Sometimes, a separate player is required to view the animation.

Compact Disc File Formats

The standard file formats for CD-ROM discs are:

HFS: This stands for the hierarchical file system. It is the standard format used by the Macintosh family of computers to access CD-ROM programs as well as other files and folders on Mac computers.

ISO 9660: This is the International Standards Organization file format for CD-ROM discs. The ISO format has been adopted by most CD-ROM manufacturers so that their discs will be compatible with most computers, regardless of the computer manufacturer. The ISO standard is also the format used for accessing Photo CD discs.

High Sierra Format: This format is part of the ISO 9660 format.

Joliet File Structure: This is an extension of the ISO 9660, and the basis for the CD Plus specification that allows multisession disc use in conventional audio CD players by placing audio tracks in the first session of the disc. The Joliet system enhances file recognition by lifting restrictions in file and directory names as well as the recognition sequence for multisession CD recording.

Photo CD Formats

Kodak's Photo CD technology was originally aimed at capturing the consumer photography market and predated the digital camera by several years. With the advent of the Photo CD, it was possible for the first time to have photographs that were taken with an ordinary camera scanned onto a compact disc through the services of the neighborhood photography store. Then, using a CD player, the photographs could be viewed on the family television set.

Rather than finding its widest acceptance in the consumer photography market, however, Photo CD technology continues to find wide acceptance in the desktop and conventional publishing markets. New software tools continue to appear that are designed to find, sort, manipulate, and modify photographic images stored on the Photo CD. The five major Photo CD formats are:

Photo CD Master Disc: This is the original Photo CD format for the consumer photographer. The disc can hold 100 images at high resolution. The images are stored at five different resolution levels, depending on the end use of the picture: 2048 x 3072 pixels is the highest resolution available for preparing color separations and other high-quality color renderings; 1024 x 1536 pixels is intended for high-definition television viewing; 256 x 768 pixels is designed for traditional television viewing; 256 x 384 pixels is made for thumbnail sketching; and 128 x 192 pixels is designed for smaller thumbnails. The master disc also functions as a digital negative, similar to a conventional film negative. The disc can be brought to the photography store and regular prints made from the slides that are stored in digital format on the disc.

Pro Photo CD Master Disc: The pro disc offers a higher level of resolution than can be found on the CD master disc. The Pro Photo CD Master Disc stores pictures at a resolution level of 4096 x 6144 pixels. Larger film formats such as 120 and 4 x 5-inch as well as regular 35-mm film are usually digitized onto the Pro Photo CD Master Disc.

Photo CD Catalog Disc: The photo catalog format is set up to handle a large number of images at lower resolution for display on regular television sets. Materials such as mail order catalogs and similar products lend themselves to this type of format because the lower picture resolution is acceptable. Print-quality reproduction is not usually achievable with the lower-resolution quality of this format.

Print Photo CD Disc: This format was developed for the color electronic prepress industry. It stores color originals in the CMYK (cyan, magenta, yellow, and black) format necessary for producing color separations.

Medical Format: This format allows data from CAT and MRI scans to be stored on the CD for later analysis or for archival purposes.

Audio Data (CD-DA), MIDI, and MP3

CD-quality audio was born in 1981, with the establishment of the audio format *Red Book* standard by Phillip and Sony Corp. (CD-DA). The quality of sound reproduction on a computer is dependent on three variables: the quality of the original sample or recording; the recording rate on the computer, in thousands of cycles per second (kHz); and the quality of the computer audio playback system. All conventional audio CDs are based on a sound sampling rate of 44.1kHz. Each sample contains 16 bits of data, which provides 65,536 different wave levels in two tracks for reproducing stereo sound.

Sound reproduction capabilities accompanied the evolution of the personal computer from its consumer introduction in 1981. The first Macintosh computers were born with sophisticated sound capabilities that were built into the system board and logic of the machine. Their Windows®-based counterparts, however, needed add-on sound cards installed on the computer's motherboard to give the computer sound recording and output options. Virtually all current PC-based computers, however, are on par with Macs as far as offering sophisticated sound input and output capabilities.

The higher the sampling rate used to digitize original audio, the better the quality of the sound will be when played back. However, higher sampling rates require greater amounts of memory to store the digitized audio. Figure 7.22 shows a comparison of different types of audio along with their sampling rates and the amount of memory required to store one minute of two-channel stereo audio.

Quality Level	Sampling Rate (KHz)	Resolution (Bits)	Bytes to Store 1 Minute Stereo Audio
CD Audio	44.1	16	10.09
ADPCM Level A	37.8	8	4.33
ADPCM Level B	37.8	4	2.16
ADPCM Level C	18.9	4	1.08
Digitized 22 KHz	22.0	8	2.52
Digitized 11 KHz	11.0	8	1.26
MP3	44.1	16	1.0

FIGURE 7.22:
Bytes needed to store one minute of digital audio

MIDI: MIDI is an acronym for musical instrument digital interface. The MIDI process is often used to enhance compact disc products and programs by adding computer-generated music and musical effects to a product. MIDI files can be stored on a compact disc or as a recorded digital audio track. If the MIDI files are not recorded in CD-DA format, a MIDI interface card is required to play back the sound files. Many MIDI sound files are available as public software on Internet bulletin board systems.

MP3: As discussed previously, MP3 is an audio compression codec based on the MPEG video compression format. MP3 can offer file sizes one-tenth the size of standard MPEG files while preserving near CD-quality sound. It accomplishes this feat by removing the digital signals that are undetectable to the human ear during the compression process. This process is called *perceptual coding*. With this compression technology the consumer can burn about 10 hours of music onto a CD instead of the roughly 74 minutes that a traditional audio CD can manage. There are thousands of free MP3 sound files and music clips available on the Internet at little or no charge.

Data Specifications of Compact Discs and Digital Versatile Discs

Both conventional CDs and DVDs have the same outside dimensions—5-1/4 inches. Other formats, such as the small Kodak 80-mm discs are designed for laptop computers and personal digital assistants.

Data Storage on Conventional CDs

On standard compact discs, data are stored on a spiral track that runs from the inside to the outside of the CD. The track spacing, or "pitch," of the track is 1.6 microns (μ); one micron equals one millionth of an inch. During manufacture, a laser burns small "pits," or indentations of varying lengths into the disc within the spiral data tracks. The untouched surface between the pits are called "lands." Digital data are

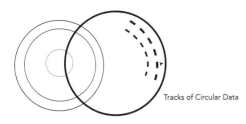

Tracks of Circular Data

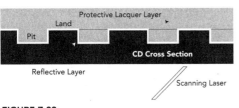

FIGURE 7.23:
0s and 1s on lands or pits of a CD

either a 0 or a 1. On the CD, the change from either a pit to a land or a land to a pit represents a "1;" the length of the path between these changes (the length of either the pit or land) equals a certain number of 0s. The arrangement of data on the typical CD is illustrated in Fig. 7.23.

As stated, the typical audio CD can hold up to 74 minutes of audio. This works out to approximately 783 MB of information. Allowing for error correction, the final disc capacity is about 680 MB.

Data Storage on Digital Versatile Discs

At first glance, CDs and DVDs are almost identical. Both discs are 5-1/4 inches in diameter, 1.2 mm thick, and rely on lasers to read data stored in pits and lands in a spiral track. However, at this point the similarities end.

DVDs were originally called "digital video disc," because the format was intended to be the primary delivery system for digitized movies shown on home TVs. Since then, other applications have moved onto the disc, and due to its potentially huge storage capacity, the "video" has been changed to "versatile."

DVDs are designed to hold a typical full-length feature film that averages about 135 minutes of screen time. Using an MPEG-2 codec, full-motion video uses about 3,500 kilobits per second (Kbps). To this, add 5-channel digital surround sound which features four directional speakers and a nondirection subwoofer channel at 384 Kbps. Again, add additional storage for multilanguage dialog tracks and subtitles for the movie and we reach 4,692 Kbps for each second (which is about 586 kilobytes, or KBps, per second) of the 135-minute movie. Multiplying all of this out gives us a capacity of 4.75GB of storage capacity required.

To make all of this information fit onto a 5-1/4 inch disc, the track pitch is reduced from 1.6 μ to 0.74 μ. Also, the pit size on the data tracks shrinks from 0.83 μ to 0.40 μ. Because a laser with a shorter wavelength is required to read the smaller data tracks, the disc platter is thinner so that the light doesn't have to travel through as much plastic to reach the data layer on the disc. The DVD specifications call for a disc only half as thick as a conventional CD, so to make up the difference, a blank 0.6-mm platter is glued on top of the DVD. To deliver the nearly 600 KBps required for movie playback, DVDs spin faster than standard CDs and must deliver a minimum of 1.3 MBps, although drives with more than twice that speed have appeared on the market already.

Although 4.7 GB is a great deal of information, the DVD specification calls for an eventual quadrupling of that storage capacity, to 17 GB. Increasing the storage capacity of DVDs is accomplished by going from single-sided to double-sided discs, and by using single- and double-density layers. In the double-density format, the focus of the read laser is changed to read two layers, the first of which is translucent instead of opaque. This enables the laser to penetrate and read two data layers instead of only one. In its double sided version, the blank plastic disc glued to the top of the conventional DVD is replaced by a second, recordable disc platter. The DVD storage capacities along with the layering options are highlighted in Fig. 7.24.

DVDs also feature sophisticated security systems that make copying the discs difficult. Look for DVDs to take over more and more data-intensive applications in the future as most computers come equipped with DVD compatible drives as the standard configuration.

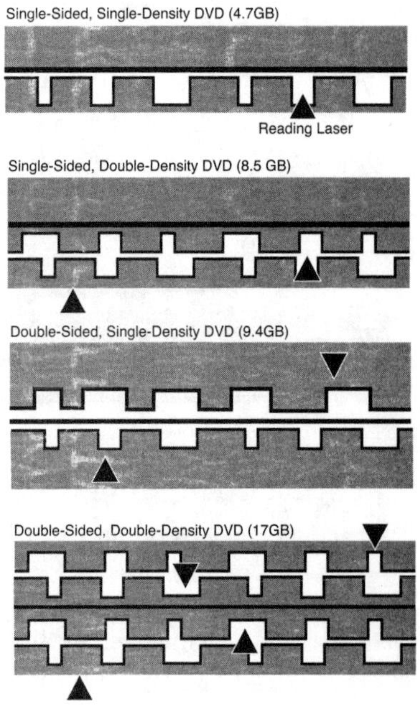

Reading Data on Compact Discs

When the CD is inserted into the drive, or reader, the data are read from below. CDs are more prone to damage from the top, or label side, than from the bottom of the disc. The plastic substrate provides more protection on the bottom of the disc than the relatively thin protective lacquer coating on the label side of the disc. Early-generation CD drives used disc caddies, into which the disc was placed, and provided a measure of protection for the CD against scratching. The caddy assembly was then inserted into the drive or reader. Modern CD drives and readers are caddyless, so care must be taken when handling the CD.

Data are read from the CD by passing light from a focused laser beam through the bottom plastic (nonlabel side) substrate of the CD. The laser light is focused on the pits and lands burned into the disc and reflected off the aluminum coating. As the laser moves across the pits and lands, the level of reflected light changes. Pits tend to scatter and diffuse the light, whereas the land surfaces reflect light with little change in intensity. A change in intensity of the light as the laser moves from a pit to a land, or vice versa, is a 1. If the intensity of the light remains constant for a certain period of time while the laser is over either a land or a pit, the light is interpreted as a 0.

To ensure data accuracy, the drive has autofocusing capability that keeps the laser at a certain distance from the reflective layer of the disc and focused on the center of the data track. Light intensity reflecting off the disc is continuously monitored. The pick-up head can be minutely adjusted to maintain proper tracking position and vertical distance from the disc by small servo-motors capable of very fine adjustment.

Single-Sided, Single-Density DVD (4.7GB)

Reading Laser

Single-Sided, Double-Density DVD (8.5 GB)

Double-Sided, Single-Density DVD (9.4GB)

Double-Sided, Double-Density DVD (17GB)

FIGURE 7.24:
Single- and double-sided DVDs

Compact Disc Erasable (CD-E) Format

Rerecordable compact discs have been commercially available since 1977. The process of erasing and rerecording CDs is based on the use of a phase change material, in which high-energy laser light is focused onto the material. When exposed to the laser, the material changes into a crystalline state. During the read process in the CD playback unit, the crystalline phase reflects light, which imitates the pits and lands of a conventional CD-ROM. Erasable CDs are compatible with existing CD drives.

Enhanced CD Format (CD Plus)

The original CD format was developed to store only audio information. An audio CD usually occupies between 50 to 60 minutes of the available 74 minutes of information space on the disc. The remaining 14 to 24 minutes of the disc are left blank. To take advantage of this unused space, which can be used to store anything from song lyrics to digital movies and other related information, mixed-mode CDs were created. A mixed-mode CD contains data on the first track and audio on the subsequent CD tracks. However, most audio CDs are not designed to skip the first information track and go to the second and following audio tracks. Playing the first track of a CD that contains conventional digital data on an audio CD player can damage some of the sophisticated stereo components. The CD Plus, or enhanced format, solves this problem by creating a multisession disc. The audio tracks are located on the first session of the disc while the remaining supplemental data are placed in the second session of the disc. Because all audio CD players are single-session readers only, the second session of the CD remains transparent to the audio CD equipment, which plays only the audio component of the disc.

Computers equipped with multisession CD-ROM drives scan the entire disc before playing anything. The computer can then be instructed to either play back the audio tracks or read the data stored in the second session of the disc.

CD and DVD Recorders (CD-Rs and DVD-Rs)

The format used by CD burners records single copies of CDs (called *one-offs*), or a limited number of CDs for both conventional CD-ROMS and DVDs. Currently, DVD recorders are limited to burning single-sided, 4.7 GB capacity DVDs. For recording programs longer than the two hours that fit on current DVDs, content producers will have to go to replicators that can burn dual-layered DVDs.

Data Transfer Capabilities of CDs

The ability of the CD drive to transfer data is a function of the following drive characteristics:

- Rotational speed of the drive
- Average access time required by the drive to retrieve information
- Data transfer rate of the drive, in kilobytes per second
- Ability of the drive to read single- and multisession discs

How quickly the drive spins the CD sets the stage for the speed of information transfer from the disc to the computer. The faster the rotation of the disc, the greater the scanning velocity of the drive read mechanism. First-generation CD drives rotate at about 530 revolutions per minute (rpm) on the inner disc tracks and about 200 rpm at the outer tracks. Double-speed drives rotate at 1060 rpm on the inner tracks and about 460 rpm at the outer disc tracks. Quad speed players rotate between 800 to 2000 rpm while 8-speed drives run between 1600 and 4000 rpm. Faster drives have correspondingly higher rpm values. When reading audio data, all drives shift back to single speed.

The difference in the rotational speed of the drive depends on where the drive's pick-up head happens to be located on the disc. To accurately read data, the drive must maintain a constant data rate moving under the pick-up head. This rate is called *constant linear velocity* (CLV). If the drive were to maintain a constant rotational speed, data on the outside of the disc would move more slowly under the pick-up head than data located on the inside tracks of the disc. To achieve CLV, the rotational speed of the disc is adjusted by the drive's servo-motor as the pick-up head moves from the outside to the inside of the disc.

To ensure an accurate data flow from the CD, data rate from the disc is compared with the frequency of a highly accurate clock built into the drive mechanism. The speed of the servo-motor is constantly adjusted based on this comparison. Current CD drives are offered with rotational speeds upwards of 50+ times faster than first-generation units (a 50 speed drive is designated as a 50X drive).

The access time on a drive depends on how far the drive pick-up head has to move across the surface of the disc to retrieve specific information, and how quickly this move is accomplished. Although the access times of current CD drives are a fraction of their first-generation cousins, they still lag behind the times offered by hard disc units.

Data transfer rates affect how smoothly a particular program runs on a CD drive. Specifications for data transfer vary based on the application. For example, an audio CD has a data transfer rate of about 176 KB per second (ps). A single-speed CD-ROM transfers data at about the same rate, but some of the data are used for error-correcting information, which results in an effective transfer rate of 150 KBps. However, data transferred at 150 KBps are too slow to run video clips and deal with large graphics files. This has led to the proliferation of high-speed CD drives, where speeds above 50X are commonplace. And, as we have seen with DVD drives, the single-speed DVD format calls for data transfer of 1.3 MBps. Drives with more than twice that delivery speed are already commonplace.

The longevity of the CD-ROM and all of its siblings speaks to the adaptability and versatility of this unique storage medium.

Single- and Multisession CDs

Single- and multisession CDs refer to how the data were originally written onto the disc during the recording process.

Single-Session CDs: A single-session disc contains one lead-in area, the program area, and a lead-out area. The data in the program area of the disc can be written either all at one time or at different writing times. Writing data to the CD at different times does not make the disc multisession. Figure 7.25 is a block diagram of a single-session compact disc.

FIGURE 7.25:
Single-session compact disc

Multisession CDs: A multisession CD has more than one lead-in area, program area, and lead-out area. Multisession discs can be written either during one writing session or at different times, depending on the features of the CD recorder. Multisession discs offer the flexibility of adding more information to the disc when it becomes necessary. An example of this would be adding 50 slides to a Photo CD that already had 50 slides scanned onto it. Figure 7.26 illustrates a multisession CD, showing the two lead-in, program, and lead-out areas that highlight recording sessions 1 and 2.

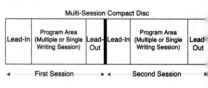

FIGURE 7.26:
Multisession CD

CD recorders are offered with 4X, 6X and 8X recording speeds, depending on the drive interface—the read rates on these units are generally higher. The recorders are available in a variety of read/write configurations, with prices starting under $300.

■ HOW CDS ARE MADE

A compact disc is comprised of a clear plastic disc, called a *substrate*. The plastic has pits and land areas that represent the digital data. On top of the substrate lies a very thin layer of aluminum that mirrors the pit and land surfaces. The aluminum provides the shiny reflective surface that enables the laser beam to reflect off the pit and land surfaces of the disc when the beam is reading the disc. A plastic coating covers the aluminum, which prevents scratching and oxidizing of the aluminum and keeps it shiny. The process of producing a CD-ROM into multiple copies is referred to as *mastering* the disc.

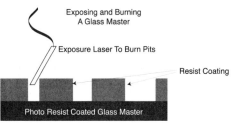

FIGURE 7.27:
Exposing the glass master

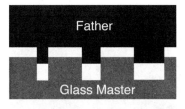

FIGURE 7.28:
Electroplating a mother disc from the father disc

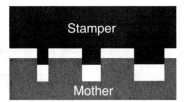

FIGURE 7.29:
Making stampers from a mother disc

Premastering the Data

Before the actual mastering process can begin, original data must first be converted into one of the standard CD-ROM formats (ISO 9660, High Sierra, Apple HFS, or DVD). This data conversion is referred to as *premastering*. Original customer data, supplied in a variety of digital-tape or hard-drive formats, is translated by the disc manufacturer onto a digital mastering tape. Once the data has been formatted, the premastering process is complete.

Mastering and Disc Production

The first step in CD production is the production of a glass master disc. Optically ground glass, with a very fine (1/10th μ) photoresist layer is exposed to a laser, which burns the pit and land patterns onto the glass master. When the disc is developed, the areas exposed by the laser are etched away and then silver-plated, leaving the actual pit structure of the disc (Fig. 7. 27).

A negative disc is then electroplated onto the original glass master. When the negative is separated from the master, a negative disc is produced. This disc is referred to as a *father* disc. Although the father disc could be used to reproduce CDs, it quickly wears out. Therefore, additional *mothers* are fabricated from the father by electroplating the father. Both of these steps are illustrated in Fig. 7.28.

A number of stampers are made from each mother image. Stampers are used to reproduce the actual pit structure onto the compact discs (Fig. 7.29).

The stampers are then used to make the actual compact discs, using an injection molding process that is similar to the one used to produce traditional long-playing vinyl records. The stamper creates the pit and land structures on the polycarbonate compact disc (Fig. 7.30).

In the final stage of the production process, the information layer of the disc is coated with a micron-thick layer of aluminum, which provides the reflective surface for the laser optical reading unit. A lacquer coating is placed over the aluminum to prevent scratching and oxidation of the aluminum coating. The disc label is then printed on top of the lacquer coating (Fig. 7.31).

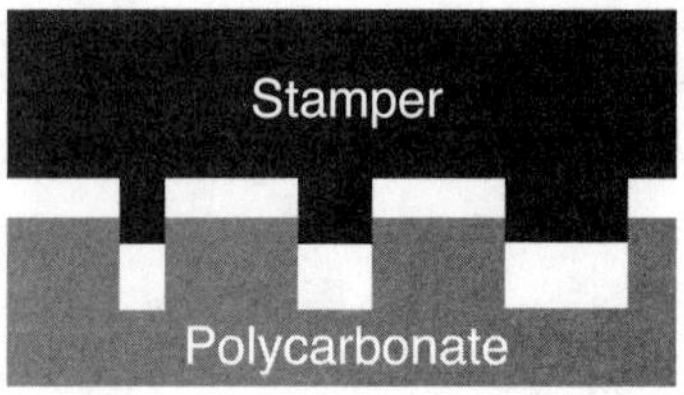

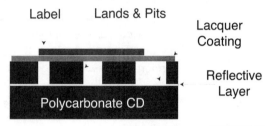

FIGURE 7.30:
Stamping the CD

Desktop CD-ROM Writers

Although master and producing compact discs is an advanced technology, systems are available that put the entire production process on the individual desktop at affordable prices. These systems are referred to as either CD-Rs (compact disc recorders) and CD-RW (rewriteable compact disc recorders) and are used for producing single discs (one-offs), and limited-run discs in a variety of computer formats. The input for these systems can come from a variety of media, including hard drives, Zip® drives, magnetic optical media, and a variety of tape drives. A desktop CD-R system is shown in Fig. 7.32.

FIGURE 7.31:
Lacquer coating and labeling

Most desktop CD-Rs offer three recording modes to choose from: incremental, single-session, and multisession. Incremental recording allows the operator to record some data, stop, and then add more information. Before the disc can be read, however, the recording session must be closed with a lead-out after the last recording increment. Single-session recording necessitates recording the entire CD without interruption. Multisession recording allows for recording data in a series of sessions that appear as separate volumes on the CD.

Desktop CD-Rs and CD-RWs record on gold media. Unlike conventional compact discs, which are silver in appearance, these units use a laser to write to the disc, which decomposes an organic dye layer placed over stationary grooves on the disc. Although they are not stamped, discs produced via a CD-R system can be read by conventional CD-ROM drives.

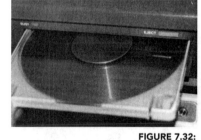

FIGURE 7.32:
Desktop CD-R

■ SUMMARY

The computerization of the graphic design and production industry has focused largely on the prepress side of the communications process. The information highway that gets much of the attention these days rests largely on the ability to convert and manipulate audio and video data in a digital format.

This chapter examined methods of digitizing a variety of data by utilizing flatbed and drum scanners, digital cameras, and CD-ROMs. The output options chosen for digitized materials depend on whether the data will be printed directly, as in direct-to-plate or direct-to-press technologies, or output to an intermediate processing stage, such as imagesetter or laser printer for proofing. The continuing evolution of CD-ROM technologies will prove to be a major force in the industry as their influence for information storage, retrieval, and multimedia increases in the coming years.

■ SUGGESTED STUDENT ACTIVITIES

1. Construct a timeline of the development of the CD-ROM. Begin the timeline with the introduction of the CD-ROM in 1981.

2. Construct a chart highlighting the binary numbering system and comparing the binary system to the conventional numbering system. Compare the same values of specific items in both binary and conventional numbers.

3. Calculate the scanning resolutions required for the following original photographs:

   A. 40% reduction at screen ruling of 133 lpi.

   B. 200% enlargement at screen ruling of 300 lpi.

   C. 33% reduction at screen ruling of 85 lpi

4. Construct a chart showing the side-by-side comparisons between conventional CD-ROMs and DVDs. The chart should highlight the four storage level options of the DVD format.

5. Compare, in chart form, the optical and interpolated resolution characteristics of five commercially available scanners. Use current computer store advertising and brochures to highlight the features and price comparisons for each of the scanners selected.

6. Using an original black-and-white or color photograph, make a series of four scans: 50 lpi, 100 lpi, 200 lpi, and 400 lpi. Using a loupe to examine the detail of each scan, compare the resolution, quality, detail captured, and overall contrast range captured in each of the scans.

Chapter 8 LINE AND HALFTONE ILLUSTRATIONS

Chapter 8 LINE AND HALFTONE ILLUSTRATIONS

Identify Different Types of Camera Copy

Calculate Enlargements and Reductions

Understand the Chemistry of Photography

Understand the Basics of Densitometry and Halftone Screen Rulings

Identify Different Types of Graphic Arts Process Cameras

Expose and Developing Line Negatives

Understand the Diffusion Process Transfer

Produce Halftones and Continuous Tone Images on a Computer

Process and Evaluating Halftone Negatives

■ INTRODUCTION

We have spent significant time in this text on the subject of how digital imaging techniques have made significant inroads into the traditional graphic arts and printing technologies. None of these inroads has been more significant or more far-reaching than the effect that digitization has had on traditional, chemical-based photographic processing used in the preparation of line and continuous-tone copy for printing.

These effects have their precedents in other, related technologies within the graphic arts. We have examined how the traditional process of using foundry type for setting text was replaced by mechanized Linotype and Ludlow typesetting machines; Linotype machines eventually gave way to phototypositors which were themselves eclipsed by laser-driven imagesetters. Following in this tradition, digital and computer-generated imaging systems have largely replaced conventional graphic arts cameras in the preparation of line and halftone illustrations. Computer-generated imaging has many advantages over chemical, or analog, photography. Film has always been an intermediate step in the production of printed images. Eliminating film handling by manipulating images on a computer screen and then sending these images directly to either film or plating on the printing press not only saves time, but eliminates the use of toxic chemical processing and streamlines the entire production process.

Silver-emulsion-based photography can still play an important role in demonstrating how images are transferred from the computer and artist's drawing board to the printing plate. The resolution characteristics of photographic film are higher than can be delivered by most scanners and imagesetters. This fact gives film a quality edge over digital techniques. The resolution of high-quality graphic arts film (called *ortho film*) is equivalent to a high-quality digital scanner operating at about 6,000 lines per inch of resolution.

Continued improvements in scanner technology will all but close the gap between the quality of digital and photographic imaging. As such, the graphic arts industry will continue to migrate toward the digital technologies and conventional photographic imaging will continue to play a small role.

Within this framework, let's look at the basic techniques used to produce traditional line and halftone images on both photographic film as well as procedures for outputting images from the computer directly on to film using digitized imagesetters. In this chapter, we will examine the use of both conventional photography as well as direct-to-film techniques used in the production of line and halftone negatives. Regardless of the method used to produce the negative, the concepts of image quality and control are the same. Quality, as usual, transcends the methodology of production.

■ TYPES OF CAMERA COPY

Original copy that is to be reproduced can be classified as either line or continuous-tone copy.

Line Copy

Line copy includes all material that is composed entirely of line or areas of single, solid tones only. Line copy contains no gradation of tone, shadows, or gray areas. Examples of line copy include typeset copy and pen-and-ink drawings. Photographs that have already been screened, either because they have been printed, or prepared for printing using screened print techniques, can also be classified as line copy.

Continuous-Tone Copy

Continuous-tone copy contains blacks and whites, as well as intermediate shades of gray, or gradation of tonal ranges. Examples of continuous-tone copy include original black and white and color photographs, charcoal sketches, and airbrush renderings that incorporate shades of gray and colors in addition to solid blacks and whites.

■ CALCULATING ENLARGEMENTS AND REDUCTIONS

The amount of available space for an illustration in a printed piece as well as the size of the original copy usually make it necessary to either enlarge or reduce original artwork and text when preparing line and/or halftone negatives. All enlargements and reductions are based on a scale of 100%, with 100% designating same-size reproductions. A line negative shot at 200% produces a negative image that is twice the size of the original. A negative shot at 50% produces copy that is one-half the size of the original.

■ PROPORTION SCALES

A proportion scale is the device used to determine the percentage of enlargement or reduction required in a particular situation, based on the size of the original and the required size of the finished copy. A rotating dial proportion scale is shown in Fig. 8.1. When working with this type of scale, the size of the width of the original copy on the inside wheel is rotated to align with the required size of the reproduction on the outer wheel. The percentage of the resulting enlargement or reduction shows through the window on the inner portion of the wheel. All proportion scales work in a manner similar to the one shown in the figure.

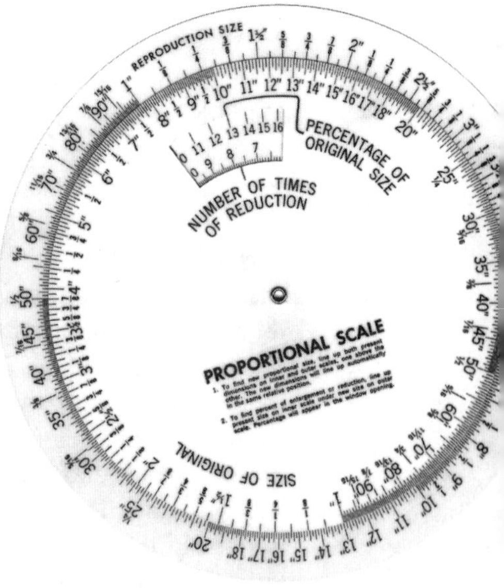

FIGURE 8.1:
Proportion scale

Computational Method

Sizes of enlargements or reductions can also be calculated mathematically, using the following formula:

$$\frac{\text{Reproduced size}}{\text{Size of the Original}} = \text{Percentage of reproduction}$$

To show how this formula is used, let's assume that an original photograph measures 6 inches wide and we wish to reproduce it at 9 inches wide. To calculate the reproduction percentage, use the above formula as follows:

$$\frac{9 \text{ inches final size}}{6 \text{ inches original size}} = 1.5 \text{ or } 150\% \text{ reproduction size}$$

■ CROPPING ILLUSTRATIONS

Most photographs contain at least some areas that are irrelevant or unnecessary as far as its intended subject matter. These unnecessary portions can be marked to be cropped out of the final negative. Cropping emphasizes the intended subject matter of the original photograph by eliminating extraneous information that otherwise captures the viewer's attention. When marking photographs for cropping, the original is covered with either a clear tissue or acetate overlay on which the cropping marks will be placed. This allows marks to be

FIGURE 8.2:
Cropping an illustration

moved or changed as necessary without marking up the original. In a digital editing program, cropping is done with a cropping tool that is used to draw a rectangle around the area of the photograph to show how it will appear after cropping (Fig. 8.2).

■ THE CHEMISTRY OF PHOTOGRAPHY

The chemical process of photography, increasingly referred to as "analog photography," to distinguish it from its digital counterpart is based on the action of visible light on a light-sensitive emulsion coated onto a plastic support base. Let's take a closer look and see what happens when film is exposed to produce a picture. The cross-section of a sheet of graphic arts film is shown in Fig. 8.3.

Graphic arts, or ortho, film is, in sensitivity terms, "red blind." Red blind film sees the color red as black, or as an absence of light. For this reason a red safelight can be used when working with ortho film in a darkroom. The ability to use a red safelight greatly simplifies film handling and processing.

Structure of Black and White Film

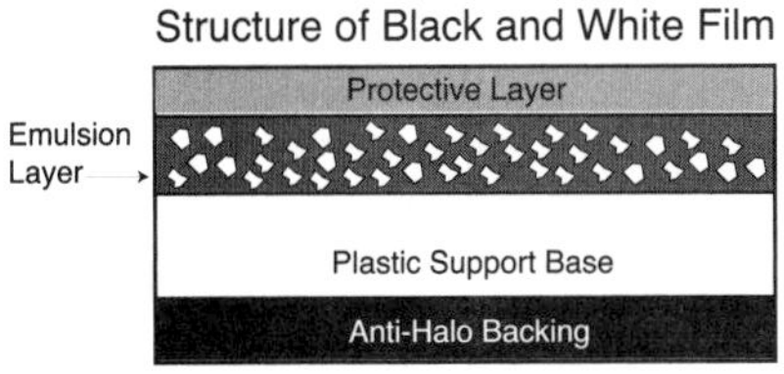

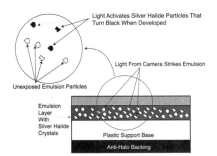

FIGURE 8.3:
Cross-section of black-and-white film

Most graphic arts film uses a film base made from relatively thin acetate plastic between .003 and .008 inches thick. The protective layer coating above the emulsion layer helps to prevent the film from scratching during normal handling and processing. The emulsion layer consists of light-sensitive silver halide crystals that are dispersed throughout a gelatinous emulsion medium. The silver halide crystals produce the final photographic image. The plastic support base is placed below the anti-halation (or, anti-halo) layer. This anti-halo layer prevents light that has penetrated through and exposed the silver halide crystals in the emulsion from reflecting off the base of the film. If this light were to reflect off the base of the film, it would re-expose the emulsion on the way back out through the film. This would produce a ghost, or halo image, hence the term anti-halo layer.

During the exposure sequence, light from the camera is reflected off the copy, through the lens system of the camera. The light then exposes the photographic emulsion as it penetrates the film. This exposure to light causes a chemical change in the emulsion of the film and produces what is known as a *latent image*. The term latent image refers to the fact that the light striking the film has been recorded by the emulsion of the film but requires further chemical processing in order for the image to become visible.

Film processing is carried out in four steps: a chemical developer; a stop bath, fixing solution, and a water wash.

In the developing process, the developer chemically "reduces" the exposed silver halide particles in the emulsion to black metallic silver (Fig. 8.4). The developing process must be properly timed so that only the silver particles exposed to reflected light during the exposure sequence are affected by the developer. Unexposed silver particles remain unchanged.

FIGURE 8.4:
Action of film developer on silver emulsion particles

The stop bath chemically neutralizes the action of the developer. Neutralizing the developer prevents further chemical activity from taking place within the emulsion once the negative has reached the proper stage of development. The nature of ortho film is such that given too much time in the developer, virtually all of the emulsion will turn to black metallic silver, regardless of how much light penetrates the film during exposure.

After the stop bath, the fixing solution loosens and begins to remove unexposed silver particles from the film emulsion (Fig. 8.5). A final water wash completes this removal process and washes away all remaining processing chemicals from the film. After washing, any remaining water can be squeegeed off the film and it is then left to dry.

Film processing can be done either manually or with automatic film processing equipment. Figure 8.6 illustrates the configuration of a typical automatic daylight film processor. These processors can be used for developing sheet film from a camera, roll film, or paper used in computer-driven imagesetters.

Daylight processors typically employ a series of transport rollers that move the film from one section of the processor to another. Note the absence of a stop bath in this processing sequence. Because the processor incorporates a variable timing mechanism and accurate control over the temperature of all chemistry, in this type of setup, chemical action taking place within the film emulsion is tightly controlled. A drying unit coupled to the processor delivers dry film into the delivery tray.

On-going technological advancements in film technology have also produced environmentally friendly films that require no developing chemicals other than ordinary water. Continuing advancements in this area will no doubt have significant impacts on film processing techniques in the years to come.

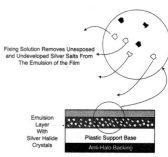

FIGURE 8.5:
Action of the fixer
on film emulsion

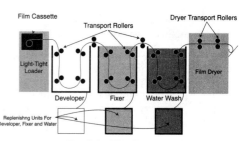

FIGURE 8.6:
Configuration of a typical
daylight film processor

Film Sensitivity

Film is rated, or classified, according to its sensitivity to different parts of either the visible or invisible electromagnetic spectrum. Some specialty films are sensitive only to the infrared portion of the spectrum. These films are typically used in applications that range from heat loss analysis of buildings to photographic satellite surveillance cameras that can take photographs through heavy cloud cover. Ortho film used in the graphic arts is sensitive to the blue-green portion of the spectrum, as discussed previously.

Figure 8.7 illustrates the entire electromagnetic spectrum. You can see from this illustration that visible light occupies only a very small portion within this spectrum.

Films that are sensitive to the entire visible portion of the spectrum, such as the black-and-white and color films used in amateur and commercial photography, are referred to as *panchromatic*, or simply *pan* films. Pan films use emulsions that are sensitive to the red, green, and blue portions of the spectrum. Color films contain a separate dye layer for each of the primary colors (red, green, and blue light). Black-and-white films are sensitive to the entire visible spectrum, as are color films, but record the three primary colors as differing shades of gray in the film emulsion, rather than as discreet colors.

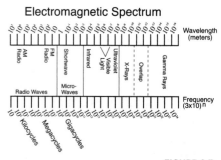

FIGURE 8.7:
Electromagnetic spectrum

Another consideration in the discussion of analog photography concerns the action of light as it passes through the emulsion of the film. Determining how much light is reflected from original copy, or is transmitted through a photographic negative, is known as *densitometry*. Densitometry is examined in more detail in the next section.

Basics of Densitometry

The science of densitometry deals with the measurement of the optical density (or the degree of blackness) or light-stopping ability of a particular tonal area of a film negative or film positive. Densitometry also deals with the density of photographic prints, paintings, and printed reproductions. The density, or darkness, of a photographic negative or positive is a result of the amount of silver dye developed within the emulsion of the film or photographic paper. In printed copy, density comes from the darkness, or light-stopping ability of the printing inks used to make the print. The final quality of a printed halftone illustration is dependent on the density of the various tonal areas in the original print as well as how accurately these tonal areas have been copied onto the halftone negative and transferred to the printing plate. A basic understanding of densitometry is necessary in order to evaluate and maximize the quality of the entire halftone photographic process. Four qualities can be measured in densitometric terms: *opacity*; *density*; *transmittance*; and *reflectance*. Each of these terms is explained below.

Opacity: Opacity is the ability of a substance (such as the developed silver particles in the emulsion layer of a piece of photographic film) to prevent light from passing through. Opacity is measured in decimal numbers ranging from 1 to 100. The higher the number, the greater the opacity, or light-stopping ability of the photographic emulsion.

FIGURE 8.8:
Taking readings with a densitometer

Density: Density is the same as opacity; however it is measured with a device called a *densitometer*. Densitometer readings use a scale with numbers from 0 to 4.0 (the higher the number, the greater the density). Densitometer readings can be taken either with an analog or digital densitometer. When taking readings, the sensing head of the densitometer is placed carefully over the exact area of the copy where the density is to be measured (Fig. 8.8).

Densitometers are available either as reflection units, which measure the negative density in reflection copy, or as transmission units, which determine the transmission density of photographic negatives. The densitometer is a quality control device. By taking measurements of density readings from different parts of a negative, a technician can compare the density readings of the negative to the original This comparison helps ensure that the maximum density range will be achieved in the final, printed copy.

Transmittance: Transmittance, or transmission, is the amount of light striking a photographic negative that actually makes it through, or penetrates, the emulsion layer in a particular section of a negative. Transmittance is expressed as a percentage of transmitted incident light (light that strikes a negative) and is a function of the halftone dot sizes on the negative. For example, a transmittance of 10% is 1/10 of the incident light, and occurs at a point in the negative with a 90% dot. Transmission readings can be taken from both photographic negatives and positives.

Reflectance: Reflectance, or reflection, is the percentage of incident light that is able to reflect off the copy (a photographic print, for example) in a particular tonal area of the photographic print. Reflectance is dependent on several variables. Among these are the brightness of illumination available when and where the print is viewed, and the type and color of the photographic paper used to make the print. For example, viewing a print in a well-lighted room will give higher reflectance readings than viewing the same print in a poorly lighted area. A perfect halftone print should have a 50% dot in the gray areas. The reflectance in this section of the print would be 50%. Conversely, an area of the print with a reflectance of only 5% (an area of the print that was reflecting only 1/20 of the incident light) would be a very dark gray or black in tone. Reflection readings can be taken from photographic prints and similar original artwork.

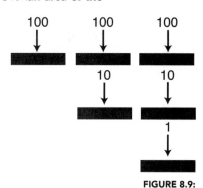

FIGURE 8.9:
Density relationship between transmission and reflection of light

Figure 8.9 shows a simple relationship between density and transmission of light. In this example, each additional layer of density reduces transmitted light by a factor of 10. By measuring the whitest white and the darkest dark area in a photographic print or reproduction using the densitometer, the overall contrast range of the illustration or photograph is easily determined. This contrast range is used to determine the proper exposure times when making a halftone negative, and it is discussed in greater detail in the next section.

With this basic understanding of the photographic print process, we'll move on to a discussion of the halftone process and how continuous-tone illustrations are prepared for reproduction.

■ HALFTONE SCREEN RULINGS

To print any continuous-tone illustration on a printing press, the picture must first be broken up into a series of dots. The halftone process is visible if you look closely at any photograph in a newspaper. Close inspection reveals the dot structure of the picture which is all but invisible when you view the page at a normal distance (between 16 to 24 inches). Because printing presses can either print solid ink, or nothing at all, the purpose of the halftone process is to convert the picture into a series of dots that can be reproduced by the press. This lets the human eye and brain interpret the picture as a continuous-tone illustration when viewed normally. Halftone screen technology will be examined later in greater detail.

Breaking a Picture into Dots

When using conventional photographic techniques to produce a halftone negative, a halftone screen that incorporates a built-in dot structure is placed over the film during the time the original photograph is exposed in the camera. This halftone screen is referred to as a *contact screen*, because, during exposure, the screen is directly in contact with the film. Early halftone screens were made from two sheets of glass with ruled lines, bonded together at a 90-degree angle. Most halftones are now produced using contact screens made from plastic. The dot structure on a contact screen is nearly clear in the center of the dot, and becomes progressively grayer, or darker, as you move away from the center.

During exposure, light reflecting from the dark, or shadow areas, of the original photograph is relatively weak. This light only passes through the center, or clearer areas, of the halftone screen dot. Light reflecting from the original in the brighter, or highlighted areas, is strong enough to penetrate the outer areas of the screen dot. This greater dot penetration through the screen produces a relatively larger dot on the negative. Light reflecting from the middle tonal areas of the original penetrates the center, clear areas of the contact screen as well as part of the grayer areas. Middle tones expose about one-half of the dot area from the halftone screen onto the negative.

FIGURE 8.10:
Comparison of dot shapes

Dot Shapes

We have established that continuous-tone illustrations are converted into a series of dots in the halftone process. There are many different halftone dot shapes available, the most common being round, square, and elliptical. Of these, the round dot is used most often. This is because the shape of the round dot enables more surface area of the halftone screen to be covered with actual dots. Greater surface area enables greater detail to be captured in the negative from the original print. Elliptical dots are preferred for facial features because this dot produces a softer transition from lights to darks as opposed to round dots. Note the difference in the areas covered by different dot shapes in Fig. 8.10.

Halftone screens are available with different sizes and shapes of dots and are categorized by the number of dots per inch that the screen reproduces. The greater the number of dots per inch in the halftone screen, the greater the detail will be in the printed reproduction. Coarse screen rulings, between 65 to 100 dots per inch, are used where detail quality is not important. Printed photographs in newspapers, newsletters, and tabloids fall into this category. Most text books use screen rulings between 133 and 150 lines per inch. Where highest reproduction detail is required, screen rulings of 300 lines per inch are common. Artistic reproductions and detailed medical photography would fall into this last category. Figures 8.11(a) and 8.11(b) compare the detail of an illustration reproduced at both 65- and 133- lines-per-inch halftone screens.

FIGURE 8.11(a):
Illustration produced at
65- line screen

FIGURE 8.11(b):
Illustration reproduced at
133- line screen

Types of Halftone Screens

Because there are many types of contact screens available, the one to use for a particular job depends on the type of copy being photographed and the effect the photographer wishes to achieve. Some of the popular types of contact screens are discussed below.

Gray Contact Screens: Gray screens are the standard contact screen. They contain a vignette dot, lighter in the center and darker as you approach the outer areas of the dot (as described previously), and are used for direct-screen halftone exposures for both black-and-white and color separation work.

Magenta Contact Screens: Magenta screens are used primarily for black-and-white copy work. They are not used for making color separations because the magenta color of the screen interferes with the color filters used in the separation process. Yellow and magenta filters are used with magenta screens to increase or decrease the contrast range of the halftone negative.

PMT Gray Contact Screens: PMT screens are used in the diffusion process transfer, or photomechanical transfer (PMT) process, for making screened paper prints (positives) from original copy. The resulting screened prints are referred to as *screened velox prints* and are used to help prepare combination negatives. The PMT diffusion transfer process is described later in greater detail.

ROUND DOT (100)   SQUARE DOT (100)   ELLIPTICAL DOT (100)   MEZZOTINT (75)

STRAIGHT LINE (62)   SUNBURST (100)   LINEN (50)   MEZZOTINT (150)

STEEL ENGRAVING (50)   WAVY LINE (60)   CONCENTRIC CIRCLE (60)   STEEL ETCH (50)

FIGURE 8.12:
Special-effects halftone screens

Autoscreen Film: Autoscreen film incorporates a halftone dot structure built into the emulsion of the film. This feature eliminates the need for the conventional halftone screen when making halftone exposures. The emulsion of the film acts in the same way as the halftone screen. It contains thousands of dots that increase in light sensitivity from the center to the outside of the dot. As with conventional dot structures, the size of the resulting dot in the autoscreen film is dependent on the amount of light reflecting from the original. Darker areas of the original areas expose only the center of the dot in the film and the lighter areas expose correspondingly larger areas of the dot pattern. Autoscreen film is available only in 133 dots per inch.

Specialty Screens: In addition to conventional halftone screens, specialty screens are available for producing unusual photographic effects. These screens are used in place of conventional screens during the exposure sequence. Some of the effects available using specialty screens are illustrated in Fig. 8.12.

Stochastic Screening

Conventional halftone screening presents an optical illusion to the viewer. When working with black-and-white illustrations, the halftone screen prints evenly spaced rows of dots that vary in size throughout the illustration, depending on the tonal area of the original. The varying size of the dots allows more or less of the white paper on which the image is printed to show through. This produces different shades of gray because the eye averages the amount of space occupied by both the white paper and the printed black dot. When working with color illustrations, the same theory of dot representation applies; however, four successive colors are printed over one another using transparent color inks. The inks act as filters to reproduce the primary colors of red, green, and blue to recreate the original color illustration (see Chapter 5 for more in-depth discussion on color generation and reproduction).

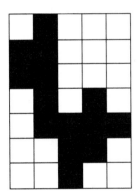 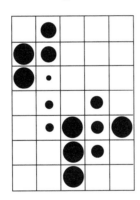

FIGURE 8.13:
Comparison of conventional halftone and stochastic screen dot patterns

Whereas conventional halftone photography uses the same number of dots in the highlight and shadow areas of the print and varies the sizes of these dots from, for example, 10% to 90%, a technique called *stochastic screening* is based on dots that are all the same size, but varies the space between the dots. Stochastic screening is sometimes referred to as *frequency modulation*, or *FM screening*, meaning that the dots vary in frequency, or number. Because stochastic screening relies on what appear to be randomly placed dots (rather than uniformly distributed dots used in conventional halftone screens), line or screen ruling terms are not applicable to the stochastic technique. Figure 8.13 contrasts the differences in dot patterns between the conventional halftone and stochastic screen process dot patterns.

One major advantage of the stochastic process is the elimination of moiré patterns. When rescreening black-and-white halftone originals or printing four-color separations, the placement of the dots is a critical factor relative to moiré patterns. If overlapping dots do not fall at just the right angle, or if they interfere with one another, then a moiré pattern will develop. Because stochastic screening uses randomly placed dots rather than uniformly generated ones, no moiré pattern can develop. A moiré pattern produced by the improper alignment of halftone dots is illustrated in Fig. 8.14.

FIGURE 8.14:
Moiré pattern

Stochastic screening has become a widely accepted standard during the past several years. Most imagesetter manufacturers have stochastic screening software either available or installed on their machines as a standard feature. Many large-format ink jet printers used for sign making and high-quality output use stochastic screening as the standard output format. Because the dot size on stochastic screens is smaller than the conventional halftone dot, it is particularly adaptable to the dry offset process, in which dot gain is minimized. However, because there are more dots, there is more opportunity for "graining" in the resulting print.

■ WORKING WITH COMBINATION NEGATIVES

When both line and halftone illustrations will be printed on the same page, there are several techniques that can be used to combine the two different types of negatives on the same page. Two of these techniques use traditional photographic and mechanical processes to prepare the pages. The third technique involves the use of software programs to assemble the different elements of the page, including text and line and halftone illustrations, on the screen-generated page. After positioning all of the text and illustrations, the entire page is output either to an imagesetter, which delivers the page on film, or it is printed on a high-quality laser printer, which outputs the page and readies it for the graphic arts camera. Outputting positive copy for photographing with a graphic arts, or process, camera is known as producing "camera-ready copy." Producing the completed pages on film by using an imagesetter is known as a "direct-to-film" procedure.

Traditional Combination Page Techniques

The term "traditional technique" for producing the printed page is now associated with the use of conventional photographic processing, as opposed to computer-image generation. There are two ways to prepare pages that contain both text and continuous-tone copy for reproduction.

The first technique produces only one negative that contains both the line and halftone illustrations. To do this, original photographs are first screened to produce halftone negatives. The halftone negatives are then contact printed to produce screened, positive prints of the original photograph. As mentioned previously, these screened prints are referred to as screened velox prints. The velox prints are then pasted up and photographed on the process camera along with the line and text copy.

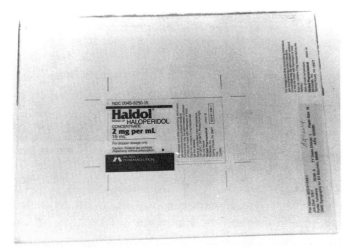

FIGURE 8.15:
Mechanical with both text and continuous-tone copy

The resulting pasted-up page is referred to as a *mechanical*, and an example is shown in Fig. 8.15.

In the second technique, the page is prepared by photographing all of the line copy and text material for the page, leaving spaces, or windows, where the halftone illustrations will go. These blocked-out window areas appear on the mechanical, or on the negative, in the exact location where the illustrations will appear. Separate halftone negatives are then pasted into the prepared line negatives in the window areas. The process of pasting negatives in this manner is referred to as *stripping-in* the halftone negative. The block-out/window technique is illustrated in Fig. 8.16.

FIGURE 8.16:
Window block-out method for stripping-in halftone negatives

Camera-Ready Copy

The great majority of copy for printing is now produced using computerized page layout programs. Text is set up in a word processing program and line art and photographs are prepared and digitized using illustration and image-editing software. These elements are then "imported" onto the electronic page. Figure 8.17 shows a completed page assembled in QuarkXPress®.

After all of the elements of the page have been positioned, two output options are available depending on the available equipment.

If conventional process cameras will be used to produce negatives for making offset printing plates, then the completed page is printed out using a high-quality laser writer, which results in a positive page print. The high quality of this print classifies it as camera ready. Camera-ready copy requires computer-driven imaging capable of delivering resolutions above 1,200 dpi. Photographic imagesetters, which can output both film negatives and paper positives with output resolutions between 1,600 to 3,000 dpi, are most often used for this purpose. This copy is then photographed using a process camera to produce the negatives required to make the printing plate. Figure 8.18 illustrates photographic positives as they are delivered by a daylight photographic processor and generated in the imagesetter.

FIGURE 8.17:
Page assembled electronically on a computer

Most often, imagesetters are used to produce photographic negatives rather than positives. As discussed earlier, the production of photographic negatives is known as a direct-to-film process and produces complete pages on a photographic negative, which are ready for plate production. Because most imagesetters can output to either film or paper, the direct-to-film process eliminates the intermediate step of photographing the page and then processing the negative, which is both time-consuming

153

and costly. In effect, traditional photographic processing procedures are completely eliminated. Using a daylight processor for film is both fast and efficient. The imagesetter can use the same chemicals to process either paper or film.

Direct-to-film processing will virtually eliminate traditional camera and darkroom processing techniques in most phases of commercial printing within the very near future.

■ GRAPHIC ARTS PROCESS CAMERAS

Although the role of the graphic arts camera continues to be deemphasized, as digital photographic techniques take over the once dominant position of analog, or conventional photography, traditional photography can continue to play a meaningful role in graphic arts educational programs. Print quality, whether achieved using a traditional or digital format, is subject to assessment procedures that are based on principles established using traditional photographic techniques.

Graphic arts cameras, referred to as "process cameras," are designed specifically for large-format photography. One method of classifying the process camera is based on the largest size of sheet film the camera is physically capable of exposing. For example, a 14 x 18 inch camera takes a maximum sheet-film size of 14 x 18 inches. Other terminology used to classify process cameras are as follows:

Darkroom Camera

These cameras are designed to be located in a light-tight room, such as a darkroom. An installation option on this type of camera is to have the film loading end of the camera installed in a darkroom, leaving the copyboard in a lighted room. Figure 8.19 illustrates a vertical process camera which is small enough to fit in a darkroom, or, equipped with a moveable film back, can be used in a lighted room as well.

Gallery Camera

Gallery cameras can be used in normally lighted rooms. This type of camera contains a removable film holder which is taken into a darkroom where the film is loaded. The film holder has a light-tight tray to protect the film when the holder is taken from the darkroom into the lighted room where the camera is located. The film holder is then placed into the camera, the light-tight tray is removed, and the exposure is made. After the exposure, the light-tight tray is then inserted back into the film holder to protect the film when the holder is removed from the camera and carried back to the darkroom. In the darkroom, the film is first removed from the holder and then processed.

FIGURE 8.19:
Vertical darkroom camera
(Courtesy Nu-Arc, Inc.)

■ EXPOSING AND DEVELOPING A LINE NEGATIVE

Exposing and developing a line negative is a five-step process:

1. Setting up the darkroom and preparing the film;
2. Making preliminary camera adjustments;
3. Placing copy on the copyboard and adjusting the camera lighting;
4. Loading the camera with film and making the exposure; and,
5. Processing and evaluating the film.

Setting Up the Darkroom and Preparing the Film

Before taking any pictures, the processing chemicals should be prepared with the film in place and ready for handling under safelight conditions.

Traditional tray-processing of film has largely been replaced by rapid-access chemical techniques relying on machine-processing of the film. Although tray development may be used occasionally, machine developing produces more consistent film quality much more quickly than hand-processing techniques.

Disposal of Photographic Chemicals

It should be noted that conventional film developers, fixers, and stop baths are classified as toxic substances. This makes their disposal subject to federal regulations. They cannot simply be poured down the sink drain. Modern darkrooms will be equipped with specially-designed holding tanks for storage of spent chemistry until it can be properly disposed of. For specific procedures regarding proper disposal, refer to the manufacturers' recommendations and the applicable Environmental Protection Agency (EPA) regulations.

Performing Basic Camera Adjustments

Camera adjustments involve setting enlargement and reduction ratios for the lens and copyboard, setting exposure time, and adjusting the lens aperture.

Enlargements and reductions are set on the camera by moving both the lens board and copyboard to their proper positions along the horizontal camera rail. Depending on the camera, either analog scales or digital readouts indicate the percentage of reproduction to which either the lens or copyboard has been set. The camera produces a 100% reproduction when the distance between the center of the camera lens and the copyboard is the same as the distance from the center of the camera lens to the film plane. The camera acts in a manner similar to a photographic enlarger that has been placed on its side. Thus, the overall size of the enlargement is set by changing the distance from the copyboard (or enlarger easel) to the camera lens (or enlarger lens). Fine focus is set by adjusting the lens board controls of the camera. The camera operator needs to remember that the gauges for both the copyboard and the lens board must read the same reproduction size; otherwise, the final size of the reproduction, the focus, or both, will be off.

The aperture of the lens works in conjunction with exposure timer settings, determining between them, how much light comes through the lens system of the camera to expose the film. Developing time for line negatives is not fixed but rather, depends on how much density, or darkness, of the emulsion layer develops. Therefore, light striking the film must be adjusted to permit the negative to develop slowly. Slowly developing negatives enable the camera operator to adjust the development process as the gray scale develops to maximize the developed negative for precise control of density. Negative density is both determined and controlled by a 12-step gray scale (discussed later) that is placed alongside the copy on the copyboard but out of the image area of the original.

Sometimes, especially when working with new film or chemistry, trial and error will determine which lens and timing settings work best and offer the camera operator the greatest degree of control over the development process. As a starting point, try setting the lens aperture to F16, with an exposure time of 10 seconds, when shooting copy at 100%. If, when developing the film, the image comes up too quickly and the development of the negative cannot be stopped precisely at any specific step on the gray scale, either the F stop of the lens should be increased (try one step up to F22), or the exposure time should be decreased (try a reduction of 3 to 5 seconds). Conversely, if the images takes too long to develop, try increasing the exposure time from 10 to 14 seconds. Subsequent adjustments will be made as new test negatives are developed.

Setting Up the Copyboard and Lighting System

Copy should be centered on the copyboard using the alignment guidelines screened onto the copyboard backing. A gray scale is placed alongside the copy and it acts as a guide during development

FIGURE 8.20: Gray scale

of the film. A photographic gray scale is shown in Fig. 8.20.

The camera lights should be positioned so that they overlap slightly with the center of the copyboard. The lights should be equally distant from the copy. Note the alignment guides on the light rails to ensure that the lighting system is properly adjusted prior to exposure (Fig. 8.21).

Loading the Camera with Film and Making the Exposures

Film is placed on the camera back with the emulsion side of the film facing up. The emulsion side of the film is the lighter, and duller, of the two sides of the film. The darker side of the film is the plastic support base. If you hold the film up to the safelight, it will be easy to see which of the two sides of the film is the emulsion, or lighter side. Also, the film will curl toward the emulsion side.

Film is usually placed on the center of the film back on the camera. Use the ground glass to check for final positioning of the film.

After the film has been positioned, the vacuum pump is turned on, and the camera back is closed and latched. The vacuum pump keeps the film firmly in place against the camera back during exposure. The sequence begins when the exposure button on the timing control panel of the camera is pressed. Activating the exposure control simultaneously turns on the camera lights and opens the shutter in the camera lens for the time set on the control. The control automatically turns off the camera lights and closes the lens shutter after the set-time has elapsed. At this point, the camera can be opened, the vacuum turned off, and the film removed from the camera and ready for processing.

FIGURE 8.21: Positioning camera lights

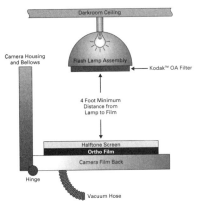

FIGURE 8.22:
Flash exposure setup

GRAY SCALE DEVELOPMENT GUIDE			
Density of Copy	Size of Copy		
	10-40%	40-120%	120-400%
EXTRA HEAVY COPY Black Bold type Etching Proofs Photographic Proofs	4	5	6
NORMAL COPY Black Type Proofs Fine Serif Proofs Pen and Ink Drawings	3	4	5
LIGHT COPY Gray Proofs Typewritten Sheets Forms with Light Lines Good Pencil Drawings	2	3	4
EXTRA LIGHT COPY Extra Fine Lines Ordinary Pencil Drawings Light Gray Copy	1-2	2	3

FIGURE 8.23:
Steps of grayscale for
different types of copy

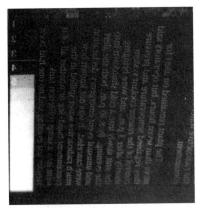

FIGURE 8.24:
Negative developed
with gray scale guide

• Main, Flash, and Bump Exposures

Most halftone exposures require at least two, and sometimes three, separate exposures to capture all of the detail in the original illustration or photograph. These exposures are referred to as *main, flash,* and *bump* exposures.

The main exposure captures the majority of the detail, highlight, and middle tones of the original copy. The flash exposure is a different process and is made by opening up the film back of the camera and exposing the film/screen sandwich to a yellow filter lamp located above the camera (usually mounted on the ceiling). The flash exposure is designed to bring up detail in the shadow areas from the original on the negative (the clearer areas on the halftone negative). This exposure enables the small dots that have begun to form in the negative to receive additional light from the flash exposure lamp to ensure they will come up during development of the negative. The flash exposure sequence is done with the camera back opened and the film exposed to an external "flash" exposure lamp. This setup is illustrated in Fig. 8.22.

The third exposure, the bump, is taken to increase detail in the highlighted areas of the negative. This exposure is made with the screen removed from the film, usually for a period of about 3 to 5% of the main exposure. The bump exposure is usually made after the main exposure. For example, if additional detail is required in the highlighted areas, a picture whose main exposure is 20 seconds might require a bump exposure of two or three seconds. Bump exposures are usually made on a trial-and-error basis.

The purpose of this halftone exposure sequence is to enable the camera to capture the greatest overall contrast range from the original copy, which is greater than the camera can capture through just the main exposure alone. Flash and bump exposures extend the contrast range of the camera. They bring up details in both the highlighted and shadow areas of the original that would otherwise be lost if only a main exposure were taken.

• Processing the Film

Film is processed using either trays or rapid-access equipment. After processing, the gray scale should be checked to ensure that the density of the film matches the required step of the gray scale. Figure 8.23 shows the grayscale steps required for different types of copy. After development, the grayscale guide on the film is developed to the appropriate step as indicated by the guide (Fig. 8.24).

■ HALFTONE PHOTOGRAPHIC PROCESSING

Although an increasing amount of halftone photography is being done digitally, the principles of halftone quality are the same whether a conventional process camera or a computer is being used. As you review this material, refer to the principles behind the halftone process and breaking a continuous-tone picture into dots, mentioned previously. These principles are also applicable whether a conventional halftone or stochastic screening process is used.

The steps involved in producing a halftone negative are:
1. Calibrating the camera with a halftone computer;
2. Determining proper exposure times;
3. Setting up the camera and flashing lamps;
4. Making the exposure; and,
5. Processing the film.

Most halftone negatives are exposed using a plastic contact screen. The contact screens have an emulsion and nonemulsion side, similar to photographic film. Contact screen will also curl toward the emulsion side. To get the camera ready for exposure, ortho film is placed on the vacuum back of the camera, emulsion side up, as in the line copy procedure. The contact screen is then placed over the film with the emulsion side of the screen against the emulsion side of the film (Fig. 8.25).

FIGURE 8.25:
Placing a halftone screen over ortho film

Note from Fig. 8.26 that the size of the contact screen must be larger than the size of the film. This size difference is necessary in order for the screen to be held in place by the vacuum of the camera when the screen is placed on top of the film and the camera vacuum is turned on. For example, when using 10 x 12-inch ortho film for shooting halftones, an 11 x 14-inch contact screen should be used, and so on.

Processing Halftone Negatives

The determining factor for achieving consistently high quality in analog photography is to eliminate as many variables from the process as possible. Serious photographers work with the same brand of film, the same processing chemicals, and photographic papers. An in-depth knowledge of your materials reduces variables and enables the technician to achieve consistently high results.

When working with line negatives, the gray scale is used to help produce uniform negative density. The gray scale helps to override chemistry temperature and film variations to produce uniform negative development. When producing halftone negatives, the gray scale is not used as a development guide. In the halftone process, gray scales are often incorporated alongside halftone images to check dot structures from highlighted to shadowed areas, but are not used as an aid in the development process.

Calibrating process cameras helps to eliminate the variables of camera lighting systems and exposure times as they relate to capturing density range during the exposure sequence. To control variations in negative density as a result of the development process, all halftone negatives should be developed for the same amount of time, with consistent agitation of the tray during the process. During the camera calibrating process (discussed later), all negatives must be developed for the same amount of time in order for the calibration procedure to be accurate. Consult manufacturers' recommendations if calibration procedures on a particular camera are required. When a camera has been calibrated, it must be remembered that if, for example, 2–3/4 minutes has been established as the developing time for processing the calibration film, then this same time should be used when developing all subsequent halftone negatives. A change in developing time will necessitate a recalibration of the camera. It's a good idea to keep as many variables as possible to an absolute minimum to achieve consistently high results when generating halftone negatives.

Although specific times may vary from one manufacturer to another, a developing time of 2-3/4 minutes is a good starting point for conventional tray processing. With automated chemical processing, development times will be based on the specific requirements of the chemistry and associated equipment.

Shooting Halftone Prints As Line Copy and Rescreening

Once a continuous-tone illustration or photograph has been screened and printed, it contains a series of halftone dots that enables it to be treated as line copy. Although the image has been broken up into darker and lighter areas via the halftone screen, in effect it represents a single tonal image. Halftone negatives can be made from these prescreened originals by treating them as ordinary line copy and photographing them on the camera without the need to use a halftone screen.

Halftone prints can be pasted up on a mechanical alongside other line copy and photographed as one piece of line copy. Care must be taken when treating prescreened halftone prints as line copy if they will be either enlarged or reduced. For example, an original halftone print with a screen ruling of 100 lines per inch reduced to 75% results in an effective screen ruling of 150 lines per inch on the reproduction. Screen sizes finer than 150 lines per inch will tend to fill in on certain types of presses and should therefore be avoided. Conversely, a 100-line-per-inch original, if enlarged to 200%, will have an equivalent screen ruling of 50 lines per inch. This produces a print with a screen ruling that may be too coarse from a visual or design point of view.

It is sometimes desirable to rescreen a halftone print using traditional halftone photographic techniques. If enlargements or reductions will result in objectionable screen sizes, or the screen pattern of the original is too fine to be reproducible on the camera while keeping the detail of the original intact, the original halftone print will have to be rescreened.

The major problem encountered when rescreening a halftone print occurs when the dot pattern of the screen used in the camera interferes with, or mismatches, the dot pattern on the original halftone print thus producing a moiré pattern (refer to Fig. 8.14). When using scanners, selecting the descreening option almost entirely eliminates the possibility of moiré patterns from appearing when the file is output to an imagesetter.

■ DIFFUSION TRANSFER PROCESSING

Diffusion transfer processing was mentioned earlier in this chapter in reference to preparing PMT negatives. The diffusion transfer process can produce either opaque, positive prints as well as screened halftone prints on photographic paper from original photographs. The resulting screened prints are referred to as screened velox prints. Once screened, these prints can be pasted up on mechanicals alongside text and line illustrations and photographed as line copy without the need for special halftone preparation techniques.

Diffusion transfer uses a special transfer film and receiving paper. The transfer film is placed in the camera just like ordinary film. If a screened velox is to be made, a special halftone contact screen is placed over the transfer film and the exposure is made. To process the print, the transfer film and receiving paper are placed face to face and sent through an activating solution in the diffusion processor. As the transfer film encounters the activating solution, the image

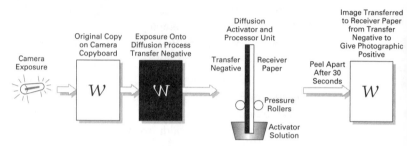

FIGURE 8.26:
The diffusion transfer process

on the transfer paper is developed and then transferred by contact onto the receiving paper. A pair of rollers in the processor squeeze the transfer film and receiving paper together. Under pressure from these rollers the image is completely transferred from the transfer film to the receiving paper. The paper and film sandwich is then peeled apart with the image now on the receiving paper. The transfer process is depicted in Fig. 8.26.

Because diffusion processing involves image transfer, the normal rules for lightening and darkening the resulting print are reversed. To darken a transfer positive, exposure time is reduced; conversely, to lighten the print, exposure time in the camera is increased. Main exposure times for diffusion process are between 10 and 20 seconds. Flash and bump exposures are not used in this procedure.

FIGURE 8.27:
Image ready for further processing

■ MAKING HALFTONES ON COMPUTERS

Producing halftone images on the computer is a two-step process: the originals are scanned, using either a flatbed or drum-type scanner. Because most scanners operate as plug-in additions to photo-editing programs, the image automatically opens up in the editing program and is ready for further manipulating. With a digital camera, the image is downloaded from the camera into the photo-editing program. This takes the place of the scanners described above. From this point on, all images, regardless of their original source, are treated in the same manner.

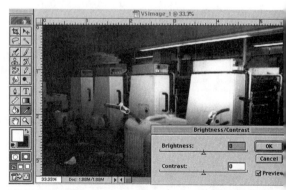

FIGURE 8.28:
Adjusting brightness and contrast

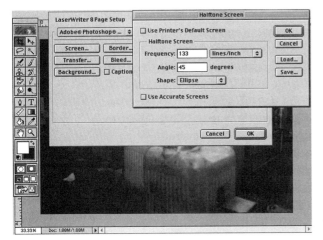

FIGURE 8.29:
Halftone screen selections

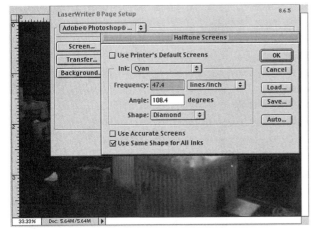

FIGURE 8.30:
Color separation screen angles

After scanning or downloading, the image is ready for further processing, as shown on the computer screen in Fig. 8.27.

At this point, changes in brightness, contrast, cropping, and color levels can all be applied to the image. The brightness/contrast adjustment control shown in Fig. 8.28 is typical of the specialty control function menus throughout an image-editing program.

Prior to outputting the image to an imagesetter or platesetter, certain decisions concerning the halftone screen characteristics must be made. Specifically, the screen angle, screen size (in dots per inch), and the shape of the halftone dot shape must be selected. These choices are made from a selection menu (Fig. 8.29).

Screen sizes and angles are particularly important when these characteristics apply to work that is to be output from the computer onto color-separated negatives. Screen angles and sizes are selected so as not to interfere with one another when color separations are overprinted on to each other to reproduce the color original. Note the selection menu options when outputting color separation negatives (Fig. 8.30).

Scanning and editing continuous-tone illustrations on a computer eliminates all darkroom steps except for film processing, which is normally accomplished using daylight film processors. Regardless of the method used to produce the line or halftone negatives or plate imaging, the characteristics that are used as benchmarks in assessing negatives and print quality cut across the technical boundaries used to produce them.

■ PROCESSING AND EVALUATING HALFTONE NEGATIVES

Evaluating halftone negatives, whether they are produced digitally or in a traditional fashion, involves an examination of the dot patterns in the negative and how these dots correspond to the tonal areas in the original photograph or artwork. Ideally, the halftone negative will enable a printing plate to be made that will print a reproduction whose overall tonal range closely matches its original.

Highlighted areas from the original should yield about a 90% dot on the halftone negative. A 90% dot on the negative should give a good, solid 10% dot on the printing plate (this figures can vary, based on press differences, from, for example 3/95 to 5/85). Conversely, shadowed areas from the original illustration should result in a good 10% dot on the negative, resulting in a 90% dot on the printing plate. Because of the pressure exerted by the rubber blanket on the offset press during printing, the ink and water used in the printing, as well as the type of paper used, halftone dots on the printing plate tend to become larger. This is called *dot gain*. When dot gain is present, a 90% dot in the shadow area on an offset plate tends to fill in and print solid black. When this happens, whatever detail was held in the shadowed area of the dot is gone. What results is a loss of detail and overall contrast range in the final print. Dot gain can be held to a minimum by having well-formed dots in both the negative and the printing plate. Middle tones in the print should range in dot size from about 30 to 70% and should reflect the overall tonal range of the original photograph or illustration.

When relating the quality of the halftone negative to the original, remember that the main exposure determines the dot size and structure in the middle tones; the flash exposure determines the dot size and detail in the shadowed areas; and the bump exposure controls detail in the highlighted areas. If a main exposure is too long, the detail in the highlighted areas of the original will be lost because the dark areas of the halftone negative will tend to close up completely and lose the small 10% dots. Thus, for larger dots in the highlighted areas (transparent areas of the halftone negative), the main exposure should be decreased. For smaller transparent dots in the highlighted areas, the main exposure should be increased. For smaller dots in the shadow areas, decrease the flash exposure. To bring up details in the highlighted areas you will need to experiment with different bump exposure times.

■ SUMMARY

This chapter covered basic photographic techniques used with the process camera to produce both line and halftone negatives. The development of these skills enables the production of high-quality halftone reproductions with an understanding of the relationship of quality control of the input process. This relationship holds whether images are produced using traditional or computer-generated techniques.

Continued advances in digitization technology will have a profound impact on traditional copy preparation skills and techniques in the coming years. Some experts predict the end of the traditional darkroom in the near future; others foresee a more gradual, extended shift in technologies. Regardless of individual opinion, there is no doubt that many fundamental changes in this area have already taken place.

For example, this textbook does not cover traditional photographic color separation camera work. Today, software technology automatically produces color separations simply by choosing the separation option. The tedious process of separating full-color originals into component negatives on a process camera using skills that took years to learn and develop has taken its place in history. Color proofing, once the domain of the color separation house or printer, can now be done on affordable dye sublimation and toner-based laser copiers with exacting results.

Traditional camera processing of line and halftone illustrations will no doubt continue as a graphic arts process for years to come. However, it is no longer the integral part of the graphic reproduction process that it once was.

■ SUGGESTED STUDENT ACTIVITIES

1. Calibrate a process camera. Using a 12-step gray scale and a reflection densitometer, calibrate the steps of the gray scale with density readings taken from the densitometer. Using the calibrated densitometer as original copy in the camera copyboard, take a series of main exposures on the camera to determine which exposure time captures the greatest overall contrast range, as determined by the densitometer. NOTE: If a reflection densitometer is not available, a Kodak® reflection density guide can be used instead. The reflection guide is a visual densitometer with holes in the middle of each step of the gray scale. To make density measurements, the tonal area of different parts of a photograph are visually matched to the tonal area of the gray scale. Although not as accurate as a reflection densitometer, the reflection guide is a good substitute when no densitometer is available.

2. Calibrate a flash exposure test strip. Using a halftone contact screen, conduct a series of test strip exposures. Under safelight conditions: Place a halftone screen over a piece of ortho film on the back of the process camera. Cover the screen/film with a sheet of white paper, leaving only a small portion of the screen/film uncovered. Turn on the camera vacuum and set the timer to 60 seconds. Turn on the flash lamp. Every 10 seconds, move the white paper over to uncover an additional small area of the screen/film. Continue until the 60 seconds of exposure time is over. Process the film for 2-3/4 minutes Evaluate the negative. Look for the strip that gives a good 10% dot on the negative. The time used to produce this dot is the basic flash time for the negative.

3. Produce a mechanical of a combination page. The page should be the first page of a newsletter, and should contain a title section, table of contents for the newsletters, two or three columns of text, and one continuous-tone illustration. The elements can be pasted up on illustration board or other similar heavy-duty backing material. The backing should be ruled to the finished size of the page.

4. Using a reflection densitometer or reflection density guide, measure the highlighted, shadowed, and middle tones of five different photographs. Determine the overall density range in each of the photographs.

5. Shoot a halftone negative of an original photograph. Evaluate the photograph and compare the density range of the halftone negative with the original photograph. How close did you come to capturing the density range of the original photograph?

6. Compare the quality of a halftone produced by conventional photographic techniques and from a digital file. Using whatever contact screens are available in the laboratory, produce a conventional halftone negative. Then, using the same original copy, bring it into Photoshop® and output the file to an imagesetter. Use the same screen size and dot shape of the contact screen in outputting the file. See if you can find any differences between the halftone negative produced on the camera from that output from the imagesetter.

Chapter 9 STRIPPING AND PLATEMAKING

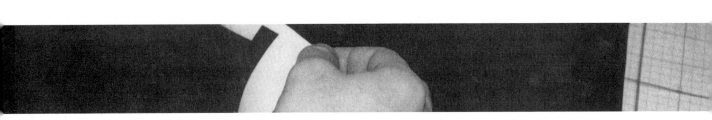

STRIPPING AND PLATEMAKING

Prepare Flats Using Goldenrod Sheets

Understand Stripping Procedures for Preparing Multi-Color and Multi-Flat Images

Place Traditional Offset Platemaking Techniques within the Framework of Modern Digital Reproduction Techniques

Examine Lithographic Plate Technology, Exposure, and Processing Techniques

Provide an Overview of Computer-to-Plate Technology

■ INTRODUCTION

The various elements of a project, including line and halftone negatives, artwork (whether generated on a computer or handdrawn), and text, come together during final image assembly. This final layout, with all of the copy set in place is called a *mechanical*. After photographing all of the copy, the negatives are positioned on a *masking sheet*. Windows are then cut into the masking sheet to enable transferring images from the negatives to the printing plate. This process is known as *stripping*. The masking sheet used to make the printing plates is called a *flat*.

Traditionally, preparation of masking sheets and flat stripping had been done by hand. Today, technological innovation and computerization are quickly eliminating these two stages in image preparation; the hand preparation of mechanicals is rarely done anymore. Instead, layouts are prepared by assembling all of the page elements on a computer using page-layout software. Once the pages are made up, there are two options: the pages can be output to digital imagesetters that produce one negative containing all of the page elements; or, the pages can be output to either imagesetters or platesetters that deliver finished printing plates. With either method, the intermediate steps of photographic processing, stripping, and even platemaking are eliminated.

Using even higher levels of technological innovation, the printer might have computer-to-press (CTP) technology in the shop. Using CTP technology, the computer outputs complete pages directly to the printing press where the plates are imaged on the press cylinders.

This chapter examines both the traditional and newer technologies associated with generating photographic images on different types of plate media.

■ THE GOLDENROD SHEET

A flat is a sheet of specially-prepared paper on which all of the negatives that make up the page are positioned. The sheet of paper is known as *goldenrod* because of its yellow color. Orange vinyl and mylar are also used for stripping both single and four-color projects. A completed flat, ready for platemaking, is shown in Fig. 9.1.

The goldenrod sheet prevents the transmission of "actinic" light. Actinic light is that portion of the electromagnetic spectrum that causes a photochemical change in photographic material. Note from figure 9.1 that a window has been cut around the boundary of the negative. When exposing the flat on a platemaker, light passes through the negative and exposes the photographic plate below. The remainder of the goldenrod flat prevents light from the platemaker from reaching the photographic printing plate. Only areas in the flat where a window has been cut allow exposure of the plate material.

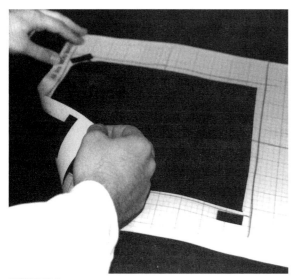

FIGURE 9.1:
Stripped flat ready for platemaking

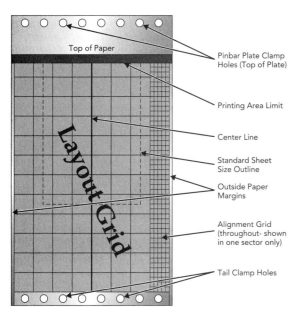

FIGURE 9.2:
Preruled goldenrod sheet

Labels on Figure 9.2:
- Top of Paper
- Pinbar Plate Clamp Holes (Top of Plate)
- Printing Area Limit
- Center Line
- Standard Sheet Size Outline
- Outside Paper Margins
- Alignment Grid (throughout- shown in one sector only)
- Tail Clamp Holes
- Layout Grid

Flat Sizes

Sheet sizes of goldenrod flats are exactly matched to the sizes of the printing plates for a variety of different printing presses. For example, an A.B. Dick Co., model #360 offset press uses a printing plate whose overall dimensions are 11 x 18-1/2 inches. The goldenrod for this press has the same measurements. An A.B. Dick Co. model #9500 series press uses plates measuring 13 x 19-1/8 inches; the flats for this press are the same dimensions.

Ruled Masking Sheets

Most of the masking sheets for small format offset presses, whose paper capacity is less than 17 x 22 inches, use goldenrod flats that come preruled, with all necessary dimension and reference lines printed on the sheet. Large format offset presses generally use unruled goldenrod. Figure 9.2 illustrates a goldenrod sheet dimensioned for a small sheetfed offset printing press.

Note the series of holes on the top and bottom of the flat in Fig. 9.2. These holes line up with the pin bar plate clamps used on the head and the tail of the plate cylinder on many small offset presses. The gripper margin, identified as a solid black bar just above the printing area limit, is about 3/8 of an inch wide on most presses. This margin represents the area at the top portion of the sheet where it is held in place by the gripping clamp as the sheet of paper is fed through the cylinders of the printing press. Because the paper is held firmly in place by the gripping clamps, this area represents a nonprinting section on the sheet of paper. For this reason, the printing area limit on the goldenrod begins directly below the gripper margin. When stripping negatives onto the flat, the top of the printed image can only come up to the gripper margin. If a particular job requires an image to be printed closer to the top of the page than the gripper margin allows, a larger sheet of paper is used and then trimmed to size after printing. Additional references used by the stripper on the goldenrod are the center line, the outside margins of standard sheet sizes of paper, and a 1/4" grid pattern. The grid makes it easier to keep all of the negatives straight when positioning them on the flat.

Page Sequencing and Signatures

One sheet of paper on which several different pages are printed is referred to as a *signature*. After the sheet has been printed, it moves to a folding machine where the sheet is folded so that all of the pages will be arranged in proper position and sequence. Depending on size, a booklet or book may contain many signatures. Signatures are often printed in 4-, 8-, 12-, 16-, 32-, and 48-page formats, depending on the sheet-size capacity of

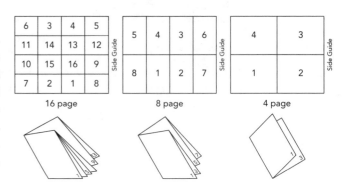

FIGURE 9.3:
4-, 8-, and 16-page signature makeup

the printing press and the length of the book or magazine. Figure 9.3 shows the folds required to make 4-, 8-, and 16-page signatures, along with the corresponding positions, or imposition, of each page on the flat, as described next.

Imposition

The placement of each image on the flat so that it will print in the right order and position is called *imposition*. Proper imposition is important because it minimizes press time, paper costs, and finishing costs (trimming and folding). Factors that affect imposition are the design of the piece being printed, the type of paper used and the availability of different sheet sizes of the paper, and the capacity of the press used to print the job. Imposition is also affected by the different types of work formats used to print the job. Some of these formats are described below.

One-Sided Imposition: This is the simplest type of imposition where one printing plate prints only one side of the sheet. This format is used on small offset presses for printing single-sided jobs.

Sheetwise Layout: This format is used to print both sides of a sheet of paper with two different images using two separate printing plates.

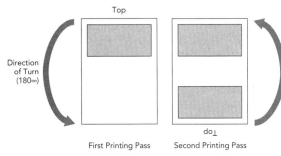

FIGURE 9.4:
Work-and-turn imposition

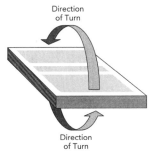

FIGURE 9.5:
Work and tumble

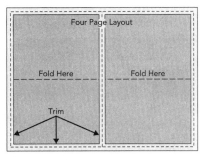

FIGURE 9.6:
Layout of 4- and 8-page booklet

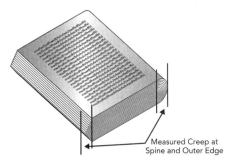

FIGURE 9.7:
Creep

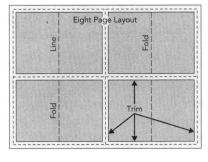

Work and Turn: In the work and turn format, one printing plate is used to print both sides of the same sheet of paper. After the first press run, the pile of paper is turned over and fed into the press using the same leading edge on the sheets (Fig. 9.4).

Work and Tumble: Work and tumble also uses one plate for printing both sides of the sheet; however, in this format, the paper pile is tumbled so that the opposite end of the sheet serves as the leading edge during the second press run (Fig. 9.5).

Figure 9.6 shows the fold and trim lines that have been marked on a typical layout for both a 4- and 8-page layout.

Creep and Bleed

Two considerations that must be taken into account before starting to strip a job are known as *creep* and *bleed*. The term bleed refers to printed images that extend beyond the edges of the page. When bleeding images are used, allowances must be made in stripping because the actual printing area of the image extends beyond the page size on the flat. Therefore, the image is stripped in slightly over the edges of the page—1/8-inch is standard. After printing, the sheet is trimmed to its finished size.

Creep describes the tendency of the center pages of a book, or series of pages in a large signature to move, or creep forward, resulting in an uneven edge before trimming (Fig. 9.7).

Creep is measured from the spine to the outer edge of the signature. Although creep is not usually a factor when printing small pamphlets or booklets, creep allowances for center signatures in large books becomes important when proper alignment of all pages in the signature are critical. The best way to make allowances for creep during stripping is to make up a dummy of the job from the same paper stock that will be used in the final print. After making all of the signature folds in the dummy, actual creep measurement can be taken and incorporated into the stripping.

■ STRIPPING PROCEDURES

In stripping, all of the assembled negatives are positioned and taped in place on a sheet of goldenrod in preparation for making the final printing plate. Sometimes negatives of each individual item on the page must be positioned separately on the goldenrod. In many instances, this type of stripping is made simpler by direct-to-film technology, which requires stripping only a single negative that contains all of the separate images, and has been generated on the computer and output on an imagesetter. Stripping takes place on either preprinted or blank sheets of goldenrod paper sized for the particular press that will be used to print the job.

Stripping a Single Page

Before starting a stripping job, the stripper will refer to a job sheet that contains all information required for the job. The stripping process usually takes place on an illuminated light table as shown in Fig. 9.8.

The light source on the table provides the illumination required to view the negatives as they are positioned on the goldenrod. Also, note the straight-edge rulers, mounted on moveable tracks on the table, which enable precise positioning of all of the page elements.

Flats can be stripped with the emulsion side of the negatives either facing up or down. Conventional stripping usually places the negative on the flat, emulsion side down, so that during

FIGURE 9.8:
Illuminated light table

platemaking the emulsion of the negative will be directly against the emulsion side of the printing plate. This arrangement results in the sharpest images possible on the plate surface. Also, the emulsion of the negative is less prone to scratching when it is face down during stripping. The following eight steps highlight the stripping process.

1. The goldenrod is carefully positioned on the light table using either a T-square or built-in adjustable rules on the light table. The goldenrod can be placed either vertically or horizontally, depending on the requirements of the job. When properly positioned, it is taped in place on the surface of the light table as shown in Fig. 9.9.

2. Critical dimension lines such as the gripper margin, paper center line, and the outside dimensions are identified and highlighted on the flat. One or two notches can be cut into the flat to highlight the leading to the top edge of the flat. This notch also reminds the stripper to place the leading to the top edge of the negatives in the proper position as it relates to the leading edge of the flat (Fig. 9.10).

FIGURE 9.9:
Goldenrod positioned
on light table

3. All negatives should be trimmed to within 1/2 inch of their finished sized. The 1/2-inch border is used to tape the negatives in place on the flat.

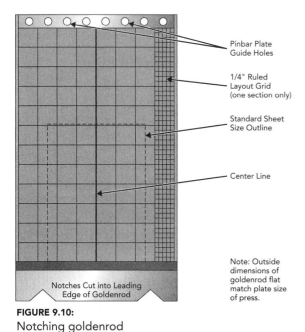

Pinbar Plate
Guide Holes

1/4" Ruled
Layout Grid
(one section only)

Standard Sheet
Size Outline

Center Line

Note: Outside
dimensions of
goldenrod flat
match plate size
of press.

Notches Cut into Leading
Edge of Goldenrod

FIGURE 9.10:
Notching goldenrod

FIGURE 9.11:
Taping negative in place
on the flat

FIGURE 9.12:
Cutting a window into a flat

4. A corner of the flat is lifted and the negative is placed "underneath" the flat with the emulsion side of the negative down against the glass screen of the light table. The negative can now be moved under the flat and into its final position. Any registration marks on the negative as well as object lines of the negative itself can be used to align the negative with the grid marks on the flat.

5. After positioning the negative, a small diamond-shaped hole is cut through the goldenrod (but not through the negative). The hole should be located over a nonimage area of the negative and cut using just enough pressure with a small knife or razor blade to cut through only the goldenrod and not through the negative. After this hole has been cut, a piece of red litho tape is placed over the hole, taping the negative temporarily in place to the goldenrod. This tape is used to hold the negative in place only while the flat is being turned and only until it can be permanently taped on the back side of the flat.

6. The goldenrod is flipped over on the light table with the underside of the flat and negative now facing up. The negative is taped permanently to the underside of the goldenrod at its four corners, using small strips of red litho tape (Fig. 9.11).

7. The flat is flipped over again, right-side up. Windows can now be cut into the goldenrod flat over the image areas in the negative in order to be able to expose the printing plate. Sometimes one window can be cut over the entire negative. At other times, when there are several smaller images, it may be more advantageous to cut out several smaller windows in the flat. The procedure of cutting windows (shown in Fig. 9.12) requires practice to ensure that only the goldenrod is cut and the negatives are left untouched by the cutting blade. Scrap negatives and goldenrod should be used so the stripper can refine the cutting techniques used in this procedure. One useful technique is to place a sheet of clear plastic or photographic film under the goldenrod, on top of the negative. This provides a layer over the film to protect it while the beginning stripper develops the necessary cutting skills.

8. Windows are cut for exposure control devices such as gray scales, dot gain scales, etc. Gray scales and the like are stripped into the flat outside of the trim size of the finished sheet of paper. In this way, the press operator can refer to them during the printing run. Afterward they are trimmed off during the finishing process. The stripper also refers to the instructions that accompany these control devices for their specific use.

◼ OPAQUING NEGATIVES

The opaquing process covers up unwanted dots and scratches on the negatives that would otherwise be exposed onto the plate and would print in the finished copies. During this process, an opaquing solution, which is a dark viscous liquid, is painted onto the negatives to cover up unwanted dust spots and scratches.

Opaquing is performed after the windows have been cut in the flat and is done with either a small brush and opaquing fluid or a special opaquing pen (Fig. 9.13). Opaquing pens are cleaner than their brush counterparts and are generally easier to use. The opaquing fluid is water soluble, and, in case of mistakes, can be removed with a cotton swab and then reapplied if necessary.

If the opaquing solution were to be applied to the emulsion side of the negative instead of the base of the negative, a layer of separation between the negative and the plate could take place, causing a distortion of the image during plate exposure (Fig. 9.14).

FIGURE 9.13:
Applying opaquing fluid to the negative

FIGURE 9.14:
Image distortion through improper opaquing

◼ STRIPPING MULTICOLOR AND MULTIFLAT IMAGES

In several instances, more than one flat may be required for a job even though the image is only one color. For example, some jobs may contain both line and halftone copy where the line copy is stripped onto one flat and the halftone negatives onto the other. These two flats, working in conjunction with one another, are referred to as *complementary flats*. Multicolor work usually requires that separate flats be prepared for each printing color. Multicolor or complementary flats are stripped following the same procedures as those used for single flat work. The methods used for aligning multiple flats so they print in register with one another are described in the next section.

Register Pins

Metal pins, called *register pins*, are used to line up multiple flats on a light table. The pins are taped to the light table. Holes are punched into the goldenrod sheets to line up with the taped pins. Using this technique, all of the flats are held in the same position in register with each other during stripping (Fig. 9.15).

Figure 9.16 illustrates a representation of a multicolor job prepared using a separate flat for each of the printing colors. After the flats have

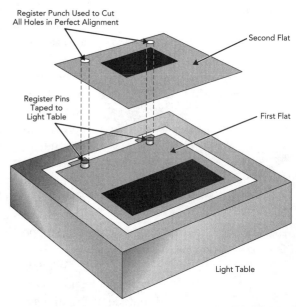

FIGURE 9.15:
Using metal register pins

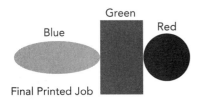

Green
Blue   Red

Final Printed Job

Registration Marks, Gray Scales, and Color Bars Removed
After Alignment in Press or During Trimming

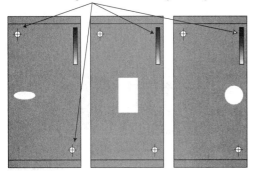

Blue Separation Flat   Green Separation Flat   Red Separation Flat

FIGURE 9.16:
Three-color job stripped on separate flats

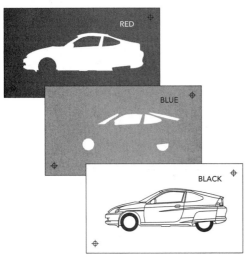

RED

BLUE

BLACK

FIGURE 9.17:
Ruby masking film for three-color printing job

FIGURE 9.18:
Cutting ruby film

been stripped, they are placed one on top of the other on the register pins on the light table to check for stripping accuracy and proper placement of all negatives.

Ruby Masking Film for Multicolor Stripping

Ruby-colored masking film is used most often for preparing multicolor printing jobs where only one flat is used for making multiple exposures onto a printing plate. The ruby film is cut by hand to expose window areas on a flat.

Most multicolor artwork requires close tolerances when preparing the flats, even if the colors don't overlap each other. Figure 9.17 illustrates how a ruby masking sheet would be used to prepare a three-color printing job.

Ruby masking film blocks actinic light in the same way that goldenrod does. Thus, the ruby film also acts like a photographic negative. The red and blue separations in Fig. 9.17 could be used to create photographic positives on the process camera, or the ruby film could be used to cover different areas of a negative. This would enable one photographic negative to be used in exposing a multicolor job.

When using ruby masking sheets, the ruby film can either be punched and placed on register pins on the light table, or it can be taped directly onto the flat. The ruby film is prepared by cutting it with a sharp knife and then peeling the film from the clear backing sheet to uncover the areas to be exposed through the flat (Fig. 9.18).

When preparing the masking film, the cut should only go through the film and not through the plastic support base of the film. After all of the cuts have been made, the ruby film can be peeled back leaving the rest of the masking material in place.

Complementary Flats

When a job calls for very tight image tolerances, it is generally preferable to strip separate flats rather than to try to strip many negatives, positioned closely together, onto the same flat. For example, jobs that contain both text and continuous-tone images that butt up, or are closely adjacent to, one another, are usually prepared using separate flats. As mentioned earlier, these flats are referred to as complementary flats.

When preparing complementary flats, register pins are used to ensure tight tolerances of all of the flats. Sometimes the two complementary flats can be taped to an underlying sheet of goldenrod to check for proper registration (Fig. 9.19).

Following the procedure in Fig. 9.19, a window large enough to expose the images on both flats is cut into a base sheet of goldenrod. When it is time to expose the plates, the goldenrod base is positioned over the plate and the first flat is folded down into position over the goldenrod window for the first plate exposure while the other flat is folded out of the way (Fig. 9.20).

When making the second exposure onto the plate, the process is reversed, and the first flat is folded out of the way and the second flat is folded down into exposure position.

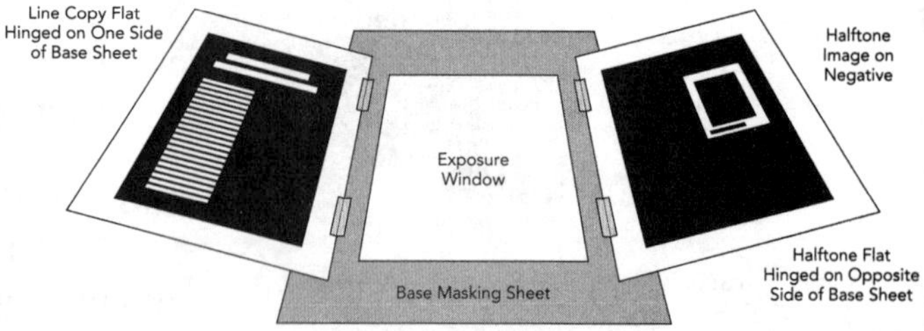

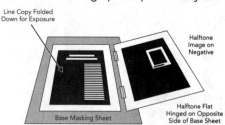

FIGURE 9.19:
Setting up complementary flats

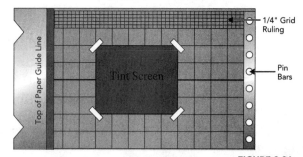

FIGURE 9.20:
Making plate exposures using complementary flats

Step and Repeat

The step-and-repeat process is used when the same image is to be printed many times on the same sheet. In one step-and-repeat method, both the front and back side of two jobs are ganged up on one mechanical layout. A second method of step and repeat involves using one photographic image, which is placed in a step-and-repeat platemaker. This special platemaker can be set to make multiple exposures at exact locations on the plate as determined by the technician. The exact locations of each exposure are set on a computer. Once adjusted, the machine will automatically move the image across the plate, making separate exposures of the image at each location.

Screen Tints

If the original artwork does not contain any screens or shades, it can be added to the job during platemaking. In Chapter 5 we saw how the proper use of tint screens can add emphasis to the printed page. Prior to platemaking, commercial tint screens are stripped into the flat for subsequent exposure (Fig. 9.21).

When adding screen tints using separate flats, the tints are positioned between the negative and the plate during a separate exposure. Commercial tint screens are available in a variety of patterns and screen sizes.

FIGURE 9.21:
Tint screen stripped into the flat

■ PROOFING THE FLAT

It is common practice to proof a flat before printing the job. Proofing ensures that all of the elements in the flat are in proper registration and that all of the scratches and pinholes in the negative have been opaqued. Also, because the flat is composed of all negative images, it is difficult to visualize what the finished job will look like in positive format. There are four ways to proof both single and multicolor flats: press proofs, photomechanical proofs, opaque proofs, and digital color proofs.

Press Proofs

Press proofs are actually small printing runs made before the actual press run of the job. Press proofs are generally reserved for long-run high quality jobs because of the expense involved in setting up the press with the proper inks and paper. To make a press proof, a plate is made from the flat and set up on the press, using the same inks and paper that will be used in the final press run.

Photomechanical Proofs

Photomechanical proofs can be used for proofing either single or multicolor jobs. In this process, inexpensive photosensitive materials are exposed through the flat and developed to offer a rendition of what the job will look like, without the expense of using the actual papers and printing inks. When making photomechanical proofs for color jobs, either color transparencies or opaque-based materials with color overlays are employed. When using color transparencies, each separate color flat is exposed onto the transparency, which develops into a specific color during the developing process. After all of the exposures have been made, the transparencies are registered and lined up on top on each other to approximate the look of the completed job.

Opaque Proofs

Opaque proofs use a heavy paper or plastic support base on top of which sensitized color sheets or toners are added to create progressive proofs of the job as each layer is sensitized and exposed. Each color requires a separate exposure and development. Each color sheet or toner represents one of the standard process color printing inks and is laminated onto the base at the end of each exposure process. After all of the exposures have been made, the finished sheets yield a high quality representation of the finished job.

Digital Color Proofs

The availability of low-cost, high-quality, ink jet and dye sublimation technology has greatly simplified the digital color proofing process. It has also made digital color proofs the method of choice for producing both color and black-and-white proofs. The digital proofing process is faster and higher in quality than either photomechanical or opaque proofs and closely approaches the quality of press proofs. Dye sublimation technology, once costing more than $30,000.00 for a high-quality output device is currently available for less than $500.00; prices on the technology continue to drop. Digital proofs, in order for to be considered contract grade proofs, must be able to be matched on the printing press. Thus, many low-cost printers cannot be used for producing contract proofs.

■ CARE OF FLATS

Many flats are used again later, and are therefore stored for archival purposes. Because the negatives scratch easily, completed flats should be stored in folders made from nonabrasive papers and placed flat down in a drawer. Storage cabinets and shelves can be purchased or built specifically for this purpose.

■ TRADITIONAL OFFSET PLATEMAKING

The earliest lithographic printing plates were handdrawn on specially prepared stones. This direct-image lithographic stone has been replaced by the modern photosensitized offset printing plate (Fig. 9.22). In this process, images from the printing plate are offset to a rubber blanket and then printed onto a sheet or web of paper as it moves through the printing press. Despite the inroads digital printing presses have made, traditional offset printing still holds a position of dominance in the printing industry.

Lithography is based on the principle that oil and water do not readily mix. The image areas on the printing plate are grease-receptive. The nonimage areas of the plate are water-receptive (hence the oil, or grease and water, components of the chemical principle). During the printing process, the plate is first wet down with a dampening solution on the press referred to as a *fountain solution*. The non-image areas of the printing plate accept the fountain solution, which is repelled by the grease-receptive image areas on the plate. As it continues to rotate in the press, the wet plate now encounters the ink rollers, where the grease-based offset ink is transferred to the grease-receptive image areas on the plate. The ink is repelled by the wet, nonimage areas of the plate. The oil and water principle underlies most of the technical aspects relating to image quality in traditional offset printing.

The original lithography stones were prepared by hand in reverse and represented the early history and primarily artform era of lithography; present-day offset plates are prepared in the positive. During the printing process, the positive image from the plate is offset on to a rubber blanket. The image on the blanket is printed in the negative, or "wrong-reading" format. As the process continues, the image from the blanket is transferred to a "right-reading" image on to the paper. This process is highlighted in Fig. 9.23.

FIGURE 9.22:
Offset Printing Plate

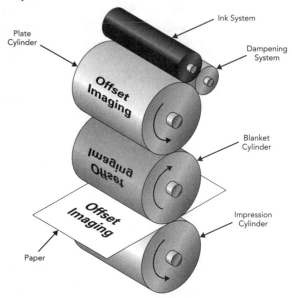

FIGURE 9.23:
Image from offset plate transferred to a blanket

Platemaking and Proofing Equipment

Traditional offset plate technology has remained relatively unchanged and continues to account for a significant portion of high-quality offset printing images. Much of the equipment used for platemaking is also used for proofing flats. Platemaking equipment consists of a light source, vacuum frame, and a sink or processor for developing and processing the plates. Computerized equipment is also used for high-volume plate processing.

The flip-top platemaker in Fig. 9.24 is equipped with a vacuum frame and high-energy light source.

FIGURE 9.24:
Flip-top platemaker
(Courtesy Nu-Arc, Inc.)

FIGURE 9.25:
Plate developing sink
(Courtesy, Nu-Arc, Inc.)

The plate exposure system illustrated in Fig. 9.24 consists of a vacuum frame and exposure light source. The vacuum pump presses the flat tightly against the plate. When the proper vacuum level is reached, the light source is energized to expose the plate. Exposure times vary for different light sources and plate materials. The technician is referred to instructions that come with the plates to determine the proper exposure times for specific plate materials.

There are several different light sources available for platemakers that provide the high-intensity light in the blue and ultraviolet portions of the spectrum that we have referred to as "actinic" light. Quartz and Xenon and metal-halide are the most popular exposure options. Stand-alone computerized control systems are also available for use on a variety of platemakers.

Although almost any type of large sink can be used to develop plates, developing sinks (darkroom sinks) are specially designed to facilitate the platemaking process. Darkroom sinks are constructed from either fiberglass or stainless steel and come with built-in drain boards. During the development process, the plate is placed on the drain board; all of the plate developing takes place in the sink. Most darkroom sinks are available with optional temperature-controlled water supplies and plate-clamping mechanisms. A developing sink of this type is shown in Fig. 9.25.

■ LITHOGRAPHIC PLATE TECHNOLOGY

There are several different types of offset plates currently in use. Most of these plates are "presensitized," meaning that the light-sensitive emulsion coating for the plate is applied during the manufacture of the plate. Plates can be sensitized on either one or both sides and are manufactured from a variety of materials, depending on the length of the press run and type of work that will be printed.

Plate Classifications

Most offset plates consist of three components: the base of the plate, or material from which the plate is manufactured; a covering over the base; and the light-sensitive plate coating.

Offset plates are fabricated from either aluminum sheet, paper, or foil-laminated paper. For press runs of more than 10,000 copies, the plate of choice is aluminum. Paper and foil/paper combination plates are used for press runs of less than 5,000 copies. The basic plate classifications are as follows:

Direct-Image Plates: Direct-image plates are usually manufactured from paper and prepared by either typing or drawing directly on the plate. After preparing, an etching solution is applied to the plate to fix the image and make the plate more water receptive. Direct-image plates are only for short run jobs.

177

Presensitized Additive Plates: Additive plates use a solution that adds a lacquer, or long-run coating, to the image areas of the plate during the developing process. Thus, this developer is "added" during plate processing.

Presensitized Subtractive Plates: In the subtractive process, the processing solution removes all of the image coating from the nonimage areas of the plate. The image coating is thus "subtracted" from the plate during processing.

Negative Acting Plates: These plates use standard negatives stripped into a flat to produce positive images on the plate. Light striking the plate during exposure hardens the emulsion, which remains as the image area after processing.

Positive Acting Plates: Positive acting plates use photographic positives instead of negatives in their preparation. Light striking the plate during exposure softens the emulsion, which is then removed during plate processing.

Surface-Coated Plates: On surface plates, the presensitized plate emulsion sits directly on top of the plate surface, as illustrated in (Fig. 9.26).

FIGURE 9.26:
Surface-coated plate

Because the photographic plate emulsion is coated directly on top of the plate, surface-coated plates are short-run plates. Under the continued pressure and operation of the printing press, the emulsion of the plate will break down, limiting use of the plate to relatively short press runs of 5,000 to 10,000 copies.

Deep-Etch Plates: Deep-etch plates feature the emulsion coating of the plate bonded onto the base metal of the plate. On these plates, the emulsion is actually etched into the surface of the plate material, making these plates more suitable for long press runs than surface-coated plates. A cross-section of a deep-etch plate is illustrated in Fig. 9.27.

FIGURE 9.27:
Cross-section of deep-etch plate

Bimetallic Plates: Bimetallic plates are made from two dissimilar metals bonded together. One of the metal layers acts as the grease-receptive image area while the other forms the water-receptive nonimage area of the plate (Fig. 9.28).

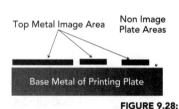

FIGURE 9.28:
Bimetallic plate cross-section

Although more expensive than other plate alternatives, bimetallic plates hold up well during long press runs and are used almost exclusively for this purpose.

Direct Photographic Plate Processing: This process uses a camera system that is loaded with presensitized plate media. The camera is also equipped with a processing unit to develop the plate. Original copy is placed on the copyboard of the camera and exposed onto the plate media, which is then cut to the proper length and fed through the automatic processor, producing a finished plate at the end of the processor. These types of plates are usually reserved for press runs of less than 5,000 impressions.

Electrostatic Plates: The electrostatic process was originally directed toward the small in-plant market and has been used to make offset plates for many years. The process uses a special image carrier referred to as a *plate master*. The image to be printed is projected onto the electrostatic master in a procedure similar to making a photocopy. As the plate is being processed, toner is applied and fused to the plate surface. Before printing with the electrostatic plate, an etching solution is applied, which is similar to the solution used in direct-image plates. The fused toner on the plate becomes the grease-receptive image area on the plate.

■ PLATE EXPOSURE AND PROCESSING

The following procedures refer to processing presensitized negative-acting subtractive (one-step) plates. The processing steps for other types of plates are similar to those described here. Before using any plate material, manufacturers' specifications should always be consulted in regard to both specific processing techniques as well as any requirements for the disposal of spent processing chemistry.

1. The developing area should be set up with the proper chemicals. Necessary materials include soft cotton litho wipes, a pad of newsprint with a top slip-sheet, and soft sponges for developing the plate.

Offset plates should be handled by the lead and tail edges of the plates only. If processing the plates in a room other than a darkroom, subdued room lighting should be used, if possible. Fresh plates, if left exposed to normal fluorescent or incandescent room lighting, will become exposed and ruined in just a few short hours. Always leave fresh, unused plates in the original package, stored in a dark, cool area, if possible.

FIGURE 9.29:
Aligning flat over the plate

2. Expose the plate on the platemaker. After removing a fresh plate from its package, place it on the platemaker, with the flat properly aligned over the plate (Fig. 9.29).

When the platemaker is first opened, and before either the flat or plate is positioned on the platemaker, make sure that the spring hinges on the frame are working properly and are capable of holding the frame in the open position while the flat and plate are positioned beneath. The goldenrod flat is placed directly over the plate and aligned along the top and right or left edges. Before closing the glass top of the platemaker, make sure the glass is clean. Smudges or bits of opaquing fluid should be removed with glass cleaner before closing the top.

After closing the platemaker's top, the vacuum is turned on and adjusted as necessary to achieve the proper vacuum setting. Too little vacuum will not hold the plate in place when the vacuum frame is rotated into the exposure position; too much vacuum will leave depressions on the negative from the rubber cushion pad on the vacuum frame.

3. Set the proper exposure time on the control panel of the platemaker. Some manufacturers may include recommended exposure times for their plates, based on the type of platemaker and light source being used. Most shops will run a series of test exposures by cutting a plate into small pieces and using a 21-step negative gray scale or plate control wedge on each of the small plate samples. Each sample is exposed for different times and then developed and examined to see which exposure time results in the proper gray scale or wedge reading. Figure 9.30 shows a 21-step gray scale developed along with the plate image as a quality control check for proper plate exposure time.

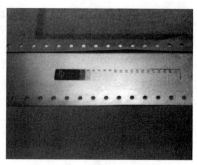

FIGURE 9.30:
Gray scale wedge on plate

After making all adjustments, the plate is exposed. If the second side of the plate will also be exposed the platemaker is opened, the plate flipped, and the second flat is placed in position over the plate for the second exposure.

4. Using the appropriate plate chemicals, the plate is developed. Before processing, make sure the work area is clean and the processing chemicals and materials are easily at-hand. If using a plate-clamping device in a darkroom sink, the plate is clamped at both the top and bottom edges. If using a pad of newspaper, make sure the top sheets in the pile are clean and also keep plate sponges or cotton pads nearby.

The temperature of the developing chemicals should be between 70 and 75°F. A small amount of developer is poured onto the plate surface. The use of a developing sponge, which is moved in a figure-8 motion across the plate with moderate pressure, helps to bring up the image evenly across the plate (Fig. 9.31). Although the specific amount of developer varies from one manufacturer to another, a small puddle about the size of a hand should be adequate. The developer should be spread evenly across the surface of the plate.

FIGURE 9.31:
Pouring developer onto the plate surface

Excess developer should be removed from the plate using a plate squeegee. Some manufacturers call for a second chemical application across the plate at this time to ensure complete development of all the plate images. Check screened halftone areas carefully for full development.

At this point, the remainder of the chemistry on the plate is squeegeed off, and the plate is washed with water. If the second side of the plate has been exposed, it should be developed at this time, following steps 1 through 4 above.

5. The plate should now either be dried and prepared for storage, or placed on the printing press if the press run is to take place immediately (press operation is explained in Chapter 10). If the plate will not be printed immediately, it must be protected and sealed to prevent oxidation from occurring on the plate surface.

Plate preservation is accomplished using commercially prepared solutions. The manufacturer's instructions should be closely followed when using any of these products. One longstanding method of preserving plates is to use a solution of gum arabic diluted 1-part gum arabic concentrate to 8-parts water. Only as much gum as will be required should be diluted. The solution is applied to the surface of the plate using soft cotton litho wipes and the gum arabic is spread from one side of the plate to the other. Allow fifteen minutes for the gum arabic to dry before placing the plate in storage.

■ COMPUTER-TO-PLATE TECHNOLOGY

Computer-to-Plate (CTP) technology is sometimes also referred to as direct-to-plate (DTP). CTP technology has made inroads into traditional plate processing, although total market penetration for CTP systems remains relatively low due to a variety of factors. Reduced platemaking costs associated with CTP systems, along with costly conventional platemaking processes such as photography, stripping, and film retouching will eventually overcome the resistance against upgrading to CTP technology. Speeding up makeready time, maximizing the old adage in the printing industry that, "the money is made on the printing press" will eventually accelerate the adoption rates of CTP technology.

The heart of all CTP systems remains the computer, operating on either the conventional PC or Macintosh platform. Outputting from the computer, the most common CTP options are as follows:

FIGURE 9.32:
Computer-driven platesetter
(Courtesy Linotype-Hell, Inc.)

FIGURE 9.33:
Polyester plate material

Dedicated Platesetters: Platesetters are based on imagesetter technology, and usually output metal plates. Platesetters, depending on the size/capacity of the unit, can run in excess of $100,000.00. A computer-driven platesetter is shown in Fig. 9.32.

This unit is similar in appearance and function to a conventional imagesetter. The material, which is a polyester-based plate media, is fed into the platesetter from a light-tight cassette (Fig. 9.33).

Plate Media on Conventional Imagesetters: When it is not practical to purchase a dedicated platesetter, an existing imagesetter can be easily adapted for CTP technology by using polyester plate media in the imagesetter in place of film. Some experimentation will be required when switching to polyester because the image densities produced on film will be different from those produced on polyester plate material. Also, different chemistry from photographic processing must be used when developing polyester plates. If possible, two daylight processors should be set up: one to handle imagesetter film output and the other to process plate output.

Toner-Based Platesetters: This technology employs converted laserprinters using conventional toners along with plate material compatible with the laser printer.

Registration errors, especially in multicolor offset printing jobs, occur in the stripping process. With CTP technology, stripping discrepancies are virtually eliminated because plate-to-plate registration is almost perfect in CTP systems.

The selection of either metal or polyester plates is primarily one of budget. Metal plates are expensive and the platesetters that image them represent a sizeable investment. Polyester on the other hand, is a stable plate material, and because it can be used effectively in imagesetters, it is an ideal transition material or primary material for print shops on a limited budget. Toner-based systems are certainly the cheapest entry into CTP technology; however, they yield the poorest overall results in terms of both plate and print quality.

Finally, the on-going move to digital plating technology is based on the continued development of user-friendly equipment and falling price levels of the equipment. As these trends continue, inroads of CTP into conventional platemaking practices will continue.

■ SUMMARY

This chapter highlighted the traditional processes of both stripping and platemaking. Also, computer-to-plate (CTP) digital plate production options were examined.

Stripping procedures are all focused around one primary objective: placing the images in the exact position required for a perfect printing run. Although minor adjustments in image position can be made once a printing plate is on the press, it is much more efficient, and less expensive, to maximize image registration on a flat. Stripping single and multicolor flats, as well as the use of complementary flats, were also detailed in this chapter.

The equipment used to produce offset printing plates, from platemakers to darkroom sinks and specialized developing materials, were also highlighted as traditional platemaking continues to enjoy a dominant role in the industry. Digital techniques, however, as exemplified by computer-to-plate systems are putting pressure on the role of traditional platemaking. The primary digital techniques were also discussed, with an insight into the digital options available based on budgetary constraints.

SUGGESTED STUDENT ACTIVITIES

1. Cut an offset plate into four pieces. Place a 21-step gray scale on the plate and make a series of four test exposures on the platemaker, one on each of the four pieces of the plate. After developing the plate sections, determine which exposure time yields the best results, as indicated by the development of the gray scale.

2. Using a pre-exposed line or halftone negative, strip the negative onto the flat, in preparation for printing the job on an 8-1/2 x 11-inch sheet of paper. During the stripping process, highlight the center and outside dimension lines of the finished sheet size. After stripping the flat, opaque any existing pin holes or scratches in the negative.

3. Using the flat stripped in item #2 above, expose and develop a printing plate. After developing the plate, coat it with a diluted solution of gum arabic and water to protect it until it is ready to be printed on the offset press (see the suggested student activities at the end of Chapter 10).

Chapter 10 PRINTING TECHNIQUES AND POST-PRESS FUNDAMENTALS

Chapter 10 PRINTING TECHNIQUES AND POST-PRESS FUNDAMENTALS

Understand the Oil and Water Principle Applied to Lithography

Examine the Operating Principles of Offset Presses, Duplicators, Single- and Multi-color Offset Presses

Provide and Overview of Offset Press Ink and Dampening Systems

Troubleshoot Image Quality

Techniques Utilized to Print Color Separations

Identify Cleaning, Storage and Maintenance Procedures Involved in Offset Press Work

Examine a Variety of Post-Press Operations

Highlight Environmental and Safety Factors in Offset Printing

◼ INTRODUCTION

Traditional offset lithography remains the dominant printing process as we enter the new millennium. Invented at the close of the eighteenth century by Alois Senefelder, a Bohemian actor searching for an inexpensive method to reproduce manuscripts, the medium began largely as an art form. Starting by placing images on copper engraving plates, Senefelder eventually focused his attention on images prepared in reverse on Bavarian limestone. The material he used for drawing the images was a mixture of lampblack, soap, wax, and rainwater.

In this traditional process, after drawing the image on the stone, it is wet down with a solution of water and gum. The stone retains moisture on the nonimage areas and repels the water from the image areas. When a fatty-based ink is applied to the stone, the still-wet stone repels the ink in the nonimage areas but accepts the ink on the image areas. By placing a sheet of paper over the inked image and applying pressure on top of the paper, the image is transferred from the stone to the paper; in this way, the lithographic process was born.

Senefelder also worked with a related process called *image transfer*, a procedure developed to simplify the preparation of negatively-imaged lithographic stones.

In this process, the work to be printed is first drawn on a piece of specially prepared proofing material using a fatty-based ink. The image from the proofing material is then transferred, or printed, onto a litho stone as a reverse image. Using the image transfer process, the original image need not be prepared in reverse, but rather is transferred onto the litho stone after being drawn as a positive. However, when preparing direct single- or multicolored lithographic prints, the original drawings on the stone must be prepared in reverse.

Throughout its history, lithography has always been a significant avenue for artistic expression. For example, the color lithographs of Currier and Ives, produced at the turn of the twentieth century, are highly prized works of art. Many artists continue to use lithography as their main medium of expression for portrait, landscape, still life, and other expressive formats.

This chapter examines traditional offset printing and equipment as well as common post-press finishing techniques.

■ THE OIL AND WATER PRINCIPLE APPLIED TO LITHOGRAPHY

FIGURE 10.1:
Image and nonimage areas
on an offset plate

The word lithography comes from two Greek words meaning, *stone writing.* From a technical standpoint, lithography is a chemical printing process, based on the principle that oil and water don't mix. Adapting this chemical principle to the offset process, the image areas on a lithographic plate are grease-based and thus repel water—the oil part of the oil and water principle. The nonimage areas on the plate are water-receptive and repel grease-based printing inks—the water part of the oil and water principle. Figure 10.1 illustrates an aluminum offset printing plate being installed onto a small duplicator. Note the image and nonimage areas on the plate.

The term *planography* is also used to describe lithographic printing. Planography, or planographic printing, refers to a process in which both the image and nonimage areas are on the same "plane," or surface, and is used interchangeably with the term "lithography."

The term *offset lithography* came into use when the process incorporated transferring, or "offsetting," the image from the original stone or lithographic plate onto a rubber blanket. The image from the blanket was then transferred onto a sheet of paper. Offset offers distinct advantages to the direct lithography process. Most important of these is the ability to prepare the original as a positive, rather than negative image, which greatly simplifies image preparation. Also, the tonal reproduction of an offset image is a bit softer than its direct image counterpart. With increases in printing speed and continued technological innovations in system hardware, offset became the dominant printing process by the mid-twentieth century and continues to account for approximately 80–90% of all printed material.

■ OFFSET PRESSES AND DUPLICATORS

A distinction is often made when describing offset machines as either duplicators or presses. The term *duplicator* refers to small-format offset machines, running sheet sizes of 11 x 17 inches and smaller, the term *press* denotes larger format machines.

Traditional offset presses can accommodate sheet and image sizes of 40 x 50 inches (or larger, in some instances), with maximum operating speeds of 15,000 impressions per hour (iph). Offset duplicators, in addition to smaller sheet sizes, usually have maximum operating speeds of 8,000 to 10,000 iph. Duplicators find their greatest application in quick print facilities where press runs are usually less than 5,000 copies. Offset presses are capable of producing finer image quality than are duplicators. Also, high-quality, full-color reproductions are reserved for presses. Duplicators can be operated by one individual with limited training whereas larger presses require extensive operator training and apprenticeship programs before a person is fully qualified and certified.

■ SINGLE- AND MULTI-COLOR OFFSET PRESSES

Offset presses are configured to run either single or multiple colors. Each additional color to be printed requires a separate *color head*, or printing unit, incorporated into the design of the press. Figure 10.2(a) illustrates a small-format, single-color offset press; Fig. 10.2(b) shows a four-color offset press.

Single-color presses can often be equipped with an auxiliary, second color add-on printing head. This second color head comes equipped with its own ink and water system, and offsets its images on the same blanket as the original press. An add-on, two-color printing head is illustrated in Fig. 10.3. When not in use, the two-color head is rotated out of position and the press operates as a normal single-color press.

FIGURE 10.2(b):
Six-color offset press
(Courtesy, SIRS Mandarin, Inc.)

Sheet-fed and Web-fed Presses

Sheet-fed and web-fed designations refer to whether a printing press uses individual sheets of paper or if the paper comes from a roll, or "web." The web designation refers not only to offset presses, but to gravure and flexographic presses as well.

Sheet-fed presses use standard and nonstandard sizes of paper. A feed-table mechanism controls the pick-up and insertion of each sheet of paper into the press. This is accomplished through the use of air and vacuum controls that are adjusted based on the size, weight, and thickness of the paper being printed. Sheet-fed mechanisms are typical in all offset duplicators and smaller-sized offset presses.

FIGURE 10.3:
Add-on, two-color printing head

Web-fed presses use large rolls of paper feeding into the press in a continuous stream, or web. The paper is cut into individual sheets after it has been printed at the

FIGURE 10.4:
Web offset press
(Courtesy, SIRS Mandarin, Inc.)

delivery end of the press by a device known as a *sheeter*. Figure 10.4 shows a web-feed mechanism on a four-color offset press.

Depending on the particular job requirements, several options are available for the web paper after printing. For example, if the paper needed to be coated with a varnish or other material, the paper would probably go to a rewinder before being coated. If the printed sheets were part of a signature of a book, the paper would first go to the sheeter, be cut into individual sheets, then sent to a folding machine to make up the signatures. The term *standard web offset process* (SWOP) is a graphic arts standard and it comes from the widespread use of web presses in commercial printing applications.

■ PERFECTING PRESSES

Perfecting presses print on both sides of the sheet of paper during a single press run. This is accomplished by the use of an additional printing head on the press for *perfect* printing. Either the individual sheet or the web of paper must be turned 180° as it travels between the two printing heads to properly position the paper.

■ OFFSET PRESS CYLINDER DESIGNS AND CONFIGURATIONS

There are three different common cylinder configurations used in offset presses. Although the design differences focus on the relationship of the cylinders to one another, the cylinders have four main functions in the printing process:

The *plate cylinder* is designed to hold the printing plate or other imaging master material.

The *blanket cylinder* receives the image as it is transferred from the printing plate.

The *impression cylinder* provides a solid surface to back up the paper during image transfer from the blanket to the paper.

The *delivery cylinder*, part of the paper delivery system, is usually restricted to high-speed, large-format offset presses. Some printers do not refer to this as a "cylinder" but rather, as part of the delivery system.

Figures 10.5 (a), (b), and (c) illustrate the two-, three-, and four-cylinder press designs.

The two-cylinder configuration is used primarily in small-format offset duplicators. The main cylinder, which functions as both the plate and impression cylinder, is twice the diameter of the blanket cylinder. During the operating sequence, the plate transfers its image to the blanket cylinder. As the cylinder contin-

Plate
Segment

Impression
Segment

Combination
Plate and
Impression
Cylinder

Arrows
indicate direction
of cylinder rotation

Blanket
Cylinder

FIGURE 10.5(a):
Two-cylinder offset press design

189

ues to rotate, the impression segment of the large cylinder comes around and backs up the blanket cylinder as paper is feeding through the press and the image is transferred from the blanket to the paper. The elimination of one cylinder in this configuration is strictly an engineering decision and in no way affects the print quality and speed of the printing press.

Three- and four-cylinder configurations are the standard in commercial offset presses. The three-cylinder arrangement is also dominant in small-format offset duplicators running sheet sizes smaller than 17 x 22 inches. The four-cylinder arrangement in Fig. 10.5(c) incorporates a fourth delivery cylinder coupled to a chain delivery mechanism. The chain delivery enables high-speed placement of the paper into a delivery bin on the output side of the press.

Most presses incorporate adjustment mechanisms that allow the plate to be moved either vertically or horizontally, as an aid in image registration. There are limitations to adjusting images in this manner and it is assumed that proper registration on the flat minimizes the need for adjustment once the printing plate has been mounted.

All press cylinders are arranged so they can be cleaned from either the front or back of the press, with safety covers incorporated into the machine design. Large presses use hinged steel grate-type covers as guards; small presses use clear plastic covers to protect the press operators. The covers and guard (Fig. 10.6),are moved out of the way during the cleaning process.

■ THE INK DISTRIBUTION SYSTEM

Ink distribution and delivery systems are designed to make available a uniform layer of ink across the entire image area of the printing plate. The system is composed of the ink fountain, the distribution rollers, and the ink form rollers. Figure 10.7 illustrates the ink delivery system on a typical three-cylinder offset press.

Note the direction of rotation of the cylinders in Fig. 10.7. Cylinder rotation is important because the plate must first pass under the dampening system rollers before being inked. Refer to Fig. 10.7 in the following discussions of the ink fountain, distribution, and form rollers.

The Ink Fountain

The ink fountain is a reservoir from which to feed ink onto the press. Consisting of a shallow tray and a "doctor" blade, ink is evenly metered out to the ink system during each rotation of the press. The amount of ink delivered by the fountain is determined by the space between the doctor blade and the ink roller sitting in the ink fountain (Fig. 10.8).

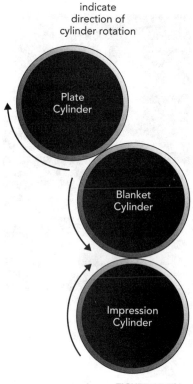

Arrows indicate direction of cylinder rotation

FIGURE 10.5(b):
Three-cylinder offset press design

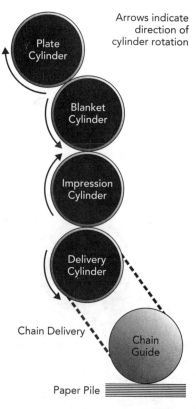

Arrows indicate direction of cylinder rotation

FIGURE 10.5(c):
Four-cylinder offset press design

FIGURE 10.6:
Protective covers on offset press

A series of screws either increase or decrease the space between the doctor blade and ink roller which determine the amount of ink in the system.

Also, an adjustable ratchet system sets the amount of rotation, or "dwell" that the ink fountain rollers turn during each press rotation. This rotation in turn determines how much fresh ink is picked up from the ink fountain by the ink roller during each revolution.

The amount of ink in the system is a critical factor in print quality. Too much ink results in an image that is either too dark or which makes it difficult to maintain a proper balance between the ink and water systems on the press. Too little ink results in light, grayed-out, or washed-out images.

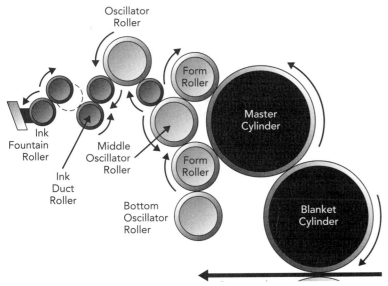

FIGURE 10.7:
Ink distribution system on three-cylinder offset press

Ink Distribution Rollers

The distribution rollers help to control the amount of ink that ends up being available to the printing plate from the ink form rollers. Another purpose of the distribution system is to grind out minor imperfections in the ink layer and further spread the ink evenly across all rollers in the system The more distribution rollers, the greater control the press operator has in balancing the ink system. The ductor roller oscillating back and forth between the ink fountain and the distribution system transfers ink from the fountain to the rollers. The large oscillating roller shown in Fig. 10.7 helps to further grind down the ink and uniformly spread it across the series of distribution rollers.

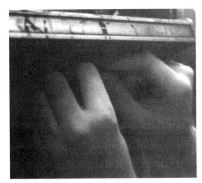

FIGURE 10.8:
Adjusting the ink fountain

Ink Form Rollers

The ink form rollers are the last in the series in the distribution system and the only ones that are directly in contact with the printing plate. By the time the ink reaches the form rollers, ink spread should be uniform, with a thickness layer optimized by the press operator.

■ THE DAMPENING SYSTEM

The dampening system provides the wetting agent, or the "water" in the oil and water principle. The water repels ink in the nonimage areas of the printing plate. The wetting agent used on many presses is referred to as *fountain solution*, which, when mixed with water extends the surface tension of the water to give it greater coating properties than just plain water. Alcohol and water are also used as a wetting agent in large-format presses. As discussed in Chapter 1, waterless offset presses do not rely on fountain solution to repel ink from the nonimage areas of the printing plate. Rather, the waterless process relies on special plates and heat-sensitive printing inks to prevent ink from adhering to nonimage areas of the waterless offset plate.

The chemical composition of the fountain solution is important in maintaining print quality. Special test kits that measure the pH (relative alkalinity) of the fountain solution should be used to maintain consistent, high-quality imaging capabilities. The dampening system is similar in roller design and configuration to the inking system, although there are generally fewer rollers in dampening systems. Dampening systems are either of the direct or combined types, usually referred to as either *conventional* or *direct*, and *integrated* or *indirect*.

Conventional Dampening Systems

A conventional dampening system delivers fountain solution to the printing plate using a roller delivery system that is separate from the ink delivery system. Figure 10.9 highlights a conventional, or direct, dampening system found on a two-cylinder press.

To help provide a constant level of fountain solution to the plate, cotton covers are installed over the water ductor and form rollers. These covers

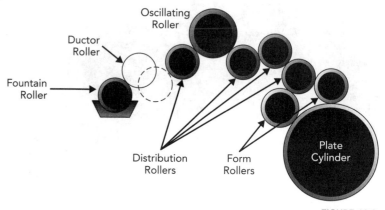

FIGURE 10.9:
Direct dampening system

are called *molleton* covers and act as small water reservoirs to help level out the flow of fountain solution in the system. The ductor roller serves the same purpose in dampening system as in the inking system: to pick up fountain solution and deliver it to the dampening system distribution rollers. The water form roller is the last in the system and applies fountain solution directly to the printing plate. Note from Fig. 10.9 that the rotation of the plate cylinder enables the plate to be dampened before being inked. This ensures that there will be sufficient wetting agent on the plate to repel ink prior to the plate being inked. Because there are no imperfections in the fountain solution that need to be ground out as there are in printing inks, there are fewer rollers in the dampening system than in the inking system.

Integrated Dampening Systems

Integrated dampening systems are also referred to as *indirect* dampening systems. These systems carry both the ink and fountain solution on the same set of rollers; there is no need for a separate set of dampening rollers as in the direct system. The integrated system requires that the printing press be inked before fountain solution is added to the water fountain. After the system is inked (including inking the water fountain roller), fountain solution is added to the water fountain. During operation, fountain solution is carried in a series of fine indentations across the surface of

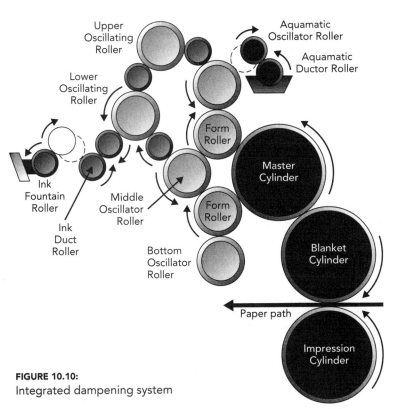

Upper Oscillating Roller

Aquamatic Oscillator Roller

Aquamatic Ductor Roller

Lower Oscillating Roller

Form Roller

Master Cylinder

Ink Fountain Roller

Middle Oscillator Roller

Form Roller

Ink Duct Roller

Bottom Oscillator Roller

Blanket Cylinder

Paper path

Impression Cylinder

FIGURE 10.10:
Integrated dampening system

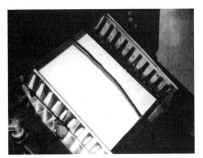

FIGURE 10.11:
Chute delivery system

FIGURE 10.12:
Chain delivery system

the water fountain and ductor rollers. Figure 10.10 illustrates the configuration of an integrated dampening system. Integrated systems are used on both small and large presses.

■ PAPER DELIVERY SYSTEMS

Paper delivery systems are designed to receive the printed sheets of paper, then jog them or otherwise ensure that they are stacked and aligned in a pile, making them ready for delivery or further processing. The two main types of delivery systems are the *receiving tray chute* and the *chain delivery*.

Receiving Tray Chute

The receiving tray chute is the simplest and least expensive paper delivery system. It is generally found on offset duplicators and smaller-format presses. The receiving tray is connected directly to the back end of the press, in line with the output from the impression and delivery cylinders. Figure 10.11 shows the setup of a typical chute delivery on a small offset duplicator. The side and back guides of the tray are adjusted for different paper sizes. The guides are also used to line up the tray properly with the position of the printed sheets as they come out of the press. Many chutes are also equipped with both side and top joggers that push up against the paper stack and keep the sheets aligned during delivery. Most stationary delivery chutes have only a limited capacity for paper and must be emptied frequently during press runs.

Chain Delivery Systems

Chain delivery systems use two chains with a series of gripper bars that grab the sheet as it leaves the press cylinders and then drops it onto the paper pile. The bars move continuously on the chains from the press end to the delivery pile, picking up and delivering paper with each rotation of the printing press. The chain delivery in Fig. 10.12 uses two gripper bars for paper delivery.

Some chain delivery systems drop the paper into a stationary tray; others incorporate a device known as a *receding stacker*. The receding stacker adjusts to automatically lower as paper is dropped into it thus maintaining an even paper height in the delivery tray. Receding stackers can also hold a large volume of paper, which reduces the number of times the receiving tray must be emptied.

Having covered the basic components of offset presses, let's move on to see how a typical job is printed.

■ PRINTING A JOB

All adjustments on the press should take place prior to printing of any job. The paper feed and delivery systems, ink, and water adjustments must be set up properly to work with one another. For purposes of this discussion, controls and adjustments refer to small sheetfed offset duplicators, although these concepts apply to large commercial machines as well and are referred to where appropriate.

Adjusting Paper Feed and Delivery

The first press adjustment prior to printing requires setting up the paper feed and delivery. These adjustments ensure that the paper feeds evenly into the press and is dropped off properly into the receiving tray. After the paper adjustments have been made, the ink and water systems are set up.

On sheetfed presses, paper is fed from a pile using a combination of air, vacuum controls, and stationary guide bars. A front paper guide bar lines up the paper evenly across the leading edge, while side guides hold the stack evenly along the length of the sheet, as shown in Fig. 10.13

The rear end of the paper feed table also uses adjustable guides to hold the paper stack firmly in place without squeezing or pinching the paper. Note the sheet feeder on a large offset press that incorporates a separate paper feed table, equipped with its own set of controls (Fig. 10.14).

After making the feed table adjustments, the delivery tray should be checked to ensure that the printed sheets will fall properly into the tray. If the tray incorporates a jogger, the adjustment of the jogger should not interfere with the paper as it comes out of the press. Some delivery systems have only one side jogger; others may have a second jogger located at the top of the tray.

Air and Vacuum Controls

A combination of air and vacuum is used to first separate, then feed, individual sheets of paper into the press. A stream of air, directed at the top of the paper pile, flutters the top sheets of paper and keeps them separated. This helps to prevent more than one sheet of paper from being fed into the press. At the same time, vacuum sucker feet pick up the top sheet and move it into the press. Air and vacuum adjustments are critical: too little air and/or too much vacuum can cause two or more sheets to be picked up at the same time; too little air and/or too little vacuum will result in sheets being either fed into the press improperly or

FIGURE 10.13:
Side and front paper table feed guides

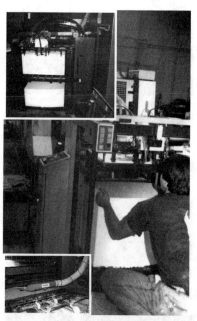

FIGURE 10.14:
Sheet feeder on commercial offset press

FIGURE 10.15:
Air pump controls

FIGURE 10.16:
Tape feed registration mechanism

not at all. Note the air pump and suction controls on the control panel of a commercial offset press in Fig. 10.15.

Adjusting Paper Registration

Proper position, or registration of the paper, is the result of two adjustments: setting up the paper properly on the feed table and making final registration adjustments on the infeed, or conveyor table, of the press, if so equipped. On some presses, the only position control adjustment for paper is the guide bar locators on the paper feed table. Other presses use a conveyor tape feed mechanism that enables the operator to make final adjustments before the paper enters the printing head. A conveyor tape feed registration system is shown in Fig. 10.16.

The incorporation of a conveyor or similar type of infeed paper registration system gives the press operator a greater amount of control in maintaining the quality and registration of the printed image than is possible with direct-feed presses. Some direct-feed systems use a micrometer adjustment on the feed table to help maximize paper position.

Double Sheet Detection

After paper adjustments have been made, paper should be fed into the press using the automatic feed controls. At this time, the press operator can make sure that all air, vacuum, and positioning controls have been adjusted properly. The actual paper for the job should be used in this final trial. Most presses have a double sheet detector that prevents two sheets of paper from being fed into the printing head at the same time. Preventing double sheets from feeding is important. They can cause subsequent misfeeds, resulting in significant press downtimes. Double sheet detectors are either mechanical or electronic, and when properly adjusted, deflect the sheets into a separate receiving tray out of the line of the normal press feed. Although the principles of double sheet detecting are similar from one press to another, specific adjustments vary by manufacturer. The operator should consult the press instruction manual regarding all adjustments.

Inking the Press

Inking the press before or after adjusting the paper feed system is at the discretion of the press operator. On presses equipped with integrated ink/water systems, the press must be inked before the fountain solution is added. One key to quality printing is to ensure there is neither too much nor too little ink on the system ink rollers. In general, running with a minimum amount of ink required to produce solid blacks is preferred.

On commercial offset presses, ink systems can be operated either manually or automatically, with minimum adjustments required by the press operator. On duplicators, ink is placed into the ink fountain after which the fountain set screws are adjusted. These screws apply pressure against a doctor blade, determining the space between the blade and the ink reservoir (Fig. 10.17).

This space in turn determines how much ink is passed from the ink fountain onto the fountain roller as it rotates within the ink reservoir. As a starting adjustment, the screws should first be tightened by hand until firm resistance is felt against the doctor blade, then backed off one-quarter turn. Ink is added to the fountain from either a can or a cartridge gun. A bead of ink should be placed on top of the fountain roller. The roller is then rotated, moving the bead from the roller to the fountain reservoir. After a sufficient quantity of ink is in the reservoir, the ink can be transferred from the fountain roller to the ductor roller to make adjustments on the fountain set screws.

FIGURE 10.17:
Ink fountain adjustment screws

With ink in the reservoir, the press is rotated by hand until the ductor roller contacts the ink fountain roller. At this point, the ink fountain roller is rotated by hand to transfer ink from the fountain to the ductor. The thickness of the bead of ink being transferred from the ink fountain to the ductor as well as the evenness of the layer of ink from one side of the roller to the other should be carefully observed.

A thin layer of ink should cover the ductor roller. If necessary, further adjustments can be made using the set screws to even out the ink layer. Once these adjustments have been completed, the press can be turned on to ink all of the rollers in the system.

When first inking any press, press operators should start with a light, rather than a heavy layer of ink. It is always easier to add ink to the system either by increasing the ratchet adjustment on the ink fountain or by opening up the doctor blade set screws, than to deal with a press that is over-inked. Inking up a small press should take from between 30 to 60 seconds. Remember that the combination of the doctor blade set screws and the ratchet control on the ink fountain determines how much ink will be delivered to the ink rollers during the initial start-up procedure.

Requirements of the job should be kept in mind during initial inking. For example, if a job requires dense ink coverage such as full-page illustrations, more ink will be needed to be delivered to the plate than with a job consisting only of line art and text. If a job has all, or most of the illustrations on one side of the page, the set screws can be adjusted to deliver a greater amount of ink to that one side of the plate. After the inking system has been set up, the dampening system can be adjusted.

The Dampening System

Fountain concentrate or other dampening solution is added to the water fountain according to the manufacturer's instructions. Duplicators use fountain solution fed from a small bottle into the water fountain (Fig. 10.18). Commercial presses use large-capacity jugs to supply the dampening solution to the press rollers.

Presses with conventional dampening systems usually have roller covers on both the ductor and form rollers. These systems need to be dampened by running the press until the mol-

FIGURE 10.18:
Small fountain solution bottle

leton rollers are damp. Integrated systems do not have covered rollers and need to be predampened for only a few seconds until an adequate amount of dampening solution is in the system.

For best quality, the operator should check the pH of the fountain solution. On a scale from 0 to 14 (0 is a highly acidic solution), offset press pH should be between 4.5 to 5.5 (slightly acidic). Also, the plate manufacturer's instructions should be consulted for recommendations regarding proper pH requirements of the printing plate. After these adjustments have been completed, actual printing of the job can start. The first step in this process is mounting the printing plate.

Mounting the Printing Plate

The plate is mounted on to the press using either a straight-edge clamp or pin-bar clamp attached to the plate cylinder. Pin-bar holes punched into the head and tail of the plate match up to pins on the head and tail clamps on the plate cylinder when mounting the plate to the plate cylinder.

After attaching the plate at the head clamp, it is advanced onto the plate cylinder until the tail clamp on the plate cylinder is rotated into position. The pins on the tail clamp are inserted into the plate in a manner similar to attaching the head clamp. After mounting the plate, a cotton pad is used to wet the plate before the press is started.

Proofing the Image

After the plate has been wet, the press is started in order to pull a press proof of the job. Press proofs ensure that the job is set up correctly and that registration of the image is correct.

On presses with combination dampening systems, the press needs only to run a few revolutions before the form rollers are lowered onto the plate cylinder. On presses with molleton-covered dampening rollers, the machine should run for about 30 seconds to allow dampening solution to penetrate the molletons before lowering the water form rollers onto the plate cylinder. With both ink and water form rollers contacting the plate, the press is run for a few revolutions and then turned off. The plate is then inspected to ensure that it is inked up only in the image areas. There should be a thin coating of moisture on the nonimage areas of the plate, which should also be clean and free of ink.

Any blemishes or ink on the nonimage areas of the plate should be removed at this time, before the final printing of the job begins. Minor corrections can be made using image removing pens. These pens resemble felt-tip markers and use a special chemical solution that dissolves the image areas of the printing plate. If image-removing pens are not available, a soft rubber eraser dipped in fountain solution can be used to erase unwanted image areas from the plate (Fig. 10.19).

If large areas of the plate are inking up in nonimage areas, check the negative and plate. Assuming that the ink and water balance is set correctly, improperly developed or outdated plates will ink up in nonimage areas due to either residual devel-

FIGURE 10.19:
Removing small blemishes with rubber eraser

oper left on the plate, or latent image areas remaining on the plate after development caused by aging of the plates or processing chemistry. If the plate was processed more than an hour before being printed, the aluminum surface of the plate may have oxidized. This causes the surface of the plate to become grease- or ink-receptive. In either of these two cases, the plate will have to be made over again.

If the press proofs check out properly and/or small blemishes have been removed from the plate, the press can be turned on and additional press proofs can be made. The printed sheets are then removed from the delivery tray for final inspection.

Press operators should get into the habit of turning the form rollers off every time the press is stopped. This keeps the plate free from roller impression marks when the press is started up again. Also, when a press is stopped for more than a minute or so, the dampening rollers tend to dry out. If the press is then started and the form rollers engaged before the dampening rollers have a chance to remoisten, the plate may completely ink up. If this happens it takes some time to clean the plate and restore the proper water and ink balance to the plate.

As the final press run begins, adjustments can be made for optimum quality by fine-tuning the ink and water balance reaching the printing plate.

Maximizing Image Quality

The distinction is made here between "wet" versus "dry" offset technology which will be covered later in this chapter. Most of the problems associated with image quality in wet offset printing relate to the balance of ink and water delivered to the printing plate. The press operator should try to achieve the best image quality using the minimum amount of both ink and water. Problems in achieving maximum image quality are also caused by other factors, including glazed ink or water rollers, improper roller pressures and glazed, damaged, or improperly packed blankets. Ink and water adjustments can only be made while the press is running; therefore, some paper waste is inevitable until the best print quality is achieved.

There are many benchmarks of quality printing. First and foremost among these is even ink coverage across the image; text should be printed in solid colors and not grayed-out. Solid colors should print with full, even intensity and coverage across the page. When printing multiple colors, each color should be in proper registration to the others. When printing halftones, there should be minimum dot gain in the picture. Dot gain comes from improperly exposed printing plates or negatives, improper pressure between the press rollers, or over-inking of the press. Any of these conditions can cause the dots to grow in size in relation to the size of the dot on the original halftone negative. There are several devices that usually accompany the printed image and act as quality control (QC) devices, allowing the press operator to continually inspect the printed sheets as they come out of the press. Almost all of the QC devices are stripped into the flat, and print outside of the main image area. They are removed during final trimming of the finished sheets. The most common QC control devices are:

> *Registration marks* placed in pairs at each corner of the illustration allow for the printing and alignment of colors in multicolor separation prints. Also, during stripping, registration marks allow for pinpoint positioning of the negative on the flat.

Star targets are placed at diagonal corners. The star target shows the amount of ink spread. As ink spread increases, the center wedge of the target begins to fill with ink. The target will also show the amount of ink slur, or line doubling on the print in addition to ink spread. Ink slur occurs in a specific direction and is indicated on the target by distorted wedges changes in the shape of the circle at the very center of the target.

Crop marks, which appear at each of the corners of the illustration are used as a guide for final trimming on the paper cutter.

Gray scales, discussed in Chapter 9, are basic QC devices that give an indication of the overall contrast range being captured by the press utilizing the halftone screen.

Color bars are used in color separation negatives to give the press operator a visual indication of the colors resulting from the overlay of transparent color separation inks.

FIGURE 10.20:
Linen tester

The use of a good quality magnifying lens, called a *linen tester* or *loupe* is an invaluable aid for close inspection of all negatives and prints, and facilitates the entire quality control process (Fig. 10.20).

■ TROUBLESHOOTING POOR IMAGE QUALITY

There are four major types of problems associated with the quality of the image in traditional offset printing. These are: image scumming, image blurring, washed-out copy, and hickeys.

Image Scumming

Scumming is a printing condition in which the printing plate picks up ink in the nonimage areas. There are two major causes of scumming: too much ink on the rollers or too little fountain solution reaching the printing plate. Too much ink is generally indicated by a loud hissing noise coming from the ink rollers when the press is running. The rollers will also take on a textured appearance from the heavy ink layer. Too little water, while almost impossible to detect visually on the rollers, will leave too little water available for the plate to repel ink in the nonimage areas, resulting in scumming.

It is usually better, from the perspective of proper press operation, to subtract ink or water rather than adding either of these to solve a printing problem. For example, in a typical scumming situation, it would be preferable to subtract ink rather than add water to clean up the plate. Remember, using the least amount of ink and water necessary to achieve the best quality result is the best solution.

However, it is not always possible to subtract ink or water in order to fix an image problem. For example, if the dampening system is not working properly, or if there is not a sufficient quantity of fountain solution available in the water fountain, then more must be added. Increasing the ratchet adjustment on the water fountain roller will increase the amount of dampening solution delivered to the printing plate.

Adjustments to clear up scumming should be made while the press is running so the operator can see the results of the adjustments being made. Sometimes, two or three dozen copies my have to be printed before final results of the adjustments are visible. Integrated dampening systems generally take fewer copies to show results than do conventional dampening systems.

Image Blurring

Image blurring is sometimes referred to as *image doubling*. Causes of double printed images may be loose blankets and excessive pressures on the impression cylinder. Before beginning the press run, the operator should check that the blanket is secured tightly to the blanket cylinder and that the impression pressure is set properly. During the press run, the operator can slowly back off the impression pressure to see if a blurred image problem disappears as the pressure is reduced. If this doesn't work, the problem probably resides in the blanket assembly.

Washed-Out Copy

Washed-out copy appears gray when it should be printing solid black. This overall gray, low-contrast appearance of the copy is almost always caused by an imbalance in the amount of ink and water reaching the plate. One early sign of wash-out is water dripping from the bottom of the roller system. In this instance, too much water in the system reaches the plate, overwhelming the inking system's ability to ink the image areas of the plate. Following preferred methodology, the remedy for this situation is to cut back on the dampening system feed controls. Wash-outs can also be caused by too little ink reaching the plate cylinder. If too little ink is suspected, the ink covering on the rollers should be inspected and the ink feed readjusted if necessary.

An additional cause of wash-out results from incorrect pressure adjustments between either the plate to blanket, blanket to impression cylinder, or both. These pressures should be checked and readjusted according to manufacturer's specifications.

Hickeys

Hickeys are small blemishes or dots that print in either the image or nonimage areas. Hickeys are caused by small pieces of paper or ink that adhere to the plate or blanket cylinder. These particles then pick up ink and transfer the image to the press sheet or they appear as un-inked small round areas within the solid image areas of the print. If hickeys are found, the press should be stopped, and the piece of ink or paper removed from either the plate or blanket. After the particle is removed, the blanket should be cleaned before resuming printing.

■ PRINTING COLOR SEPARATIONS

If a single-color offset press will be used to print a three- or four-color separation job, certain orders of the color printing sequence yield better results than others. The tried-and-true method for printing color separations is to go from light to dark inks, beginning with yellow, then magenta, cyan, and black ink. If the color separation is combined with conventional text and/or line drawings to be printed in black on the same page as the separation, then the color sequence would be to print black first, then yellow, magenta, and cyan.

A third sequence of printing uses cyan first, followed by yellow, magenta, and black. Because the cyan printer often best represents a conventional halftone picture with the greatest amount of detail of all the separation colors, this detail is apparent on all of the remaining color prints and makes registration of the following colors somewhat easier.

Regardless of the sequence used in process printing, it is important to clean the press completely between colors to prevent contamination of any ink with the color that preceded it. One method that reduces ink contamination is to clean the press after one color has been printed, ink the press with the next color to be printed and immediately clean it up before printing that color, then re-ink the press. This method preconditions the rollers to the next color of ink and is referred to as *color wash-up*.

The use of presses equipped with more than one head for color printing greatly simplifies the color separation printing process. Because of the expense involved in press setup and operation, short-run, full-color printing represents a significant inroad for digital printing presses and copiers. Although long-run (more than 1,000 copies) full-color printing is still done largely by conventional offset, the short-run color market is undergoing a continuing shift to digital output.

■ CLEANING, STORAGE, AND MAINTENANCE PROCEDURES
Cleaning and Storing Plates

After the press run has been completed, the plate must be taken off the press, cleaned, and coated with a preservative if it is to be used again. Treated in this manner, offset printing plates will last many years. Improperly cared for, the plate will be useless in only a few hours after it has been taken off the press.

After printing, the plates should be cleaned with press wash, using a soft cotton cloth to prevent scratching. After cleaning, the plate should be coated with a solution of gum arabic and water that seals the plate, allowing the solution to air dry on the plate. After drying, the plates should be stored in a folder or protective sheet to prevent scratching. Gummed plates can be stored either flat in drawers or hung vertically in a plate cabinet.

It's always a good idea to expose and process an offset plate just before it will be printed. The procedure eliminates storage and preservation problems. However, if a plate must be exposed several hours or days before it will be printed, it must be preserved using gum arabic. When the plate is to be printed, the gum arabic can be removed with either water or fountain solution using cotton litho pads. The plate can either be in a plate sink or mounted on the printing press. After all of the gum has been dissolved and removed, the plate is ready for printing.

FIGURE 10.21:
Installing clean-up mats

Cleaning a Press

Several different methods can be used to clean presses. No matter which is used, cleaning an offset press is always a dirty job.

One effective method for cleaning is to use clean-up mats. The clean-up mat is attached to the plate cylinder in the same manner as a regular plate (Fig. 10.21).

Before cleaning begins, the ink fountain is removed from the press and cleaned separately. The water fountain should also be drained and removed for cleaning at this time. If the press uses a conventional dampening system, the water form rollers should be in the "off" position before cleaning. If the press uses an integrated, or combination dampening system, the water fountain must be drained before cleaning the press.

The clean-up mat is the same size as the press's printing plate and is made from a highly absorbent material, similar in appearance and texture to a desk blotter. The mat is installed onto the plate cylinder. Once installed, the press is turned on, the ink and water form rollers are turned "on" and blanket wash is sprinkled across the main oscillating roller. The blanket wash will begin to dissolve the printing ink and work its way through the roller distribution system to the form rollers and eventually on to the clean-up mat. In this way, the mat will quickly turn the color of the ink being cleaned and will have to be changed frequently during this process. The operator will notice that after the fourth or fifth clean-up mat, the rollers will become cleaner and the clean-up mats take longer and longer to become soiled with the ink/blanket wash mixture.

Cleaning an offset press is never an easy job, whether it is a small duplicator or large web press. Note the use of protective gloves during the clean-up process on the two-color sheetfed commercial offset press shown in Fig. 10.22.

Clean-up mats can be used on both sides and should not be thrown away if they are dirty on one side only. After they dry out, they can be turned over and used again. After the rollers have been cleaned, the ink and water fountains should be reattached to the press. If a film of ink still remains on the rollers, it can be removed by hand with a soft cloth and blanket wash.

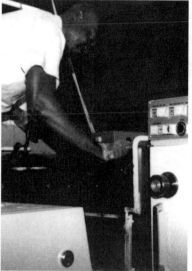

FIGURE 10.22:
Using gloves when cleaning a press

Maintenance Procedures

Offset presses require a regularly scheduled maintenance program to maximize their efficiency and minimize mechanical problems. All manufacturers have maintenance schedules for their machines that should be carefully followed.

Important maintenance procedures focus around lubrication of the chain delivery system, roller and motor bearings, and maintenance of the air blower assembly. Many electric motors are equipped with factory-sealed bearings that are lubricated for the life of the motor and require no regular attention. However, paper lint and dust can clog the air cooling fins and openings on the drive and compressor motors. The motors should be inspected frequently and any lint build-up removed to prevent the motors from overheating. Roller bearings are accessible under the protective cover of the machine and require frequent lubrication to perform properly (Fig. 10.23).

If the press incorporates a chain delivery, the chains should be lubricated frequently with a high-tack chain oil and kept free of lint and other objects that could otherwise cause the chains to jam or jump out of timing.

Most presses use solid-state sensors for detecting double sheets and paper jams. These sensors, because of their proximity

FIGURE 10.23:
Lubricating roller bearings

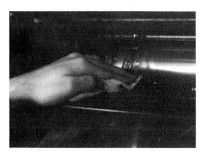

FIGURE 10.24:
Cleaning press sensors
after a press run

FIGURE 10.25:
Computerized industrial
paper cutter

to the feed and delivery systems, will accumulate dirt and paper lint and should be cleaned after each press run (Fig. 10.24).

■ POST-PRESS OPERATIONS

A wide variety of finishing and binding operations occur after a job has been printed. Finishing techniques such as trimming, scoring, embossing, and laminating as well as different binding techniques for combining multiple pages into signatures are some of the more common finishing operations. We will look at some of these operations in more detail. Some of these processes are performed on the printing press using specialized equipment; others require separate machines.

Paper Cutting

Most printed material has been trimmed at some point during its production. Almost all of the production-sized paper cutters presently sold are microprocessor-controlled (note the digital control pad in Fig. 10.25) and are available as either floor or table models.

The paper cutter in Fig. 10.25 can be programmed, through its built-in microprocessor, to automatically move and cut the paper for more than 3,000 total cuts in any specific sequence. Some systems are also available with built-in video monitors that enable the machine operator to track the cutting details of any specific job. Large-format paper cutters are usually hydraulically operated and are capable of producing several hundred pounds of force per inch over the length of the cutting blade. Small air jets built into the cutter table help the operator move heavy paper stacks across the surface of the machine. Built-in safety features automatically shut down the cutter for a variety of machine malfunctions and operating conditions. However, as with all power equipment, the operator must exercise great care during operation if accidents are to be prevented.

For smaller jobs, a tabletop cutter is an ideal choice. Small tabletop cutters are

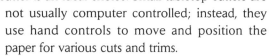

not usually computer controlled; instead, they use hand controls to move and position the paper for various cuts and trims.

Folding, Scoring, and Perforating

Many modern paper-folding machines are multifunctional and perform a variety of finishing operations simultaneously. For low-run requirements, a tabletop paper folder is standard equipment in many offices and small print shops. When larger printing jobs require controls that allow for simple or complex folding operations at speeds that range from 2,000 to more than 20,000 sheets per hour, a folder such as the machine shown in Fig. 10.26 is called for.

FIGURE 10.26:
Large capacity paper folder

The unit in Fig. 10.26 goes one step further, combining folding capabilities with scoring, perforating, and creasing. Note the counter at the top of the machine to keep track of finished copies.

Jogging

Joggers are used to evenly align all of the sheets of paper in a paper stack. All paper should be jogged before being loaded into a printing press. This helps to eliminate misfeeds due to misaligned paper on the feed table. Also, paper should be jogged before being trimmed to ensure accuracy of the trimmed sheets. Joggers come in different sizes and work by rapidly vibrating the paper pile against a top and bottom stationary guide. The vibration evenly aligns all of the sheets in the paper stack in only a few seconds. The jogger pictured in Fig. 10.27 is a small tabletop unit that handles sheet sizes up to 17 x 22 inches.

FIGURE 10.27:
Tabletop paper jogger

Collating

Collating is the process of placing all printed pages in the correct order or proper sequence. Collating can be done either on a printing press equipped with a built-in collator or with a separate collator unit. Built-in copiers have become virtually standard equipment on high-end office copiers and digital printing presses. On duplicators and commercial offset presses, collating is usually done as a finishing process because even a single sheet may contain two or more pages that must first be trimmed before they can be collated. Collators can be purchased as simple multibin systems or as multifunction controlled units such as the one pictured in Fig. 10.28, which not only collates, but folds and stitches as well. In this unit, the sheets travel from the in-feed top to the folder at the top of the machine, then to the collating unit located on the left side of the

FIGURE 10.28:
Multifunction collator

unit. These machines incorporate automatic miss, double sheet, and jam detectors to monitor the paper-feed and collating operations, and will shut down the collator if any problems develop.

Die-Cutting

Die-cutting is the process of cutting shapes from paper or cardboard using special, preformed steel cutting dies. For example, the envelope must first be die-cut into the specific shape before it can be folded and glued to its final, familiar shape. Die-cutting is a process external to the printing process and is usually done after the sheet has been printed. Die-cutting forms are made by cutting the pattern for the shape of the cut into a piece of plywood and then inserting specially manufactured steel cutting dies into the space left by the teeth of the saw as it cuts through the wood (called a saw kerf). Figure 10.29 shows a simple geometric form designed to cut out lightweight paper shapes.

Note the foam rubber lining the steel die in Fig. 10.29. The rubber is used to prevent the paper from sticking to the die

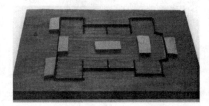

FIGURE 10.29:
Die-cutting rule in die-cutting form

FIGURE 10.30:
Die-cutting form locked up
in a press chase

FIGURE 10.31:
Electronic counter on offset press

FIGURE 10.32:
Coated cards on conveyor belt

FIGURE 10.33:
Tabletop thermography station
(Courtesy Sunraise, Inc.)

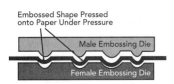

FIGURE 10.34:
Principle of embossing

after it has been cut. In Fig. 10.30, a die-cutting form, used to cut out a box window from a sheet of paper, is locked up in a press chase before the die-cutting operation begins.

Counting

Most printing presses and finishing machines such as stitchers and collators have built-in counters. Sometimes secondary portable counters are also used to give a precise count of the number of pamphlets, pages, or individual sheets actually produced after the finishing processes have been completed. The counter in Fig. 10.31 is built into the control panel of a sheetfed press to keep track of finished sheets.

Thermography (Raised Printing)

The thermography process produces a raised surface on conventionally printed material. For this reason, thermography is sometimes referred to as *imitation engraving*, and is widely used in the printing of a variety of invitations, business cards, and specialty items. In the thermography process, a resin powder is applied to the wet printing ink on a freshly printed job and then heated. Under the influence of heat, the resin powder melts but remains raised from the surface of the paper, leaving a raised letter in both appearance and feel.

Thermography units come in both tabletop and floor-model units. In Fig. 10.32, thermography power has been applied to the freshly printed piece, which is then placed on a conveyor belt. The belt carries the powder-coated piece under the heating unit, which heats and melts the powder, leaving the raised image of the type or illustration that was coated with the powder. Figure 10.33 illustrates a wide-format (12-inch) tabletop thermography station.

Large, production-model units apply the resin powder to the printed form, vacuum off the excess powder, and deliver the finished sheet automatically. Thermography powder comes in a variety of colors as well as clear resin. The availability of clear resin enables the printer to either keep the original color of the ink or change it, based on the color of the powder selected.

Embossing

Embossing produces a raised image on a sheet of paper with the use of an embossing die. A common example of embossing is the seal used by a notary public when notarizing a document. The principle of the embossing process is shown in Fig. 10.34.

Embossing is a finishing process often used in the production of high-quality printed material such as corporate and business stationery, as well as specialty marketing brochures and literature. Embossing is an external process using male and female dies to make the raised designs on the paper.

Numbering

Many items such as theater, movie, and stadium seating tickets require that each individual ticket be numbered. Printing presses can be equipped with numbering machines, or the process can be done manually after the tickets have been printed and trimmed. When the numbering requirements of a job are demanding, a large-format numbering machine may be required. Numbering machines of this type can handle multiple numbering heads. Some of these units can also score, slit, and perforate in addition to numbering. Larger units can number several thousands of sheets per hour and are usually microprocessor-controlled.

Drilling

Drilling holes in paper for use in either conventional looseleaf binders or other types of binding systems continues to be a widely used bindery technique. Paper drills are available as either single- or multiple-spindle machines, as shown in Fig. 10.35.

The drill bits incorporate a tapered shank that holds the bit firmly in place in the drill chuck. The drills are available in a variety of sizes.

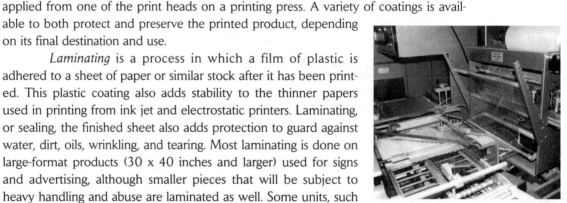

FIGURE 10.35:
Multiple spindle paper drill

Coating and Laminating

For a variety of reasons, many jobs need to be coated after they have been printed. For example, art reproductions are sometimes given a protective varnish coating after printing to both preserve the appearance of the image and give it an authentic, painted look. Coatings are usually applied from one of the print heads on a printing press. A variety of coatings is available to both protect and preserve the printed product, depending on its final destination and use.

Laminating is a process in which a film of plastic is adhered to a sheet of paper or similar stock after it has been printed. This plastic coating also adds stability to the thinner papers used in printing from ink jet and electrostatic printers. Laminating, or sealing, the finished sheet also adds protection to guard against water, dirt, oils, wrinkling, and tearing. Most laminating is done on large-format products (30 x 40 inches and larger) used for signs and advertising, although smaller pieces that will be subject to heavy handling and abuse are laminated as well. Some units, such as the one shown in Fig. 10.36, can handle both shrinkwrapping and laminating chores.

FIGURE 10.36:
Large-format laminator

Laminators can also be used for image transfer. These machines enable the transfer of images produced by electrostatic printers to both rigid and flexible base materials, depending on the end use of the product. Signs, banners, and a variety of outdoor use printed products benefit from this image transfer process.

■ BINDING TECHNIQUES

A variety of techniques is used to bind the pages of a document together. The four major binding methods are: edition binding, perfect binding, plastic binding, and side and saddle stitching. Most large printing facilities have a variety of binding equipment located either in the pressroom or in adjacent areas to facilitate the binding of documents after they have been printed and finished.

Edition Binding

The hardcover textbooks with which we are familiar are examples of *edition bindings* (sometimes referred to as Smyth Sewn). Edition bindings are made up of several signatures that are first sewn together. After sewing, a hardcover is glued onto end sheets that hold the cover in place. The end sheets are either sewn or glued onto the signatures so that the cover is connected to all of the signatures in the book. Edition bindings are the most expensive types of bindings and are usually reserved for text, relatively expensive books and books with high page counts. In Fig. 10.37, signatures for an edition binding are folded, assembled, stitched, and completed automatically along one continuous production line. Working in this way, one technician can keep the production line operating by ensuring that the feed bins along the line are continuously filled.

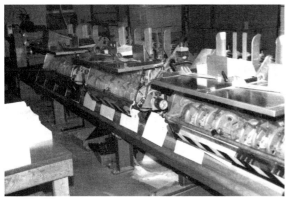

FIGURE 10.37:
Gathering and assembling signatures
Courtesy SIRS Mandarin, Inc.

Perfect Binding

Perfect binding is a padding process. In perfecting binding, the spine of the book is first trimmed and then inserted into a binding machine where a special flexible binding adhesive is heated and applied to the book spine. While the glue is still wet, the cover is then glued onto the spine of the book.

The perfect binding process is fast, durable, and inexpensive. Typical perfect binding machines can bind several hundred books per hour. The typical paperback book, phone book, and Yellow Pages® are examples of perfect bound documents that hold up well to rough and sometimes abusive treatment. For small perfect binding jobs and making pads, tabletop padding presses can also be used.

FIGURE 10.38:
Plastic binding document

Plastic Binding

Plastic binding is a popular method for binding small reports, presentations, and similar documents. The plastic binding "combs" come in a variety of colors and sizes, depending on the thickness of the document to be bound. A small office-sized binding system includes a machine for punching the holes as well as a unit to insert the plastic combs into the document after the holes have been punched. Plastic-bound documents have a neat, finished appearance, are inexpensive to produce and easily put together (Fig. 10.38).

The holes that are punched in this system are rectangular and match the shape of the plastic binding combs. For small, short-run jobs, manual hole punchers, which are capable of punching between 10 to 15 sheets of paper at a time, are generally used (Fig. 10.39). For larger jobs, an automatic hole puncher is usually required. After the holes have been punched, the plastic binding combs are manually inserted into each document (Fig. 10.40).

FIGURE 10.39:
Plastic binding hole puncher

Side and Saddle Stitching

Of all the methods of putting two or more pieces of paper together, stapling is still the simplest and cheapest method available. Stapling a document through its side (side stitching) or stapling a signature through the center fold (saddle stitching) continues to be a primary binding technique. Stitching machines are available for either manual or automatic stitching operations. Small, electrically operated stitchers can perform both side and saddle stitching operations on pamphlets and books up to about 1/4-inch thick. Larger and thicker documents require a heavy-duty stitching machine such as the one shown in Fig. 10.41.

Printing plants that require complete bindery operations use integrated machines that combine many of the functions we have seen, including folding, scoring, perforating, collating, and stitching, into one bindery production unit.

FIGURE 10.40
Manually inserting plastic binding combs

■ ENVIRONMENTAL AND SAFETY FACTORS IN OFFSET PRINTING

Operating an environmentally safe facility should always be the first consideration in any workplace. Continued improvements in both products and production technology continue to have a major influence on all facets of the graphic arts industry. The federal Occupational Safety and Health Administration (OSHA) is responsible for setting and enforcing safety guidelines in the workplace. OSHA conducts regular inspections of all workplaces to ensure safety code compliance. It has enforcement powers that range from fines to plant shutdowns in instances of regulation noncompliance.

FIGURE 10.41:
Heavy-duty stitching machine

Environmental considerations fall into several major categories that all graphic designers and printing technicians should be aware of: noise levels, odor, chemical safety, indoor and outdoor air pollution, and hazardous waste management. These areas are not mutually exclusive and there is often a great deal of overlap between them.

Noise Levels

Whereas graphic design studios are quiet work environments, virtually everything in a pressroom and printing production facility makes noise. Printing presses and folding equipment are the major contributors of noise pollution within this setting.

The standard unit of noise measurement is the decibel. One decibel (dB) is the amount of sound that is barely audible to the human ear. An increase of 10 dB indicates a doubling of sound intensity. Continued and regular exposure to sound intensities of 90 dBs will eventually cause hearing loss. Exposure to sound levels of 130 dBs can cause immediate and permanent hearing loss. If a particular workplace has consistent noise levels of 85 dBs, then all workers must be tested with audiometers on a regular basis. If exceptionally high noise levels are suspected in a particular workplace, the area should be tested and appropriate actions taken to minimize worker exposure in those areas of the plant.

Chemical Safety

Individuals working in a printing production facility are continually exposed to potential health threats from the chemical compounds in printing inks, solvents, darkroom chemicals, and other assorted cleaning solvents. The Hazard Communications Standard of OSHA requires that plant management keep all workers informed of the appropriate methods to be followed for the handling, use, and storage of hazardous chemicals. This includes a responsibility on the part of management to maintain a current inventory of all chemicals and to generate a written policy statement and list of procedures to follow when workers use potentially dangerous and/or toxic chemicals.

All chemicals must be properly labeled, with the appropriate material safety data sheets kept on file for all materials. The material data sheet for a specific product is divided into separate sections that contain the following information:

- The manufacturer's name and address
- The hazardous ingredients contained in the product
- Physical data, including boiling point, percentage of volatile compounds, etc.
- Fire and explosion information
- Health hazard data concerning inhalation, skin contact, etc.
- Reactivity data concerning the chemical stability of the material
- Spill and leak procedures to be followed
- Special protection information regarding ventilation requirements, exhaust, and general mechanical requirements
- Special precautions to be taken concerning storage and handling
- Cautionary information regarding empty containers and chemical emergencies
- Shipping data and precautions
- Any miscellaneous product and safety data

Indoor and Outdoor Air Pollution

As commercial buildings continue to become more energy efficient and tighter in their construction characteristics, indoor air pollution is on the increase. The energy conservation characteristics of a building that are designed to minimize heat loss also limit the number of normal exchanges between the inside building air and the outside air. Whereas normal building construction allows five or more complete air exchanges in a building each hour, energy efficient construction characteristics limit air exchanges in these structures to fewer than one or two per hour. Under these conditions, odors and fumes within the building can accumulate to unacceptably high levels.

OSHA has established guidelines that list the upper limits, in parts per million (ppm), for most pollutants. The higher the upper limit for a particular substance, the less hazardous it is. Also, the guidelines specify which vapors must be exhausted to the outside air from within the workplace.

Because individual reactions to any substance will vary, both material safety data sheets and written procedures for dealing with problems should be posted and known to all employees and plant managers.

Hazardous Waste Management

Every chemical that enters the printing plant must eventually leave the plant in one form or another. If the chemical does not become part of the printed product, or leaves the plant as a vapor, it becomes waste material that must be dealt with. The Environmental Protection Agency (EPA) lists four characteristics, any of which qualify a substance as hazardous waste. These characteristics are:

1. A liquid having a "flash point" of less than 140°F. The flash point is the lowest temperature at which a substance will ignite when exposed to an open flame
2. A substance deemed to be corrosive, with a pH of less than 2.0 or greater than 12.5
3. Unstable, potentially reactive products
4. Toxic substances

After any of the chemicals fitting the above guidelines have been used, they must be labeled, stored, and disposed of in a manner approved by the EPA. Most print shops now follow two basic philosophies regarding hazardous waste:

1. If it is not used or made, it need not be disposed of
2. Once generated, hazardous waste must be stored and disposed of in the proper manner

Also, alternate chemicals and materials such as soy-based inks, water-based plate processing systems, and fountain solutions that do not contain alcohol are presently available and can greatly reduce the amount of toxic material generated by a print shop. Many new materials designed to reduce the amount of toxic and hazardous waste generated in the production process are continually being developed to maximize worker safety.

■ SUMMARY

The actual process of offset printing, though familiar to most graphic arts and printing technology students, is often foreign to many graphic designers, artists, and illustrators. Based on the oil and water principle, roller configurations and press cylinder designs all influence the quality of the final printed piece.

The material presented in this chapter serves as a preparation for beginning experiences in offset printing. Knowing how to set up the paper feed, ink, and dampening systems on an offset press enables you to take those first hesitant steps into the fascinating world of watching a graphic design become a printed reality.

All the processes covered in this chapter, from press configuration to finishing operations and binding techniques, enable the designer or printing technician to communicate across traditional work boundaries. This facilitates the entire production process from initial design thumbnail sketches to the finished printed product.

■ SUGGESTED STUDENT ACTIVITIES

Suggested activities in this chapter are continued from the suggested activities in Chapter 9, and are aimed at providing students a variety of experiences in the operation, troubleshooting, and maintenance of offset duplicators.

1. Set up an offset duplicator for printing. Included in this exercise is the loading and setting up of the feed table with 8-1/2 x 11 inch paper, inking the press rollers, and adding fountain concentrate to the water fountain. The press should be run for a few minutes, during which time the paper feed should be checked for proper feed and delivery positioning. The ink rollers should be completely covered with a thin layer of ink, and the water system should be dampened and ready to go.

2. Take the printing plate produced in Chapter 9, mount it on the plate cylinder of the offset duplicator, and remove the gum arabic coating from the plate using cotton litho wipes and fountain solution.

3. Pull two press proofs in preparation for a printing run.

4. Set the press counter and print 100 copies of the job.

5. Set up the duplicator to print an additional 50 copies of the job. After approximately 10 copies, lift the water form rollers off the plate cylinder. Note the progressive scumming of the copy with the absence of a dampening solution. Before the copy turns completely dark, turn the water form rollers back on and note how the copy clears up.

6. As the press continues to run, lift the ink form rollers off the plate and note the changes in the copy as it becomes washed out. Turn the ink form rollers back on.

7. Turn off the press, and, using an image removing pen, erase a small section of the image on the plate cylinder, turn the press back on, and after several copies have printed, note the changes made by the image removing pen.

8. Turn off the press and remove the plate. Prepare the plate for preservation by first cleaning the plate with blanket wash and then gum the plate. Clean the blanket cylinder of the press with press wash.

9. Using clean-up mats, clean the press by first draining the fountain solution and removing the ink fountain. Note how many clean-up mats are required to get the press rollers clean. Clean and replace both the ink and water fountains.

10. Lubricate the press. Apply oil to the chain delivery system, if so equipped, roller bearings, and other identified oil points on the press. Service the air/vacuum system by checking the compressor glass for water—drain if necessary. Oil any motor bearings and wipe down exterior surfaces of the press.

Chapter 11 DESIGNING FOR PRODUCTION

Chapter 11 DESIGNING FOR PRODUCTION

Apply the Graphic Design Process

Design Logotypes

Design Effective Newsletters

Design Display Advertising

Design Catalogs

■ INTRODUCTION

This chapter presents an in-depth study of several common graphic design projects. It further explains the special characteristics of each. We begin with a brief review of the graphic design process that has been emphasized throughout this text, and then address the following areas: logo design, newsletter design, advertising design, and catalog design. Web page design is then thoroughly discussed in Chapter 12. Each area focuses on the particulars relating to the individual topic and the decisions made by designers in choosing the best means of communicating their clients' messages.

■ APPLYING THE GRAPHIC DESIGN PROCESS

The process of graphic design problem-solving was addressed at length in Chapter 4. In review, the process is a series of steps to assure that your design will satisfy both your individual client's needs and your own creativity. The basic steps include defining the problem; developing and setting up a budget and schedule; gathering information; creating several ideas from thumbnail sketches to final comps; presenting your ideas to the client; evaluating those ideas with the client; making necessary changes; producing the design; and making a final evaluation of the design project. By following this process in any design project, you build in ways to check your progress and evaluate your work. It is recommended that the design process be used in the following examples, although we will not list all of the steps here.

■ DESIGNING LOGOTYPES

Logo design is usually the first project that new designers attempt. Whether given as an assignment in high school or done for a friend's band, a logo is an important design element. It functions as a simple visual reminder of the group it represents. Logo design has been covered extensively in the history of graphic design and it con-

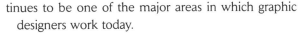

tinues to be one of the major areas in which graphic designers work today.

When creating a logo, it is important for the designer to remember that the image will be used in various applications, from business cards to (possibly) the tails of airplanes. Therefore, the designer must create an adaptable design, one that looks good whether reproduced at one-half of an inch or ten feet wide. Most good logos are kept simple so that detail will not get lost by scaling the logo. Figure 11.1 shows an example of how a well-designed logo will reproduce at various sizes without losing its impact.

There are two basic kinds of logos: image-based and typographic. Each type has its own unique characteristics, and both kinds may be used together in a single design.

Image-Based Logos

Image-based logos can be broken into three categories: pictograms, ideograms, and abstract logos. Each has its own unique characteristics, and some logos may fit into more than one of these categories at a time.

• Pictogram Logos

A *pictogram* is a simple representation of any single thing—be it an animal, the sun, or an object such as a tool. This basic representation gives a direct interpretation of the design.

Although pictograms date back to early cave drawings, it is unlikely that they were used for advertising at that time. Instead, they were a way for early humans to visually communicate with one another. Pictograms were often part of ritual celebrations.

When choosing a pictogram logo, it is important to ensure that the chosen image will represent an organization in a positive light and that the image directly relates to the company. For example, if you are creating a logo for a company that only deals in one item, such as a publishing company that produces books, a logo with a book would be appropriate. The pictogram is widely used today; two examples are shown in Fig. 11.2.

• Ideogram Logos

The *ideogram logo* is an image that represents an idea, illustrated through the use of a picture. The typographic symbol "$" is not a picture of the American dollar, yet it is immediately recognized as representing it.

Ideogram logos are more difficult to design than pictograms because each person will not necessarily read the ideographic image in the same way. It is important, therefore, to do more research in the design and presentation stages of projects that involve ideograms.

FIGURE 11.1:
A well-designed logo scaled to many sizes retains its identity

A good example of a current ideogram logo is the one for AT&T (Fig. 11.3). Designed to represent lines of communication encircling the globe, the logo uses the visual imagery of a sphere with lines across it. The sphere does not read as the earth directly, but the abstract elements are used to imply a larger idea.

Abstract Logos

Once businesses moved into a corporate structure where many different kinds of businesses were owned by one large company, designers found it increasingly difficult to use pictograms to represent the entire corporation. One single image could not represent a corporation whose subsidiaries might include the manufacture of foodstuffs and clothing as well as distribution of movies and communications, for example. Abstract logos could be created to give the corporation a dynamic look, without featuring the image or idea of any single product.

Figure 11.4 shows two abstract logos. Notice how simple design elements are combined in unique ways to create these two different logo designs.

Although abstract logos are the most common type in use today, the root of their design is not always pure abstraction. In some cases, the designer will take an image and abstract it. In the design shown in Fig. 11.5, the eye element was abstracted for a visual arts organization.

Typographic Logos

Often a designer will choose not to use an image logo at all but chooses instead to design a logo by creating a unique version of the company's name (Fig. 11.6). These typographic logos communicate the name of the company as the most important feature.

When designing a typographic logo, the designer must find a typeface that will capture the personality of the company. This can be done either by creating the type from scratch or by modifying an existing typeface. The designer should not simply take a readily available typeface and set it without modification because such a logo would be too easy for others to reproduce on a computer. An existing typeface should be modified so that it can be used only in its modified form (Fig. 11.7). This can be

FIGURE 11.2:
Examples of pictogram logos:
Logo for Atlas Jewelry
Logo for Microcar & Minicar Club, Inc.

FIGURE 11.3:
Logo for AT&T
(Saul Bass and Associates)

FIGURE 11.4:
Abstract logos work best when created from basic geometric elements

FIGURE 11.5:
Abstracted image logo

RENNSPORT MOTOR WORKS
Service • Modifications on BMWs and other fine cars

FIGURE 11.6:
Typographic logos

ATLAS
Original Type—DIN Neuzeit Grotesk BC

ATLAS
Modified type as logo

FIGURE 11.7:
Modification of an existing typeface

scanned or saved as an EPS file for use by others at the company without giving them the ability to alter it easily.

Logo Production

The final production of logos is done either on a computer or by hand. Logos created on the computer are done using a drawing program such as Adobe Illustrator®, where the final design can be saved as a separate file and given to the client. Type used in such a way should always be converted to outlines because the client's company may not have the needed font loaded on its computer. Converting to outlines will also make it more difficult for someone other than the designer to make changes to the logo. Handdrawing may be necessary for certain designs. Handlettered logos are then scanned and digitized so they can be easily placed in other documents and scaled to size quickly.

■ DESIGNING EFFECTIVE NEWSLETTERS

Newsletters are typically in-house publications for companies and special-interest groups and are created to disseminate information to a specific group of people. They may range in size from a single sheet to a multiple-page document. Most often they have to be created on a small budget and are published on a regular basis. Because of this, the designer must create a flexible layout that can be quickly produced with each new issue. Many designers produce the initial structure, or format, for the newsletter and have someone at the company change the information each time.

What Should Be Included

Items to include in a newsletter vary according to content, but the same design elements are used in most newsletters. The following sections review some of the most important elements.

• Grid Structures

The starting point in the design of a newsletter is the development of a grid system. With this grid, you will set up the number of columns, width between columns, and margins. Any repeating elements, such as page numbers, volume number, and date are also positioned at this time.

The first step is to find out the amount of copy that will be set. Although exact word count will vary each issue, basic information will help to determine how many pages will be needed. At the same time, a tentative budget should be made up. Find out how many copies will be printed and get estimates to find out how many pages and what kind of printing the client can afford.

Once it has been determined what you will be able to produce, based on the budget, use the proper paper size for the newsletter to begin the grid design.

The first step in creating the grid is determining the page margins. *Margins* are the space left on the top and bottom and left and right sides of the page. If you are creating a multiple-page newsletter, the margins usually mirror themselves across a two-page spread. Elements such as the page number, issue date, and volume number may be placed in the margins. These usually also mirror their positions across a spread, as shown in Fig. 11.8.

Grid columns help in placing text. The most important decision in creating columns is the amount of the space between columns, referred to as the *gutter*. Too little space does not provide enough of a visual break when reading. If a narrow space must be used, a break can be created by the use of a vertical rule, as shown in Fig. 11.9. Too much space will create a visual separation between columns, resulting in copy that appears to be disconnected and not part of the same story, as shown in Fig. 11.10.

A well designed grid will provide flexibility for many successive layouts. For example, although you may be using only a two-column format for most text, by creating a four-column grid you build in additional ways in which the grid can be used. This allows for flexibility in illustration placement. Figure 11.11 shows several layouts created from the same four-column grid.

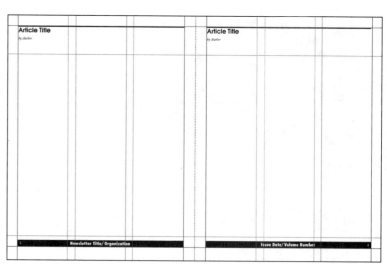

FIGURE 11.8:
A grid design for a two-page spread

When two columns of text must be laid out in close proximity to one another, a vertical line, or *rule*, should be used to separate them. The rule gives the reader's eye a stopping point for the end of each line in the first column. Without a rule between these two columns, it would be difficult to see where the first one stopped and the second one started, and the reader would visually connect the lines of one column to the next. This would result in illegibility. Rules should be used as subtle elements, as shouwn here. They should not overpower the text.

FIGURE 11.9:
Use of a vertical rule to divide two columns

When you are designing two columns of type with a gutter between them, it is most important to give enough space to that gutter. Too little space results in the lines of text running into each other across the columns. Too much space separates the columns into two distinct blocks of text. When this happens, the columns appear unrelated and the text becomes two distinct blocks. It will be difficult for a reader to connect the two columns across this "visual break". Columns should be spaced to appear natural in reading from one to the next.

FIGURE 11.10:
Too much space between columns results in a visual break separating the two columns

FIGURE 11.11:
Various layouts created from a four-column grid design

• Nameplate

The *nameplate* (sometimes referred to as *flag*)—the name of the newsletter—is positioned on the first page. It is either designed by you or provided by the client. The nameplate creates a personality for the newsletter and although its position on the page may vary, as seen in Fig. 11.12, it is the highest priority element on the first page. The nameplate may be just a name, but it usually also includes a line of explanation, such as "The Newsletter of the [name of organization]." The nameplate tells the reader what the newsletter is about.

Designing a nameplate is similar to designing a typographic logo. It should have its own unique character and communicate the personality of the organization.

FIGURE 11.12:
Two examples of nameplate layouts

• Text, Headings, and Subheadings

After the grid design has been completed, some thought should be given to the type that will fill it. Text type should be chosen so that varying amounts of copy will fit in from issue to issue and still be easy to read. After receiving the copy for the first issue, try setting it in several different typefaces to see not only how it looks, but also how much room the copy set in each typeface requires. When the same copy has been set in various typefaces, you will be surprised to see that some of typefaces, because of the x-heights of the fonts selected, take up much more room than others.

Once the text type has been chosen, the type for headings and subheadings is selected. This type is normally bolder than the text in order to stand out from it. Often, designers use a bolder version of the text font for headings, but other times a different font is chosen to contrast with the text. Figure 11.13 illustrates examples of both approaches applied to subheadings.

For headings, experiment with the size of the type as well as the font. Depending on the length of the titles, it may be necessary to use a more condensed font than that used for text so that the titles will fit properly in the space available.

• Boxes, Shading, Tints, and Contrasting Elements

Articles such as charts and sidebars must be separated from the main text. There are various methods by which to do this. An outlined or shaded box will help to separate specific text, even though it is in the same font as the body copy. When using color, the shading can be made into a tint of color to separate the box.

Another way to separate one text element from another is by a contrasting typeface or setting. In the example in Fig. 11.14, text has been separated by using different sizes and weights. In Fig. 11.15, the text is separated by the use of different leading.

• Artwork

Artwork (photographs or illustrations) may be placed on the page in several ways. To maintain a strict grid, artwork can be placed to align directly to the grid (Fig. 11.16). For a more informal look, text can be made to flow around the image, as displayed in Fig. 11.17. Many times a designer will combine both techniques in the same piece.

Less important images can be screened into the background with text flowing over them, as in Fig. 11.18 (if you choose to do this, be careful not to make the image too dark or it will be difficult to read the text over it). Also, remember that the image will function more as an effect than by showing any detail. If the image has to be shown in detail, it may be possible

Subhead

In this example, the subhead is in a heavy weight of the body text. By using a typeface from the same family, you can be assured that your subheads and text choices will work well together. This is the safest way of choosing text, headings and subheads that will work well together.

Subhead

In this example, the subhead is a contrasting typeface to the body text. In using a serif body face and a sans serif bold subhead, the subheads stand out more than they would by using a typeface in the same family as the body text. Be sure to pick typefaces that work well together in this case.

FIGURE 11.13:
Two appreaches to subheadings

Sidebar A

Here, two columns of text with different purposes (not meant to be read together, but one as a supplement to the other), are separated by character weight. The text on the right, often referred to as a sidebar, needs to be distinct from the body text. This is one way to accomplish this.

The typeface here is a bolder version of the body copy, but set in the same point size and with the same leading as the body text.

FIGURE 11.14:
Text separated by size and weight

Sidebar B

Another two columns of text with different purposes are separated by leading alone. This is another way to accomplish this. By the lines of type not being in line with one another, the two paragrahs stay distinct. Be sure that enough leading is given to separate the two while mainting readability.

This paragraph is in the same point size and weight as the body text, but stands on its own due to the difference in leading.

FIGURE 11.15:
Text separated by different leading

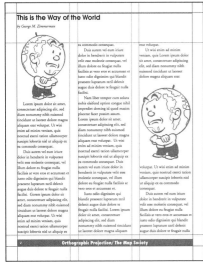

FIGURE 11.16:
Artwork aligned to the grid

FIGURE 11.17:
Text flowing around an image

FIGURE 11.18:
A screened background image

to place the full image on the page and use a portion of it as a background screen (Fig. 11.19).

It is very important to include a credit line for the photographer or illustrator of each image. There are several ways to do this. Among the most popular is placing the name in small type along the side of an image, along the bottom of the page, or in the page gutter (the meeting point of two pages in a spread). Credits can also be listed on one of the back pages of the newsletter with references to the pages on which they appear.

• White Space

In any page layout, it is crucial to balance the text with white space. This allows the reader a visual break and can help to balance a composition. In Fig. 11.20, two examples of a newsletter layout are shown. In the one on the left, very little white space was left. In the one on the right, white space was used to balance the composition.

Newsletter Production

Newsletter production has become much easier with the advent of the computer and page layout programs. By using a page layout program, it is a simple job to set up a grid or template and position text and illustrations. The computer also allows changes to be made quickly when needed.

Extra care in proofing the newsletter for typographic errors must be taken—it is often the designer's responsibility to make sure the final job is correct before sending it to the printer.

■ DESIGNING DISPLAY ADVERTISING

Newspaper and other display ads make up a large part of the work of many design studios. They are quick to produce, and because many businesses need to run them weekly or monthly with only slight changes, display ad work is often steady repeat business.

Although display ads vary from business to business, some of the most commonly used elements and options are presented here.

Basic Elements

Most display ads contain information about the business, such as the logo, address, telephone number, and business hours. One or more featured items may also appear in the ad, such as goods on sale or new items in stock.

Figure 11.21 displays a promotional ad for an eyeglass store. In it, the logo is featured at the top, with a line of copy about the store. This is a simple ad to produce.

Callouts, Artwork, Prices, and White Space

Ads usually contain elements such as photographs of the products advertised, prices for each item, and callouts for item information. Balancing these elements within the given space can be a challenge for even an experienced designer. It is important to prioritize the elements to create a design that makes efficient use of the space, allowing enough white space to keep the ad from becoming cluttered.

Figure 11.22 shows an ad for a supermarket. In this instance, the designer must prioritize the different elements so that each item is readable. This ad is more of a design challenge because the various items are competing for the reader's attention. Notice how the typography helps to separate the items and prices from one another.

Layout Options, Column Designs

When creating an ad for a newspaper or magazine, the designer has to work strictly within the standards of that publication. Before beginning to design, the specifics of column width and total ad height must be known. Often clients will be aware of these requirements, so ask them first. Newspapers charge for space by the column inch, so be sure to design your ad to fit within the client's budget.

When designing the ad, consider where it will be placed. If possible, pick up a copy of a previous issue of the publication to see what other ads appear in the section where your client will be advertising. This will help you make design decisions that allow your ad to stand out from the other ads on the same page.

Advertising Production

The production of ads involves combining many different elements. It is important to work out design ideas through thumbnails and rough form to explore how these various elements will relate in the final ad. As production time for ads usually is limited, a computer can greatly assist in the process. Commonly, laser prints will be acceptable for final artwork to be reproduced in newspapers, due to the relatively low quality of newspaper printing.

FIGURE 11.19:
Use of a repeated image for a background screen

FIGURE 11.20:
Comparison of white space as shown in two layouts

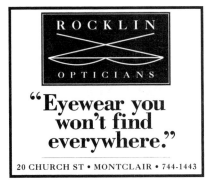

FIGURE 11.21:
Newspaper promotional display ad

For printing photographs, most newspapers use a large screen of 65 to 100 lpi for best reproduction. Newsprint absorbs ink and finer screens will clog when printed, leaving blotches and other inconsistencies in the printed photo or illustration.

■ DESIGNING CATALOGS

Designing a catalog is a complex task that involves the coordination of many different parts into a cohesive whole. Because of this, there are important design decisions to be made during the process.

What Should Be Included—Choosing a Format

Like other design projects, the initial client meeting will help to determine many factors, including the type of catalog, what products will be featured, and the budget available for photography, illustration, and printing. Because catalogs are time-driven pieces, due dates for the finished design should be set at the initial meeting.

Hot Dog or Hamburger **Silver Medal Rolls**	12-oz. pkg.	**.99**	Any Variety, Ice Cream **Kobbler Cones**	1.5 to 5-oz. pkg.	**1 99**
Specialty **Dessert Shells**	4-oz. pkg.	**.99**	Plus Deposit Where Required **Popsi 3-Liter**	2 btls.	**$3**
Any Variety Reg. or Mini **Yahara Pita Bread**	8-oz. pkg.	**.99**	Vanilla, Chocolate or Strawberry **Wafer Cookies**	6.2 oz. bags	**1 99**
Any Variety **Cheese Wads**	24-oz. pkg.	**.99**	You Know—For Kids **JuiceUP**	4 pack	**$2 49**
12 pack **HighLife German Muffins**	24-oz. pkg.	**1 29**	6.5 to 7-oz box Any Variety **Kobbler Eat'Ems**		**1 69**

FIGURE 11.22:
Typographically complex advertisement

Combining Text and Graphics

When designing a catalog, the designer will be working with other professionals, and good communication with everyone involved in the project is necessary. The most important people in this group are the photographer and the copywriter, whose combined work will be the backbone of the design. Open communication with both of these professionals is essential to prevent problems in getting all of the elements together on time.

The photographer is responsible, under your direction, for providing shots of all of the items to be displayed in the catalog. For a large catalog, this could mean choosing from hundreds of photographs. It is important that these photos have a consistency of color, lighting, and style, and it is the designer's responsibility to see that these prerequisites are met.

The copywriter will be working with the client on item descriptions and prices. This copy is subject to change at any time during the process. When designing a catalog, you must be prepared to make copy changes up until press time.

Format Considerations

To keep the catalog design flowing smoothly, the designer should develop a flexible grid system in which to work. As explained in the newsletter section, catalog design also uses the grid as its foundation. Designing a grid that will adapt to the many different kinds of elements to be employed in the catalog will save you time later in the process.

The designer needs to know whether the photographs will appear in boxes or be silhouetted. Silhouetted photos require a special setup to make the silhouetting process easier, and this should be discussed with the photographer. The photographer should be given a rough comp of the catalog before shooting begins so that each photo can be shot specifically for its placement within the catalog.

Catalog Production

The production of a catalog involves dealing with each of the various elements and personnel discussed thus far. Although text and page layout may be accomplished through use of the computer, the quality of the reproduction for color photographs in a high-end catalog may need to be done at a prepress facility for the best quality scans. In a case where the photographs or transparencies for the final scans will be provided to the prepress facility, the designer will scan in the images to use as placed FPO (for position only, as discussed in earlier chapters) scans that later will be replaced by the printer.

When creating the preliminary layout on a computer, you can scan in a low-resolution version at 72 dpi for display and cropping purposes. This will save disk space, as the low-resolution scan will create a small file size and can be given to the printer in a laser-printed version of the document. The scans will give the printer the necessary information on cropping and silhouetting

FIGURE 11.23:
A 300 dpi scan (top) compared to a 72 dpi FPO scan

only. The photographic images, provided as 4 x 5 inch transparencies by the photographer to the printer, are scanned on the printer's high-end equipment to the specifications of the rough layout. FPO files cannot be used for final output, of course, because of their low resolution. Figure 11.23 shows the quality of a 300 dpi scan compared to a 72 dpi FPO scan.

Another way of showing an FPO image is to paste a photocopy of the image, scaled and cropped, into a separate photocopy of the mechanicals. Whether scanned or photocopied into position, this dummy copy of the document provides printers with the visual information they need to produce the job accurately.

The final typographic layout of the catalog may be given to the printer on disk, electronically via FTP, or provided as a series of printed mechanicals. (Today, catalogs are often produced on CD-ROMs for distribution, rather than being printed in hardcopy form.) Photographs and illustrations are given to the printer as the actual artwork or in photographic transparency format for scanning into the layout on high-end equipment.

■ SUMMARY

In this chapter, we discussed many of the challenges each of these specific design jobs creates for the graphic designer. With a good understanding of the graphic design problem-solving model, you should be able to handle any production problems you will face as a graphic designer.

■ SUGGESTED STUDENT ACTIVITIES

1. Make a list of the one image you think describes you best (it could be a particular car, a sporting event, a style of music, or any other thing you feel people would remember you by). Then design a logo for yourself based on that image. Make sure the logo can be read well at small and large sizes, and that it is simple and clearly designed.

2. Create a newsletter for a club or activity at your school. Meet with other students to decide what kinds of information should be contained in it. Then create a style—through the use of type and imagery—that best communicates what your department is about.

3. Design (or redesign) an ad for a local small business. Adapt the same ad to work as a small-space ad, a single-column ad, a full-page ad, and a billboard. Be sure to keep the feeling of the ad consistent across all the different sizes.

4. Sell yourself! Create a catalog for all the items you carry with you each day. Include everything you have on you or carry with you—from your clothes to your tools to your pocket change. Decide how to illustrate the items (through drawings, photographs, or illustrations) and how to combine the various elements into sections and page layouts. Be sure to include descriptions and prices for each item. Name the catalog after yourself.

Chapter 12 WEB DESIGN FUNDAMENTALS

Chapter 12 WEB DESIGN FUNDAMENTALS

Understand Web Design

Examine Variables in Web Viewing

Investigate Site Planning

Examine Site Construction

Understand Site Testing

Examine Methods of Updating the Site

■ INTRODUCTION

Good Web design involves an understanding of the Internet—both its advantages and limitations. The Web is a platform unlike any others that designers are used to, and the variables and structure of the Web require special techniques to create in this medium. In this chapter you will be introduced to some of the basic factors involved in the design of Web pages and sites.

■ WEB DESIGN

Web site design is a rapidly growing area of work for graphic design firms. Designing for the Web creates new challenges for the graphic designer, but it still relies on the traditional communication design process. Web design goes from concept to execution in the hands of the designer. Unlike printed pieces, the designer can create the final site in-house and then may provide it to the client in only electronic form. Because of this, special care must be taken during each stage of the process to assure a good working site.

Web sites are displayed on the computer so it is easy to check how they will look at any stage of a project. An important thing to remember, though, is that while designers often work on large screens and have their monitors adjusted to view as many colors as possible, many people viewing the Web will have smaller monitors set at lower color resolutions. What does this imply? That the designer should try to make the Web site work across the many variables that can occur when the site is viewed.

■ VARIABLES

Variables of the Web include computer platform, color viewing, browser type and version, browser settings, browser plug-ins, window size, and download times.

Computer Platform and Color Viewing

There are two primary computer platforms: Macintosh and PC. The Mac has a basic palette of 256 colors and the PC also has a basic palette of 256 colors. The 216 PC colors, however, are not the exact same ones as on the Mac, and the palette that can be seen on both machines without dithering is only 216. This limits the use of color by the designer to the 216 colors that can be seen on both platforms.

Browser Type and Version

Several different browsers are available to view the Web. Browsers such as Microsoft Internet Explorer® and Netscape Navigator® are used to translate the Web information (a programming language known as hypertext markup language, or HTML) into viewable pages. Each browser has regular updates to add new features, but the designer cannot be sure that the viewer will always be using a current version on their machine. It is important to be aware of changes to a browser and make note of what features will and will not work with any given browser.

Browser Settings

Individual users can control specific settings, such as typeface, point size, and background color on their browser. Although it may be helpful for some people to be able to make the typeface larger on screen or choose an easy-to-read typeface, this ability to change the designer's preferences can lead to the destruction of a well-thought-out design. If the designer is aware that these changes can be made, he or she can take steps to make sure that, if they are, the design will stay relatively intact.

The viewer also has the option to turn off images on the Web, and is then able to look at pages in a text-only format. This greatly speeds up download times but can cause a page that relies only on pictures to turn invisible on the web. It is a good idea to repeat key categories of information as text under the pictures so that someone with images turned off on their browser will still be able to navigate your page.

Browser Plug-ins

Some special Web features are not provided by the makers of the browser, but may be available as "plug-ins" from the manufacturer of the feature. If the plug-in is not loaded on the viewer's computer, however, the feature cannot be seen. Care should be taken on the designer's part to only include a special feature if it is necessary to the content of the page, not just as a decoration. This will keep people from either having to get the plug-in or feeling "left out." Some designers create two options for viewing a page—one with the plug-ins and one without so those who want the information can see it without needing the plug-in.

Window Size

On a 13-inch monitor, the maximum viewing size for a Web page is only 8-1/4 wide by 4-1/8 inches high. This is small! Although larger monitors have a large viewing area, and more and more people are now using 17-inch monitors, the size limitation is still a challenge for a designer. To make the most of the space, designers must try to work so that their design can still be seen on even the smallest monitor. You should try to avoid, whenever possible, making it necessary for the viewer to scroll to see an entire image or to read text horizontally.

Download Times

As the computer reads the images and text on your Web site, information from a Web server (where the site's files are kept) must be downloaded to the viewer's computer. To keep the download times as short as possibly, it is important to take steps to minimize download times. This can be done by making the file sizes of images as small as possible while retaining a good image quality. Programs such as Adobe Photoshop® and Adobe ImageReady™ contain tools to help designers produce good quality images at small file sizes. The good thing about the Web is that images need only be 72 dpi to look good.

■ SITE PLANNING

A good Web site requires a good plan. In site design, a plan takes on two parts: part 1, the development of content and part 2, the site map hierarchy.

Part 1: The Development of Content

Content is what the site is all about—the purpose of the site and the information that will be found on it. Content may be given to you by the client or developed with the client. Because the creation of Web sites is a new experience for most clients, it is essential for the designer to stress the importance of developing relevant content for the site. In other words, the client must first decide what the purpose of the site is. Will it be used to sell products? Will it be an informational site? Will it be a promotional site? Will it be a combination of these? A Web site cannot be "all things to all people," as many clients would like them to be. Having a strong content-driven site will determine its ease of use for a visitor and will help to bring them back again. A site that is confusing or does not contain what it appears to will ultimately fail.

For example, let's say you are hired to create a site for a company that has an established chain of retail stores. The site could possibly have many purposes: as a simple site to provide store locations and hours; as a "sale flyer" to tell people of special offers available at the stores; as a full-service online store that allows people to order products online and have them delivered to their homes. The client needs to carefully think through these options and consider the impact each will have on business. Will the site provide driving instructions to the store from any location? Will customers be given special online sales not available to the general public? Could increased use of the online buying services cut into the profits from the retail stores? Although the designer cannot answer these questions for a client, it is important to make the client aware of their options in developing content for the site.

Most important is that the site works well for the purpose it was created. A site that gives incomplete information or sends mixed signals of its purpose will not be visited often.

It is also important that the purpose of the site is focused during the content development stage and that it is carefully reviewed as the site is updated. Because the web is an ever-changing medium, unlike a printed piece, its content can be easily forgotten during subsequent redesigns.

Part 2: The Site Map Hierarchy

As we know from previous chapters, hierarchy is the relative importance of various elements to one another. In a Web site, this hierarchy relates to how the individual Web pages relate and connect to one another. Due to the amount of information you can fit onto one Web page without requiring too much scrolling, Web sites have many linked pages—each with its own primary focus and content. How these pages relate to one another becomes a crucial job for the designer to assist the viewer in navigating the site easily. The overall hierarchy is often referred to as a *site map*. Often, the designer creates an actual page of the site map and includes it in the site to aid in navigation.

FIGURE 12.1:
Web site map

Unlike a book or magazine, Web pages may be connected to one another in a nonlinear manner. It is easy to jump from one page to another without having to "page through" information irrelevant to the viewers' needs. These connections are worked out through a diagram showing each page of the site and its relation to the others. Some Web design programs have the ability to create a "dummy site" using files without content to experiment with various ways of developing the hierarchy of the site. Figure 12.1 shows an example of a Web site map.

Creating a site map before the site is designed, following it closely, and making changes as needed during site construction will allow the designer and client to understand the various ways in which viewers will be able to travel though the site. The site map could be compared to a "road map" for a journey through the site. It assists people in finding their way without getting lost and frustrated.

■ SITE CONSTRUCTION

After the two previous planning stages are completed and approved by the client, it's time to have fun! After all, designing the site is why you were hired in the first place. However, designing for the Web has its own set of rules. Let's examine them here.

Use of Color

As mentioned previously in this chapter, color use is limited to 216 "clean" colors (those that will be displayed without dithering on a monitor set at 256 colors). Many design programs, such as Adobe Illustrator® and Photoshop®, that designers are familiar with for creating print graphics, have palettes or palette options that restrict your usage to the Web-safe colors. Be sure to only use these colors in your designs for optimum results. Of course, if you include a gradation in your design, even with use of Web-safe colors at either end of the gradation, the center will dither due to the mixing of color. Therefore, it is important to set your monitor at the resolution of 256 colors when you are designing. This will allow you to see the dithering of the graphics as you create them.

Image File Types

Most graphics on the Web are either JPEG or GIF formats. JPEG format is used when saving photographic images, as it will best represent the colors of the original image on the Web. JPEG files can be compressed at different rates to decrease the file size while increasing download time. How much compression you wish to use depends on how high quality of an image you desire. Figure 12.2 shows a comparison between a JPEG image with low compression (resulting in a larger file size) and one with high compression (resulting in a smaller file size). Note the differences in quality of image (remember that these are 72 dpi images, which will look fine on the Web but will look pixellated in print. Also note that the file sizes and download times are given for the image in color.) The left image is 38K and would take 8 seconds to download. The image on the right is 2K and would take 1 second to download. You will see that the image on the right has become

FIGURE 12.2:
The image on the left is a JPEG saved with low compression
The image on the right is a JPEG saved with high compression

distorted, with uneven banding. These distortions of the image are referred to as *artifacts* in JPEG images and should be avoided when possible. It is best to vary your image compression settings until you have an image that will download quickly and be of reasonably good quality. Programs such as Adobe ImageReady® let you see what the final result will look like while you have the image onscreen and let you compare the original image with the final "optimized" one.

GIF files are created for solid color graphics such as logos, line drawings, or type. In most instances, a GIF file will download faster than a JPEG, but GIF does not work well for photographic images, as shown in Fig. 12.3.

Image Sizes

The term *image sizes* refers to the actual size of the image, not the file size as discussed above. When working for the Web, always create the final image at the size you want it to be displayed onscreen. Although most Web design programs allow

FIGURE 12.3:
The image above saved as a GIF

you to resize the image within the program, making an image smaller in a Web design program should be avoided. This is because even though the image may be made smaller in the Web design program, the file size remains the same and the image will take longer to download than if it were reduced in an image-editing program. When you are dealing with many images on a page, an extra second for each image to download can mean the difference between a viewer waiting or leaving!

Typeface Choice

Choosing typefaces to use in your Web site is more of a challenge than it is when designing for print. The availability of the typeface depends on the font being installed on the viewer's computer and not yours! This means that although you may have many fonts installed on your computer, most viewers may have many less and will probably not have any specialty fonts outside of the installed system font base, which varies from platform to platform and between operating systems. Standards for most systems include Helvetica and Times, and these are the typefaces you'll find most often on Web sites for body copy.

There is another way, however, to include specialized typefaces without having to worry whether or not the viewer will have them installed. This is by converting them to graphics and placing them as such. This too has its drawbacks. The download time will be increased and if the viewer has image display turned off in the preference options, the type will be missing from your page! Because of this, most Web designers will repeat the important text placed as images in a small type size at the bottom of the page. This allows the text to be displayed even when the image display is turned off, and the repetition is barely noticeable.

Page (Window) Size

Pages for the Web are measured in pixels (or dots), of which there are 72 to an inch (72 dpi). The maximum size that can be seen on a 13-inch monitor without scrolling, as mentioned previously in this chapter, is 8-1/4 inches (595 pixels) wide by 4-1/8 inches (295 pixels) high. If you want everyone to be able to see your site without having to scroll, then each of your Web pages needs to be these dimensions. Does everyone use this as a standard? Of course not. You've probably seen many sites that are much larger, but you may also notice that many professional business sites use the width specified above on at least the home page. This gives a good impression of the site to viewers with 13-inch monitors and only requires scrolling on later pages. This is a good format for you to follow to give a professional look to your site.

Many students may have a difficult time thinking in pixels. To make your Web design process a bit easier, we've included a "pixel ruler" on page 235, for you to photocopy, cut out, and use when designing for the Web.

Design Style

The style of a Web site is where the designer gets to apply his or her talents. The overall look of the pages, color choices, design elements, and images that make up Web page design are applied just as they would be to any other graphic design piece. It is helpful to first design a master template, either as a sketch or as a Web page, so that repeating elements are consistent throughout the site. Attention needs to be paid to type style and size for repeating elements. Even though color choices are limited, the range of available colors allows a wide variety of looks for your designs. Often, picking a few colors to make up a master palette can aid in keeping a consistent look throughout the site. Be sure to use the same colors on each page for text links to be clicked on. There are actually three colors used for each link: the color of an unused link (before it is clicked on); the color for an active link (while it is being clicked on); and the color for a visited link (after it has been clicked on). The colors chosen for each should make visual sense so that visitors will be able to access where they have been on a site.

■ SITE TESTING

After a site has been designed and constructed, it needs to be tested to make sure it works correctly. The first step in this process is commonly done on your computer by opening the site in your browser and checking to see that all the images are loaded, that the links work correctly, and the text is easy to read. If you've used any special animations or video, you should also check to see if they work. With animation, the timing can be somewhat deceiving when looking at the site on your computer. They will run faster than if loaded on a remote server.

The next step involves loading the site onto a remote server and checking it in a browser. For a full test, this should be done in several browsers (Netscape Navigator® and Communicator®, Microsoft Internet Explorer®, and America Online® being the most common). Image alignment, type position, and color representation should be noted in each browser and adjustments made as necessary.

Sites should also be looked at on both a Macintosh and a PC platform. It is interesting to note that while most Web sites are created on Macintosh computers, the majority of viewers see them on PCs. You may also want to check the site on a WebTV platform, as many people are now using their televisions to surf the web. Be sure to check type size and resolution on all platforms.

Once a site has all the bugs worked out of it, it can be loaded onto the server that will support the site. Unlike most graphic design projects, in Web design this does not necessarily mean the project is over.

■ UPDATING THE SITE

Web sites change often. The information changes, the design may change, and someone needs to do the work involved in making these changes. Some design studios charge a monthly fee to their clients to make the needed changes to the site. Other changes, such as copy changes, may be done in-house by the client. Some changes may happen automatically through the use of *scripting*. This allows a programmer to create a code, or script, that can constantly change information linked to the site from other sources, such as a database. Graphic designers are not usually involved in the writing of scripts, but work with a programmer to create them. Some designers, who want to specialize in Web design, however, are learning the scripting process in order to have more control of the site.

It is important that the designer of the site have input on how the site will be managed and changed over time. Because Web pages can be changed easily, they can also be altered—with negative results to the design concept. Designers should be clear about how the site should look when it is created. The more the client understands *why* the design of the site needs to be a certain way, the less likely the site will be negatively altered by someone other than the designer making major changes to it.

■ SUMMARY

Web design is a relatively new area for graphic designers and design students. It has, and is, changing rapidly. New programs are allowing designers to work faster and with better results than ever before possible. The nature of the language that makes up the Internet, HTML, is constantly being edited and expanded, which allows more and different kinds of information to be displayed on the Web. Where it will take us is anyone's guess!

■ SUGGESTED STUDENT ACTIVITIES

1. Find three Web sites: one that you like because of the content alone, one that you like because of the design alone, and one that you don't like. Discuss how each works—its strengths and weaknesses—and discuss how ideas used from examining the good sites could be used in making the bad site better.

2. In your browser preferences, turn off the display of images and surf through your favorite sites. Discuss how (or if) they work without the visual information.

3. Using the 216 Web-safe colors, create two color palettes for two different Web sites. The first palette should be composed of subtle colors to achieve a calming effect. The second palette should be chosen to work for an exciting, active look.

4. Choose a subject with which you are familiar. Create a site map hierarchy to determine how many pages would be needed to provide someone unfamiliar with your subject with all the information you know. Use the site map to also determine how the pages would be linked so that a viewer could easily navigate your site.

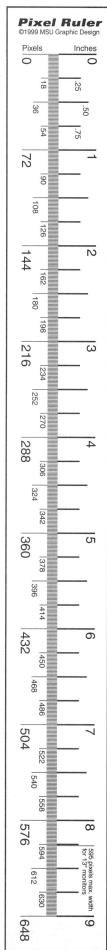

Pixel Ruler
©1999 MSU Graphic Design

Chapter 13 FUNDAMENTALS OF INTERACTIVE MULTIMEDIA DESIGN AND PRODUCTION

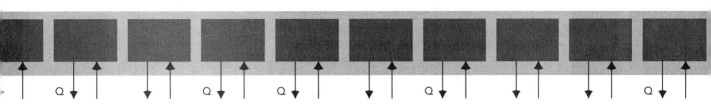

Chapter 13 FUNDAMENTALS OF INTERACTIVE MULTIMEDIA DESIGN AND PRODUCTION

Understand the Components of Interactive Multimedia and the Hardware Requirements for Successful Multimedia Projects

Develop an Appreciation of the Design and Production Skills and Associated Teamwork Required to Design Multimedia Projects

Develop the Ability to Produce Flowcharts for Major Multimedia Program Elements

Develop an Awareness of the Various Design and Production Stages Required to Produce Multimedia Titles

■ INTRODUCTION

The availability of modern, high-speed computers has nurtured the growth and development of interactive multimedia applications. Early on (ten years ago), the main use of multimedia was to mimic, on a crude scale, some of the special effects and presentation capabilities that were available only to films and television. In time, increases in computer processing speed were matched by increases in multimedia application program sophistication. Today, programs such as Macromedia Flash®, Director®, and Authorware®, enable creation of everything from the production of corporate training programs to powerful interactive games and sophisticated simulators in a multimedia environment.

The skills required to produce multimedia presentations cut across several disciplines. Material must be researched, sequenced, and written, and graphics must be prepared. Audio and video production, once the sole domain of specialists, can now be created, edited, and presented by anyone with an AV-equipped desktop computer. Small multimedia programs can be put together by one well-trained person; larger, more complex programs require a production team.

In this chapter, we will examine the core elements of multimedia and the requirements for producing a multimedia title. Once you have a knowledge of the skills and materials needed to create and produce multimedia programs, learning and working with the authoring software will be the next stage in multimedia production.

WHAT IS INTERACTIVE MULTIMEDIA?

Multimedia is the combination of text, audio, graphics, and video combined into one application and presented to the viewer. Not all multimedia programs will have all of these elements, but most will. For a program to be truly multimedia, it needs to contain more than just text and graphics; otherwise, it is simply an illustrated text.

When the viewer decides what material in the program will be viewed, and in what sequence it will be viewed in, the program becomes interactive. Interactivity is not limited to a viewer selecting specific portions of the program to look at. For example, responses to test questions, or entering information such as a name, address, and phone number is also a form of interactivity. Video games are highly interactive, as are corporate training programs that provide an overview of company policies to new employees.

Whether training astronauts on a space shuttle flight simulator, playing the latest video game, or exploring a museum through the use of a virtual reality tour, the ever-expanding, constantly changing world of interactive multimedia is a welcome communication tool for everyone.

LEVELS OF INTERACTIVITY

A *taxonomy*, or classification system, is sometimes used to describe the levels of interactivity present in a multimedia program. This classification system was originally developed to analyze titles recorded on video discs, and is presented here for general information. For each level, the video disc player is assumed to be the primary delivery system for the program.

Level I Interactivity: Only a small amount of user control is available, usually limited to stopping the program at specified places to search for other chapters or frames on the disc.

Level II Interactivity: Under level II control, the user can stop the program at certain places in the program and enter information, in response to questions, through a keypad. The viewer makes choices, causing the program to branch to specific locations and execute responses such as testing questions and keeping track of right and wrong answers.

Level III Interactivity: A computer takes over control of the video disc player in level III titles. Level III incorporates both audio and video, operating under instructions from an authoring program that controls the audio, video, and graphic images. It has a high level of user-controlled instructional capability, and the computer tracks all user responses and movements.

Level IV Interactivity: The highest degree of interactivity, including 3-D and virtual reality. Level IV is descriptive of the typical video game.

■ HARDWARE REQUIREMENTS FOR SUCCESSFUL MULTIMEDIA

Up-to-date computer technology is currently measured in months. A computer purchased at the beginning of the year will be eclipsed in processing power and system capability by the end of the same year. Not only do hardware configurations undergo significant changes, but software packages designed to maximize audio, video, and Internet delivery of multimedia programs are upgraded constantly. Minimum requirements for computer systems are recommended within this context of an ever-changing technological landscape. What is purchased today will be adequate for a year, strained to the limits of its capabilities after two years, and technologically obsolete after three or four years. System recommendations are given for both PCs running Windows® as well as Apple Macintosh® computers. The computer systems as recommended will serve for both the authoring and playback of interactive multimedia.

Although Macintosh computers were originally the machines of choice for multimedia authoring, both Macs and PCs now serve equally well for both authoring and playback tasks. The two computer platforms are not interchangeable, however, for either authoring and/or playback. System differences, from the way discs are formatted to operating system-level instruction sets and font incompatibilities, require that multimedia titles be customized to run on either computer platform. Instructions for enabling cross-platform use must be consulted in the authoring program manuals when the authoring process begins.

PC Platform Minimum System Requirements
- Pentium II® or equivalent processor with a minimum clock speed of 400–500 MHz
- Windows® 98 or Windows® 2000 operating system
- 8-GB hard drive
- 32-bit sound card with MPEG level 3 audio
- 128-MB system RAM
- 3-D capable video card with 12 MB video ram
- DVD drive with 24X+ CD playback capability
- 250-MB Zip® drive

Macintosh Minimum System Requirements
- 333 MHz G3 processor
- MAC OS 8.5
- 12-GB hard drive
- 128-MB system RAM
- 3-D capable video card with 12-MB video ram
- DVD drive with 24X+ CD playback capability
- 250-MB Zip® drive
- MPEG level-3 audio card

Note from the suggestions above that digital versatile disc (DVD) units are recommended instead of conventional CD drives for both PC and Macintosh computers. It is assumed that DVD drives will replace conventional CD drives in the coming years as the standard CD configuration in all computers. Because DVDs read and playback conventional CDs and incorporate the technology for high-level audio and video playback, they are the drive of choice.

■ STORAGE SOLUTIONS FOR MULTIMEDIA TITLES

The storage space requirements for multimedia titles have increased exponentially with the growth in volume and sophistication of materials. The most popular options for storing multimedia are conventional audio CDs, DVD discs, hard drives, and Zip® disks. Although the technology of each of these storage media was discussed in Chapter 7, we will detail their storage properties here as they apply specifically to multimedia.

Interactive multimedia in the 1980s and early 1990s were produced primarily on video discs. Although the access capabilities of video discs are relatively slow compared to modern computer hard drives, these titles had relatively little video and audio, making the video disc player adequate for these unsophisticated programs. The inadequacy of the video disc player became apparent as program complexity increased. Presently, video discs lack the access and storage capabilities required for most multimedia applications.

The conventional compact disc is the most utilized storage medium for multimedia titles at the present time. The CD however, has reached its physical and technological limits. Originally designed for audio playback, the versatility of the CD has enabled it to expand as an all-purpose storage system, but new multimedia requirements call for more than the CD can deliver in its present form. Zip® media, while continuing to grow in popularity, storage capability, and speed, still lacks the storage capacity and drive access times to adequately back multimedia audio and video tracks. Conventional hard drives are large enough and fast enough for running virtually all multimedia applications. Most multimedia programs are authored using conventional hard drives. Also, they are often used as file servers for running multimedia titles over corporate and educational local area networks.

DVD discs will eventually become the storage system of choice for most multimedia titles. They have the capability to combine storage capacity, drive speed, portability, and economies to ensure their widespread use in the coming years.

■ TECHNICAL SKILLS REQUIRED
TO PRODUCE MULTIMEDIA PROJECTS

The production of any multimedia title requires the application of considerable skills that overlap many traditional disciplines. The production of multimedia titles that incorporate text, audio, video, and sophisticated graphics requires skills not only in the creation of these inputs, also in the manipulation of the software packages required to assemble these components into an interactive multimedia title. Hence, those involved in multimedia production must have different skills. Job titles required for multimedia fall within the categories of project director, curriculum and material specialists, audio and video engineers, writers, graphic designers and illustrators, and software engineers/multimedia authoring specialists.

Large multimedia projects usually require assembling a production team whose members possess the above skills as well as marketing specialists to develop a marketing and sales plan for the project. Because marketing any multimedia title involves successfully competing for limited shelf space at the retail level, a good marketing plan is a key component to its success. Smaller projects, depending on the degree of complexity, can be produced with fewer specialists. We will take a closer look at some of the skills required for each of these projects.

Project Director

As with all group efforts, there needs to be a team leader; one person who assumes a major portion of the responsibility for getting the project done. The project director may also wear other hats in the production process. For example, the project director may also be the curriculum specialist or graphic designer. The director's accountability runs from assembling the production team to ensuring that the final program is completed within the limitations of the time and money allocated.

Curriculum and Material Specialists

The title "curriculum and material specialist" is not limited to people who specialize in producing educational multimedia material. Curriculum and material specialists focus on answering the following four questions:

1. What is the major objective of the title?
2. What material will be included?
3. In what sequence will the material be presented?
4. Are there age appropriate considerations involved?

Determining the major objective of the title is the most important step in beginning the production process. If the objective of the title is to create a program that acquaints new workers with personnel procedures and employee benefits, the corporate training nature of this project will give it a very different look from a video game or entertainment package. Everything in the program should be designed to reinforce the personality of the company. For example, the graphic overview of a small company, where everyone is on a first-name basis with management and the dress code is casual, will have a different look from a large, formally run corporation where most employees do not know everyone. Again, keeping the objective of the title in focus is of primary importance.

Curriculum and material specialists, by determining the material to be included in the title, may also help to identify the other personnel that may be required as production continues. For example, if a video sequence welcoming new employees by the president of the corporation is to be included, a video specialist to tape and edit the welcoming video sequence will be needed. If new employees are to be able to recognize the supervisors in the company, pictures of the supervisors will need to be incorporated into the program, requiring the services of a conventional or digital photographer. Historical and/or background material necessitates research time. Sources of information need to be identified and located. Perhaps an historical perspective of the business can be given by interviewing the founder of the company. This interview will require the services of an audio engineer to produce the broadcast quality audio required for the program. Original drawings, backgrounds, and artwork will require illustrators and graphic designers.

The key function of curriculum and material specialists is their ability to organize and sequence material. This involves establishing a framework for the program, setting up the branching options and feedback systems, as well as the overall look and feel of the program. Specialists are often selected that are familiar with the subject matter of the project and have worked on similar titles in the past, thus helping to facilitate all phases of the production process. For example, if the target audience of the title is first- and second-grade elementary school students, then all text, illustrations, and navigation controls throughout the program need to be age appropriate for 5- to 7-year olds. Curriculum and media specialists help to focus all efforts of the production team, helping to ensure a successful project.

Writers and Text Editors

The amount of text in any multimedia project will vary. When the project calls for a great deal of text, the services of a professional writer or text editor is usually required.

Writers and editors take all of the material gathered by researchers and media specialists, and, following an outline established by the production team, write the "screen play," or content, of the program.

In addition to creating the text that appears on the screen, all material must be edited for spelling, age appropriateness, grammar, and general readability.

Many specialized subject areas tend to have their own "vocabulary," which makes it difficult for those outside the subject area to understand basic ideas and concepts. Writers and editors help to make complicated, specialized vocabularies understandable to larger audiences. Good writing is often taken for granted because it is usually seamless to the reader; however, good writing is an integral component of most multimedia titles.

Audio Specialists

It takes more than a tape recorder and microphone to record sound that will meet the demands and specifications required by digital multimedia. Many variables can enter into the process of recording, digitizing, and editing sound samples: What sampling rate should be used for voice samples and/or for music samples? What audio capture cards should be used to capture the best sound quality—8 bit or 16 bit? Can the sound sample be compressed while retaining good quality and, if so, what compression factor should be used? How do you minimize aliasing, quantizing, and clipping when editing digital sound samples?

Two major factors that influence the quality of recorded sound are the equipment chosen to do the recording and the sampling rate or resolution of the sound clip. Many titles also contain multiple sound tracks that place increased demands on the processing capabilities of the computer. If you are familiar with solving these problems, you are qualified to record your own sounds. If not, you will need the services of a sound engineer who is thoroughly familiar with basic acoustic concepts as they apply to recording and editing sounds on the computer. Thus, sound engineers are often part of the multimedia production team whenever quality sound is required.

Video Specialists

No other technology has had such a dramatic impact on interactive multimedia as that of video recording and playback on the computer. Similar to the questions raised by audio specialization, it takes more than a high quality camcorder to produce video that will successfully integrate into the typical multimedia presentation. The variables affecting the production of quality video for multimedia uses include:

- How does recording speed affect the quality of the digitized video?
- What software packages area available for digitizing video from standard format VHS cassettes?
- Will an AV computer be required for best results or can an add-on video capture card be used?
- What video capture cards will work best on a specific computer?
- What is the best way to synchronize the audio track to the video track?
- How are additional audio tracks added to the original video sound track?
- What software packages are available for editing video and how do you choose the best for your purposes?
- Will artificial lighting be needed to record a video sequence or will natural lighting be sufficient?

Again, if you know the answers to these questions you can record your own video; otherwise, include a video specialist in the production team.

Graphic Designers and Illustrators

Graphic sequences and illustrations have become a basic element in all multimedia projects. Projects such as video games and entertainment titles display almost 100 percent graphic content at any one time. All titles also require a graphic interface that helps to draw the viewer into the program, is intuitive for fostering interactivity, and uses illustrations that help the viewer visualize a variety of content and concepts.

Although mentioned together, graphic designers and illustrators perform different functions in multimedia production. Graphic designers are responsible for assembling all of the elements on the screen; illustrators are called on to provide the special graphic elements, backgrounds, and drawings required in the program. For example, animated sequences require many drawings—sometimes twenty-five or more just to produce one second of screen animation. However, these job titles are not necessarily mutually exclusive: graphic designers are often illustrators and vice versa. The fundamental concept to remember is that special skills are required to both design a page, whether that page is electronic or in print, as well as to create the illustrations that help bring a subject to life.

The production team is almost complete. Two more specialists are needed to bring the project to life: the multimedia author or software engineer who can manipulate the computer code required to make everything work and a marketing/sales coordinator to ensure commercial success.

Authoring/Software Engineer

The mechanics of assembling the text, graphics, audio, and video elements onto the structural framework of the interactive computer program is the job of the program author or software engineer.

The term, "author" does not refer to the creator, or author of the multimedia title in the traditional sense. Rather, it refers to the process of taking the individual components created by the writers, graphic designers, illustrators, and audio and video specialists and putting them in place to produce the interactive multimedia program. Sometimes, authoring involves working from commercially available software packages such as Macromedia's Authorware® or Director®, wherein the individual elements are assembled in the appropriate places within the program. At times, commercially available software packages may not be able to perform the functions required for the project. In these instances, a software engineer is required to create the computer code necessary to create the multimedia program.

One key function of the authoring process focuses on avoiding the reason that most multimedia CDs are either returned to the place of purchase or sent back to the program developer: They simply do not function and work the way they were intended to. This happens because, although most titles are developed and authored on high-end computers, most end users will be running the program on much less powerful computers with limited processing speed and memory. This virtually ensures that the program will not live up to expectations. Program authoring or computer coding must be developed for the lowest common user-user denominator. Final field testing will determine if this goal has been met satisfactorily.

Marketing Director/Sales Coordinator

To ensure commercial success, the sales of multimedia programs should be directed by marketing and sales people familiar with the prospective audience for a title as well as the best way to promote its sale. Because access to shelf space at the retailer is a major limiting factor for program success or failure, the services of a professional marketing and sales team are almost always included in the production group.

■ DESIGNING AN INTERACTIVE MULTIMEDIA PROJECT

In the design phase of the project, decisions affecting everything, from the look and feel of the program on the opening screen to how the branching options of the program work, are made. In this phase, the production team assembled for the project will have a chance to work together as a group, perhaps for the first time. Not all of the decisions are necessarily made by the production group; many will be made by the project director. The important decisions to be made during this phase are examined in the sections following.

Selecting the Program Interface

The program interface is a combination of the screen images and actions that must be incorporated to run the program. Different types of programs have different interfaces. For example, a video game will offer vivid graphic images along with options for selecting sound level, types of tools to be used, and levels of difficulty for the player to select. A corporate training program designed to introduce company employees to a new e-mail program will focus on training exercises designed to familiarize people with the new program procedures. Educational titles are organized to present information in a sequential format with tests and statistical analysis to keep track of viewer learning. These interface formats are not mutually exclusive. Educational titles are sometimes presented in video game format; training programs often use graphics, animation, and cartoon-type figures to help get the point across. The selection of the program interface determines, more than any other decision, the look, feel, and operation of the multimedia program.

Program interface and design strategy are also affected by the data delivery system used including individual computer hard drive, corporate or educational intranet, or the Internet. Running a program from the computer hard drive or CD-ROM requires a different packaging strategy from running the same piece from the Internet or a local area network (LAN) server. Strategies for Web design are discussed later in the section entitled "Design Strategies for Web Delivery."

Specifying Content

Questions to be considered here include: How much text will the program contain? What types of screen backgrounds, if any, will be used? Will original video sequences with synchronized audio be needed? Will the program be narrated, or will screen titles be used to guide the viewer through the program?

The production team works to specify all of the content needed to produce the title within the requirements of the target audience identified. At this stage, the graphic designer begins to focus on the graphic interfaces required for the screen designs. The illustrator may begin thumbnail sketches for the drawings needed in animation sequences as well as other original artwork. Writers, working in conjunction with audio engineers will plan the narrative sequences and interview key subjects or personnel to be included in the program. As work progresses and content is identified, the software engineer or multimedia author will start to set up the basic framework for the program so the production team can begin to get an idea of what the title will look like as the framework begins to fill in. The use of any material for which permissions will be required should be identified, and the process of requesting permissions should begin. Any costs or special conditions associated with reproduction rights of all material should be handled as early in the process as possible. Should there be a problem with reproduction rights for any material, other plans can be made while still in the early stages of production.

Decisions may be made to change some content as production of the title progresses. The production process should be flexible enough to allow for some change in content, especially in the early design and production phases.

Establishing Flowcharts for Major Program Elements

Flowcharts, also called *navigation charts*, are valuable visualization tools used to help design multimedia programs. As the navigation of the program takes shape, it becomes a framework, or outline, on which to build the specific elements of the program. A flowchart illustrates the major elements of the program and how they interact with other program elements. Producing a flowchart is the first step in identifying not only major program components, but the navigation pathways in the program as well. All branching options, enabling the viewer to move within the program, should be identified in this charting process.

The flowchart in Fig. 13.1 shows the major elements of an educational compact disc entitled "The World of Tropical Forests." This title focuses on teaching middle school students about the various types of forests found in the tropical regions of the world, including rain forests.

Multidirectional arrows in the flowchart show how the branching and other interactive elements are set up to allow movement back and forth between and within sections of the program. If tests or other measurement instruments are incorporated

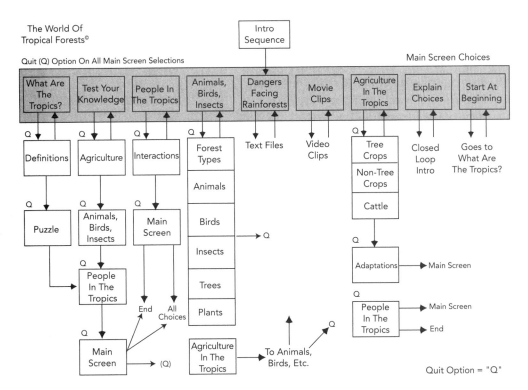

FIGURE 13.1:
Flowchart of "The World of Tropical Forests"

into the program, their location and function within the program should be identified. For example, some titles require that the viewer pass a competency test, or be able to identify specific items, before proceeding from one section of the program to another. A mechanism for matching test responses against a threshold, which will enable the viewer to proceed, should be located within the flowchart along with decisions enabling the viewer to repeat certain sections of the tests if necessary. The more detailed the flowchart, the easier it will be to assemble the elements of the program during the authoring process.

Creating Storyboards

A storyboard is a thumbnail sketch of the multimedia project. Storyboards are an integral component in film production and are also used by multimedia producers to visualize all sections of the program. Figure 13.2 shows the storyboard created for an introductory section on tropical forests of the world. Storyboards are not always required for multimedia projects; their use depends on how complex the program will be and how much artwork needs to be created. Storyboards work well with graphic intensive programs; flowcharts work best with interactive training and educational titles. When the design phase of the project is completed, production can begin.

■ DESIGNING MULTIMEDIA PROJECTS FOR NETWORKS AND THE INTERNET

Both LANs and the Internet offer convenient access to an almost unbelievable amount of information. When multimedia projects are designed to run on either corporate, government, or educational networks or on the Internet, certain design considerations must be met if the program is to run properly. The main limiting factor in delivering information across either LANs or the Internet is the operating speed of the network. Let's take a look at some of the design considerations and constraints to be examined when creating multimedia titles for both LAN and Internet delivery.

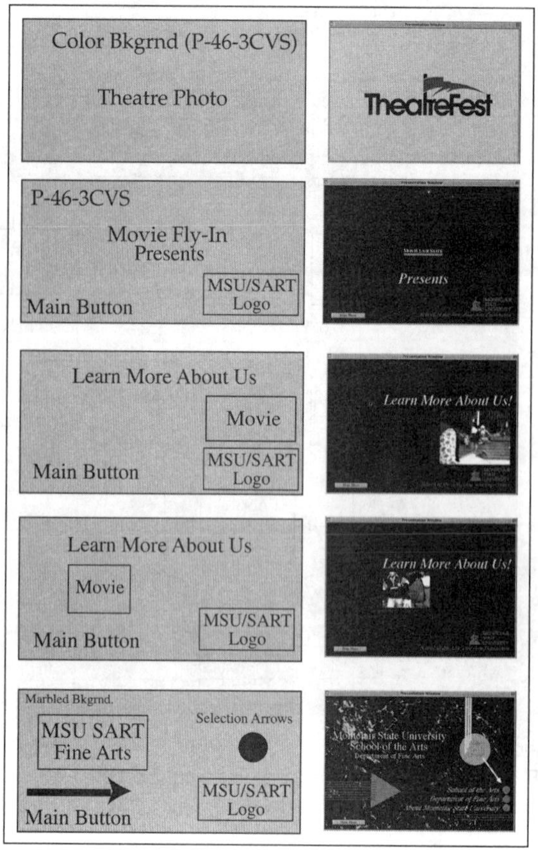

Data Transmission Speed

Although the speed of microprocessors continues to increase, a computer can only interpret and display information after it has been received and placed into computer memory. When running multimedia pieces on corporate and educational networks (Intranets), most multimedia programs treat the LAN servers as additional hard drives on the computer. If packaged properly, information is downloaded from the multimedia piece to the computer as needed. This process is called *streaming* and will be discussed in more detail later. However, it is the speed with which the computer receives information that determines how effectively it will be displayed onscreen.

FIGURE 13.2:
Multimedia storyboard

The Internet is generally slower in delivering information than either LANs or Intranets. This is because most people dialing into the Internet on phone lines use modems running between 28,800 to 56,000 bits (K) of information per second; 112,000 K modems are just becoming available as of this writing. T1 lines, typical of intranet connections found in corporate and educational networks, are capable of processing up to 3 million bits (megabits) per second; cable modems offered by cable television providers are capable of running between 1.5 to 3.0 megabits per second. However, actual data download times are far slower. For example, during peak usage times when traffic on the Internet is at its highest, transmission rates can drop to as low as 200 to 300 bits per second using phone modems, and between 80 to 100 KB/s on T1 and cable modem lines. This often translates into having to wait for more than 30 seconds to download a 60 K file when using slower phone modems. Cable modem upload and download times are also affected by the number of people subscribing to the service. In some areas, upload and download times on cable systems must be artificially capped in order to maximize use of the system for all subscribers. Upload and download times are also limited by the equipment at the other end of your connection. It does little good to have access to high-speed T1 lines on your computer when the server at the other end of your connection is limited to 28,800 KBs. As with many technologies, it is the weakest link that defines system capability.

Streaming Technologies

When using streaming technology, a multimedia piece is divided into segments that are downloaded individually. The advantage of streaming is that the program can begin to play as soon as the first segment is downloaded onto the user's computer. There is no need to wait for the entire program to download before starting to running the program. In this way, streaming enables large multimedia programs, over 35 MB in size, to run effectively. Many multimedia authoring programs incorporate streaming capabilities that enable any size program to be broken into streaming segments. This allows the program to be played over both Intranets and the Internet. Streaming is flexible in that it supports full-featured programs that contain text, graphics, audio, video, data tracking and database management. Depending on the features of the authoring software, the program can be set up to retrieve information from the Internet, go to various uniform resource locators (URLs) on the Internet and exchange information among various program users and a file server. The main limitation of streaming technology is the speed of the network delivering the multimedia program.

Design Strategies for Web Delivery

Designing multimedia programs that will run successfully on the Internet revolves around developing strategies to limit download times. Viewers who must wait too long for graphics or other information to be displayed will often leave the program. The program should be designed so that as information is being downloaded, or streamed, the viewer is engaged in some activity within the program. Interactivity requires far smaller file sizes than large graphics and sound clips and also keeps the viewer busy while other data are being made available.

Long download times are also encountered when the multimedia program contains large color graphics. Rather than relying on standard 8-bit graphic images, authors can experiment using 4-bit or 1-bit images. When using 1-bit (black-and-white) images, the creative use of foreground and background colors can be most effective in overcoming the limitations of black-and-white illustrations. Changing scanned color photos from RGB (millions of colors) to indexed color (256 colors) also helps to minimize file sizes. Picture files should be saved as JPEG and solid graphics as GIF formats to minimize the file sizes of all graphic images.

For efficient operation, keep sound and movie files as small as possible. This is accomplished by using small presentation window sizes and Web-compatible sound and video file formats.

Once the program has been completed, a test run should be done. If the program will be mounted on a file server, a complete field test under actual network delivery conditions should be performed. If the program will run over the Internet, it should be mounted and accessed via the user's Web browser to determine actual download times under a variety of network delivery conditions and then revised as necessary.

■ AUTHORING THE PROGRAM

Having made all of the basic decisions regarding program content, design strategies, etc., the authoring of the title can begin. There are two types of software packages used to author the majority of interactive multimedia titles: flowline and stage-metaphor programs.

In flowline logic, all of the elements that will appear on the screen are placed on a linear flowline. As the program runs, it encounters each element or action on the flowline in sequence and the program continues on through all of the elements in the program. To illustrate this concept, examine the flowline displayed by Macromedia's Authorware® shown in Fig. 13.3.

The flowline in Fig. 13.3 illustrates an introductory sequence for a multimedia piece entitled "The World of Tropical Rainforests." Note that the sequence contains a music background clip that plays in the background as a series of six pictures come up on the screen that introduce the title to the viewer. After the pictures have been displayed, the program display stops at the main screen, where the viewer can make choices about what to view next.

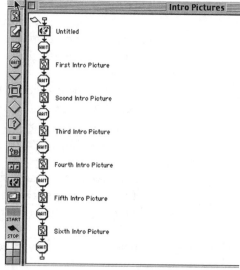

FIGURE 13.3:
Flow-line multimedia program

Every facet of this introductory sequence is tightly controlled by the program within the flowline. For example, the length of time each picture remains on the screen is set at three seconds, controlled by a "pause" command that sets the length of time the picture remains on the screen (Fig. 13.4).

In the logic of the flowline, the computer first encounters the audio icon that instructs the computer to play a background audio clip. Then it displays the first picture, continues to move to the pause command icon, where an instruction set is given to keep the picture on the screen for three seconds, then moves on to the next picture. However, each picture must be erased before the next picture is displayed; otherwise, all of the pictures will be displayed on the screen at the same time. Erasing each picture is controlled by an "erase" icon that erases the picture from the screen, allowing the author to select any erase options in the process (Fig. 13.5).

Placing a display icon that contains a picture, followed by a pause command that instructs the computer to leave the picture on the screen for a specified period of time, then on to an erase icon that removes the picture from the screen, presents the basic command structure for displaying and erasing graphics automatically on the computer. Placing an audio icon first on the flowline enables the background sound to start playing before the first picture is displayed

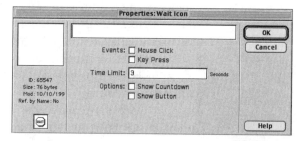

FIGURE 13.4:
Pause command structure

on the screen. The sound clip continues to play until the main selection screen is displayed. Controls for the audio icon are illustrated in Fig. 13.6. Note that the author can set everything from the playback speed of the audio clip to deciding if the audio clip plays continuously with other items as they are displayed or plays by itself.

The introductory sequence ends with the display of the main selection screen. This screen showing the viewer choices, is shown in Fig. 13.7.

When reaching this screen, the viewer selects a topic for further investigation by pressing the mouse button when the mouse is over the appropriate picture icon.

FIGURE 13.5:
Erasing icon controls

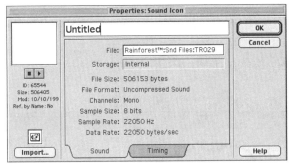

FIGURE 13.6:
Audio icon controls

The main screen must contain all of the instructions necessary to guide the viewer through the program. Regardless of how intuitive a programmer thinks a selection screen might be, it is absolutely necessary to supply the viewer with a complete set of instructions that explain what program options are available, what actions are required, and where the program will go if specific actions are taken. Most programs require the mouse button to be clicked while the cursor is over a picture or written command in order for the program to proceed. Because the main screen requires that a decision be made by the viewer in order to proceed, the icon that contains this information is named, appropriately, a decision icon. The flowline representation of a decision icon is shown in Fig. 13.8.

Each icon within the decision structure represents one of the viewer choices displayed on the main selection screen. These icons are called map icons, and they contain the program contents of each of the selections. For example, if we view the contents of the map icon labeled "introductory sequence," we see the flowline showing how the introductory sequence has been assembled from the graphic, video, and audio components (Fig. 13.9).

Although the logic of working with a flowline authoring program is intuitive, it still requires practice in order to gain a high degree of expertise in its use. There are icons available to the author to place on the flowline that enable the construction of the most complex interactive programs. For example, the icons within Macromedia's Authorware® are shown in Fig. 13.10.

Flowline-based authoring programs such as Authorware® work best when used to assemble interactive training and educational programs where tight control over timing is not required and only a limited number of elements are displayed on the screen at any one time. However, when authoring interactive programs such as video games and simulations, display timing must be tightly controlled and several dozen different graphic and text elements may be displayed simultaneously. A stage, or movie, metaphor authoring software program such as

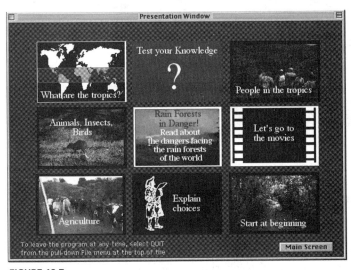

FIGURE 13.7:
Main selection screen

Macromedia Director® is the preferred authoring program in these cases.

Stage metaphor programs such as Director® set up the authoring environment by making the multimedia author a "movie" director, capable of moving elements of the movie cast on and off the stage as the "movie," or program, requires. Movie timing is tightly controlled by setting the number of frames per second that the movie, or program, will display. For example, setting the movie timing at 30 frames per second controls members of the cast, such as pictures, animation, and audio and video sequences, to within 1/30th of a second. Although tighter control of timing is available within the program, most end-user computers will probably not be able to simultaneously display three dozen graphic elements, controlled to limits greater than 1/30th of a second—always remember end-user limitations!

We will take a closer look at the stage and casting authoring environment as shown in Figures 13.11–13.15. Assume we are putting together an introductory program sequence consisting of five objects made up of four geometric shapes and one text element. We want each object to appear on the screen in sequence. To do this, each picture becomes a member of the "cast." Cast members can be photographs, video and audio sequences, text, illustrations, or anything else that will appear on the screen as part of the program. When called upon to "act" or to be on stage, a cast member is moved from the casting area into the "score." When placed in the score, the cast member is displayed on the "stage," or computer screen. The casting box, along with the five cast members that have been moved onto the left side of the stage, are shown in Fig. 13.11.

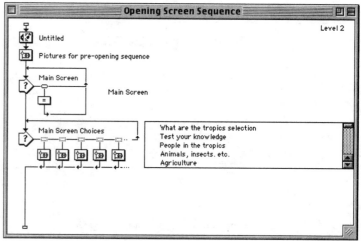

FIGURE 13.8:
Decision icon on flowline

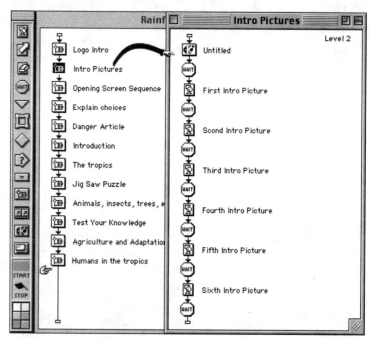

FIGURE 13.9:
Map icon contents of introductory sequence

FIGURE 13.10:
Authorware®
icons

In the casting box, each cast member is represented as a small thumbnail sketch, making it easy to identify each of them at a glance. A cast member becomes active when it is moved from its individual casting box on to the stage to become part of the movie score. Figure 13.12 shows the transition box that enables the author to determine how a particular cast member will appear when it first comes onto the stage. In this instance, cast member #1 will dissolve onto the stage during a two-second sequence as indicated in the frame property transition dialog box.

In Fig. 13.13, all five introductory pictures, representing cast members #1 through #5 have been brought into the score. Because a transition of two seconds has been set for each of the five cast members to "dissolve" onto the stage, with the movie timing set for 15 frames per second, the entire opening screen is set to display for approximately one second after all of the five pictures have been placed onto the screen. The score shows each cast member placed in a separate "sprite channel" for the 30 frames of the movie score. Note the placement of each of the five objects in successive channels; that is, cast member one is placed in sprite #1, channel #2; cast member #2 is placed in sprite #2, channel #3, and so on. This arrangement allows for each of the cast members to appear on the screen, one at a time in succession and enables the dissolve transition to work for each member of the cast.

Programs such as Director® are capable of playing multiple audio tracks. Audio clips, ranging from musical backgrounds to narration sequences, are also first saved as cast members and then placed into the score from the casting box. In Fig. 13.14, a musical clip entitled "Intro. AIF" has been selected in the import dialog box and will become cast member #20.

The true power of a stage-metaphor program such as Director® lies in the programming codes and scripts that can be made to control all phases of interactivity and animation within the multimedia title. The logic behind scripting codes tells the program how to behave when a certain condition, or series of conditions, take place. For example, Fig. 13.15 illustrates the scripting code that tells the program to play a video clip when the mouse button is clicked while on cast member #1. To make this interactivity work, the scripting code (called "Lingo" in Director®) identifies the outside boundaries of cast member #1 on the screen so when the mouse cursor moves over its boundaries and the mouse is clicked, the program automatically moves to the video segment of the score identified by the programming code, in this instance the movie entitled "Intro Movie."

Similar codes control sounds made by the program when certain actions take place. For example, a video game might require a sound to be made when one of the figures hits the ground. In this instance, the boundary areas of the ground are identified so that when one of the figures overlaps, or falls on to the ground area, the program executes a specific sound. The sound in this instance is also a cast member. Other sounds and special actions are programmed to take place in a similar manner.

There are literally thousands of different types of actions that can be controlled by powerful scripting codes used in both flowline and stage-metaphor authoring programs. Although we have examined only a few of them in this chapter, adeptness in their use requires extensive practice with both types of authoring programs.

■ MULTIPLATFORM CONSIDERATIONS

To distribute a multimedia program that will run on both the Macintosh and PC platforms, it must be packaged separately for each system. For example, if a multimedia program has been authored on the Macintosh platform, it must be "packaged" with special runtime, or projection files, that will enable it to run on PCs. Conversely, authoring on the PC platform requires that runtime programs and projectors be packaged with the completed multimedia file that will allow it to run on Macintosh computers. Although many multimedia authoring programs are available for both Macintosh and PCs, cross-platform operation can only be achieved by packaging the completed program with the necessary runtime files and programs.

Cross platform system incompatibilities show up in differences such as palette colors in illustrations and inconsistencies in text and placement and position on the screen. When authoring any multiplatform program, it is good practice to package it for the other computer platform at regular intervals throughout the authoring process. Running the programming on the other platform helps to identify system differences, and if possible, make adjustments as the authoring process progresses. This procedure will help to minimize any surprises once the authoring is completed and the title is ready for duplication and distribution.

■ FIELD TESTING THE PROGRAM

A comprehensive evaluation of any title begins with setting up a complete field testing program. This phase of production is critical. Despite the care and attention to detail in authoring, problems are inevitable because it is almost impossible to anticipate all of the actions of the viewer. Although the programmer visualizes what actions should be taken by the viewer, it is difficult to ensure that the viewer performs the actions as they are envisioned by the programmer. In the field testing stage, these problems are identified and eliminated. The more comprehensive the testing and evaluation, the more likely it will be to catch and rectify all problem situations.

FIGURE 13.11:
Introductory pictures in a cast

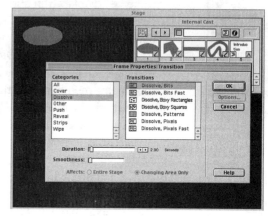

FIGURE 13.12:
Cast member #1 scored for 2 seconds

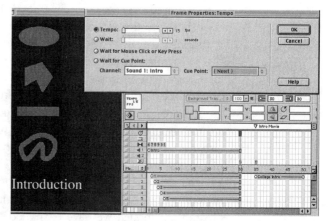

FIGURE 13.13:
Cast members #1–#5 scored in six sprite channels

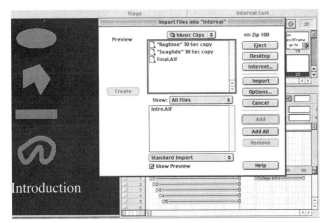

FIGURE 13.14:
Introductory pictures and audio scored for
nine seconds at ten frames per second

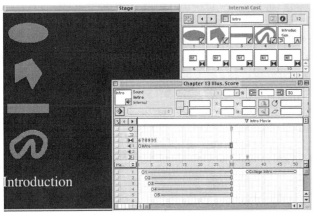

FIGURE 13.15:
Scripting code for interactivity

Problems in multimedia programming can, and usually do, appear anywhere: video sequences that end before they are supposed to; programs that do not go to the branching location when the proper button has been pressed; audio sequences that either start or end too early; graphics that take too long to display on the screen; and lines of text that do not display properly.

The key to setting up a good testing and evaluation program is to make sure that testing and evaluation is done by the end users, on computers that are typical for the intended audience. For example, if a program is an educational title designed for early elementary school students, then evaluation copies of the finished program should be made available to first- and second-grade elementary school students. Their reactions to the program should be carefully recorded. Ask questions and make observations such as: What did they like about the program? What didn't they like about the program? Were they bored or did they lose interest in the title too quickly? Did all of the branching options work as planned, or did the students find the instruction sets too difficult to follow?

Field evaluation will quickly reveal if the title, as originally designed, requires too much processing power from a typical end-user computer. Video sequences that either start or end too quickly and lost sections of audio clips are indications that information from the program is coming into the computer's central processor faster than it can be interpreted and displayed. Video clips authored on a computer with a processing speed of 400 MHz will not display with the same speed and quality as on a computer running the same video clip with a central processor speed of only 133 MHz. Incompatibilities of this type may require a redesign of the original multimedia program via the authoring software; for example, video sequences may need to be reworked by reducing the size of the playback window or by slowing down the frame-per-second playback rate from 15 to 10 frames per second. Audio sequences can often be fixed by lowering the recording sampling rate or by using a higher compression ratio. Although these changes may adversely affect the quality of the playback, they will enable the program to effectively run on lower-end computers that were not originally accounted for when the program was being authored.

Redesigning for Optimum Performance

After problems with the program have been identified by the field tests, the program goes back to the production team and authors for reprogramming and repair where necessary. The cycle of field testing and program redesign may need to be repeated several times before the production team is satisfied that the program functions as intended. What makes this testing stage of the process so critical to the final success of the effort is that once the production team signs off on the testing, any errors that may have slipped by will appear in all final duplicated versions of the title. You simply can't fix misspelled words and broken branching links on a duplicated compact disc. Again, it must be determined that the programs performs as advertised on a typical end-user computer. Even though minimum computer requirements are usually printed on the jackets and boxes of multimedia titles, the program should be designed to perform satisfactorily on the widest range of computers without sacrificing the program's operation.

■ SUMMARY

In this chapter we examined the basic ingredients that go into creating exciting, well-planned and well-produced interactive multimedia program content. It was not the intention of this chapter to present instructions on the actual production of multimedia titles; rather, the basic aspects and stages of the multimedia production process were highlighted.

Effective multimedia runs the gamut from a simple presentation of subject matter to a small class of children and authored by only one person, to creating a complex video game that requires the combined efforts of a production team for completion. Whatever the size or complexity of the program, keep in mind the basic steps to follow in designing and producing any multimedia project:

- Select an appropriate interface and delivery system
- Specify program content
- Implement a flowchart/storyboard for the program
- Author the program carefully
- Field test and reengineer the program where necessary
- Market the program according to a predefined strategy

Advertising not withstanding, all multimedia authoring programs have significant learning curves. Simple presentations with a low level of interactivity can be assembled in a relatively short time; significant interactivity incorporating graphics, video, and audio requires substantially more time to master the authoring program capabilities. However, spending the time required to learn interactive multimedia authoring techniques is a worthwhile investment. The concepts identified in this chapter will help guide your multimedia project to a successful conclusion.

■ SUGGESTED STUDENT ACTIVITIES

1. Select two commercially available interactive multimedia programs. For each of the programs do the following:

   A. Determine the authoring software used to produce the title.

   B. Create a flowchart of the basic elements of the title.

   C. Identify all of the interactive elements contained in the program.

   D. Identify the elements that make up the marketing strategy for selling the program.

2. Design an interactive media title of your own choosing. After coming up with the general idea of what the program will contain, do the following:

   A. Outline your program in storyboard format. In this storyboard, include all of the elements that will appear in your program.

   B. Identify the market you have designed your program to appeal to.

   C. Come up with a preliminary design for a CD jacket cover for your multimedia program.

Final Thoughts

We have prepared this text guided by the on-going influences of globalized and electronic commerce, and unlimited access to information on the part of increasing numbers of people worldwide. How do students, and on a broader level, educational institutions at all levels, deal with some of these trends?

- Specific models of personal computers will, in all likelihood, be out of production within 6 to 12 months after their purchase, and will become technologically obsolete within the following two years.
- Software applications will be updated approximately every 12 to 16 months.
- Once students have mastered the fundamentals of specific software programs, they will welcome, rather than fear, updates and revisions to the programs they are using.
- Much of the technical information learned during a student's undergraduate college education will become obsolete within 5 to 7 years after graduation. This "half-life" of relevant information will continue to decrease in the coming years.
- The average person might change not only jobs, but also entire careers, several times during their working years.
- Increasingly affordable digital printing technologies will continue to decrease the importance of out-sourcing agencies. New demands will be placed on existing and new personnel to broaden their range of skills related to both design and production in the graphic communications industry.

Within this complex technological landscape, the authors' solution to overcoming these obstacles is to approach subject content with an emphasis on learning concepts and solving problems rather than presenting specific skills to be mastered. For example, how object-oriented graphic design software programs function rather than emphasizing specific skills used to draw a circle or a square, are presented in this text. In this instance, knowing what the computer program is doing is more important than mastering a specific skill. Once concepts are fully understood, skills can be learned in any applications program, and on any operating platform.

However, this philosophy does not diminish the importance of acquiring the skills necessary to create, design and produce effective communication projects. Within this text, considerable space is devoted to the technical aspects of computer and photographic imaging, composition and printing. Skill acquisition, however, must always take place within the overall context of technological change and evolution. One need only think back to the venerable Linotype Operator, a backbone of the graphic arts industry for almost a century—a job category that disappeared practically overnight when the first photographic and software-driven typesetting machines were introduced.

During the preparation of this text, many decisions were made regarding the information to be included as well as that which is best left to upper level curricula. For example, what problems do graphic designers face when meeting a client for the first time? Once the problems have been identified, guidelines can be established by the designer to help ensure successful completion of the job. We have offered some suggestions in this regard. Effective learning takes place, and problems can be successfully solved by first discussing these highlights which, hopefully, will enable the designer to construct his or her own solution to a wide range of problems with a built-in flexibility not otherwise possible.

Although sometimes difficult, the authors are confident that this text contains material that is appropriate for not only beginning graphic design and printing technology students, but also for student interested in the communication arts as well. We welcome any comments or suggestions that students or teachers care to share with us to improve this text in future editions.

Martin Greenwald and John Luttropp
Department of Fine Arts
Montclair State University
Upper Montclair, N.J. 07043

e-mail addresses:
LuttroppJ@mail.montclair.edu
GreenwaldM@mail.montclair.edu

Web Site:
www.montclair.edu/design

Appendix I

Professional Design Organizations and Associations

American Center for Design
233 East Ontario St.
Chicago, IL 60611
312 787-2018
www.ac4d.org

American Institute of Graphic Arts
164 5th Av.
New York, NY 10010
1-800 548-1634
www.aiga.org

Art Directors Club of New York
250 Park Ave. South
New York, NY 10001
212 674-0500
www.adcny.org

Graphic Artists Guild
11 West 20th St.
New York, NY 10011
212 463-7730
www.gag.org

Graphic Arts Technical Foundation
200 Deer Run Road
Sewickley, PA 15143-2600
1-800-910-GATF
www.gatf.org

Society for Environmental Graphic Design
401 F Street NW, Suite 333
Washington, DC 20001
202 638-5555
www.segd.org

Society of Publication Designers
60 East 42nd Street, Suite 721
New York, NY 10165
212 983-8585
www.spd.org

Type Directors Club
60 East 42nd Street, Suite 721
New York, NY 10165
212 983-6042
www.tdc.org

Society of Illustrators
128 E. 63rd St.
New York, NY 10021
212 838-2560
www.societyillustrators.org

Society of Children's Book Writers and Illustrators
8271 Beverly Blvd.
Los Angeles, CA 90048
323 782-1010
http://www.scbwi.org

Appendix II
Relevant Web Sites

Design Collections

Cooper Hewitt/National Design Museum . . . . www.si.edu/ndm
Cooper Union Herb Lubalin Study Center. . . . . www.cooper.edu/art/lubalin
Museum of Modern Art. . . . . www.moma.org
National Graphic Design Image Database . . . . http://ngda.cooper.edu
Design Archive online at RIT. . . . . http://design.rit.edu

Design Tools

Apple Computer. . . . . www.apple.com
Adobe (Illustrator®, Photoshop®, ATM®, etc.) . . . . . . www.adobe.com
Canon (copiers and printers) . . . . www.usa.canon.com
Epson (scanners and printers) . . . . www.epson.com
Hewlett Packard (printers) . . . . www.hp.com
Macromedia (Dreamweaver®, Director®, etc.) . . . . . www.macromedia.com
Quark (XPress®) . . . . www.quark.com
Wacom (drawing tablets) . . . . www.wacom.com

Stock Illustration Sources

Illo . . . . www.illo.com
Artville. . . . . www.artville.com
The Ispot . . . . www.theispot.com
Images.com . . . . www.images.com

Stock Photography Sources

Archive (historic photos) . . . . www.archivephotos.com
Comstock . . . . www.comstock.com
Digital Vision. . . . . www.digitalvisiononline.com
Corbis Images . . . . www.corbisimages.com
FPG International . . . . www.fpg.com
Image Bank . . . . www.theimagebank.com
Photodisc. . . . . www.photodisc.com
Photo Japan. . . . . www.photojapan.com
Phototake (medical and scientific photos). . . . . www.phototakeusa.com
Stockbyte. . . . . www.stockbyte.com

Appendix III

Suggested Readings

Adobe Creative Team, Andrew Faulkner. *The Official Adobe Print Publishing Guide.* Adobe Press

AIGA. *Graphic Design: A Career Guide and Educational Directory.* AIGA Press

Aker, Sharon Zardetto. *The Macintosh Bible.* Addison Wesley Publishing

Berger, John. *Ways of Seeing.* Penguin Books

Bierut, Michael; William Drenttel, Steven Heller & DK Holland, ed. *Looking Closer: Critical Writings on Graphic Design.* Allworth Press

Bierut, Michael; William Drenttel, Steven Heller & DK Holland, ed. *Looking Closer 2: Critical Writings on Graphic Design.* Allworth Press

Bierut, Michael; Jessica Helfand, Steven Heller & Rick Poyner, ed. *Looking Closer 3: Classical Writings on Graphic Design.* Allworth Press

Blackwell, Lewis. *20th Century Type.* Rizzoli

Carter, Rob, Philip B. Meggs, Ben Day. *Typographic Design: Form and Communication, 2nd Edition.* John Wiley and Sons, Inc.

Clark, Paul and Julian Freeman. *Design: A Crash Course.* Watson Guptil

Dondis, Donis A. *A Primer of Visual Literacy.* MIT Press

Ewen, Stuart. *All Consuming Images, Revised Edition.* Basic Books

Ewen, Stuart and Elizabeth. *Channels of Desire: Mass Images and the Shaping of American Consciousness.* University of Minnesota Press

Foote, Cameron. *The Business Side of Creativity: The Complete Guide for Running a Graphic Design or Communications Business.* W. W. Norton and Co.

Friedman, Mildred. *Graphic Design in America: a Visual Language.* Harry N. Abrams, Inc.

Gottschall, Edward M. *Typographic Communications Today.* MIT Press

Graphic Artists Guild. *Handbook of Pricing & Ethical Guidelines.* Graphic Artists Guild

Heller, Steven, ed. *The Education of a Graphic Designer.* Allworth Press

Heller, Steven and Teresa Fernandez. *Becoming a Graphic Designer: A Guide to Careers in Design.* John Wiley and Sons, Inc.

Heller, Steven and Karen Pomeroy. *Design Literacy: Understanding Graphic Design.* Allworth Press

Hollis, Richard. *Graphic Design: A Concise History.* Thames & Hudson, Ltd.

Landa, Robin. *Graphic Design Solutions, 2E.* OnWorld Press

Landa, Robin. *Thinking Creatively: New Ways to Unlock Your Visual Imagination.* North Light Books

Lupton, Ellen and J. Abbott Miller. *Design Writing Research.* Kiosk

Lyons, Daniel J. *Graphic Communications Dictionary.* Prentice Hall

McCreight, Tim. *Design Language.* Brynmorgen Press

Meggs, Philip B. *A History of Graphic Design, Third Edition.* John Wiley & Sons, Inc.

Oldach, Mark. *Creativity for Graphic Designers.* North Light Books.

Perkins, Sean, ed. *Experience.* Booth Clibborn Editions

Rand, Paul. *A Designer's Art.* Yale University Press

Rogondino, Michael and Pat. *Process Color Manual, 24,000 CMYK Combinations for Design, Prepress, and Printing.* Chronicle Books

Romano, Frank J. *Pocket Guide to Digital Prepress.* Delmar Publishers

Roth, Laszlo, and George L. Wybenga. *The Packaging Designer's Book of Patterns.* John Wiley and Sons, Inc.

Spencer, Herbert. *Pioneers of Modern Typography, Revised Edition.* MIT Press

Spiekermann, Erik and E.M. Ginger. *Stop Stealing Sheep and Find Out How Type Works.* Adobe Press/Prentice Hall Computer Publishing.

Tambini, Michael. *The Look of the Century: Design Icons of the 20th Century.* DK Publishing

Wheeler, Susan G. and Gary S. *TypeSense: Making Sense of Type on the Computer, Second Edition.* Prentice Hall

Wilde, Richard and Judith. *Visual Literacy: A Visual Approach to Graphic Design Problem Solving,* Watson Guptil Publications

Graphic Design/Production Glossary

8 bits: 8 bits of computer information is equivalent to one byte. One thousand bytes equals one kilobyte (Kb).

42-line bible: So named from the number of lines of text on each page, the 42-line bible was published around 1455, by Johann Gutenberg.

actinic light: Light within the ultraviolet portion of the visible spectrum that causes a change in photographic emulsions.

additive primaries: The primary colors of projected light: red, green, and blue.

Adams press: The first steam-powered printing press developed in America, by Isaac and Seth Adams in 1830.

algorithm: A mathematical formula, or plan, used as a framework to build a computer software application program. Software interpolation programs used by scanner manufacturers to increase scanner resolution are all based on mathematical algorithms, which enable the software to "fill in the blanks" and increase the resolution of a scanned document.

Altair® 8800: The first personal computer to gain any degree of public acceptance, based on an Intel Z-80 microprocessor, and offered to computer and electronic hobbyists only in do-it-yourself kit form.

analog: Term used to describe the natural world—shades of gray rather than black and white and subtle variations of virtually all phenomena. Analog data is the opposite of digital data.

ascender: The part of a letter that rises above its x-height, as in the letters b, d, f, h, l, and k.

Authorware®: Program produced by Macromedia, Inc., used primarily for authoring multimedia training and educational materials.

autoscreen film: Orthochromatic film that incorporates a halftone screen built in to the emulsion of the film. This film can be used to shoot halftone images without the use of a conventional halftone screen.

baseline: The imaginary reference line that defines where a line of type rests.

bi-metallic plates: Offset printing plates manufactured from two different metals which are bonded together, giving the plate long-run characteristics.

binary system: Numbering system used to describe digital data, based on 0s and 1s.

bit-map images: Bit-mapped images are sometimes called "computer raster images." Pictures in bitmap are made up of individual dots or pixels, and commonly generated in paint and image editing programs.

blanket cylinder: The rubber-lined cylinder on an offset printing press on which the image is printed from the plate cylinder. The blanket cylinder then "offsets" its image on to a sheet of paper, giving the printing process its name.

bleed: Images that extend beyond the edges of the printed sheet, running to the very edge of the paper.

blurring (image doubling): Image blurring is sometimes also referred to as "image doubling." Causes of double printed images may be loose blankets and excessive pressures on the impression cylinder of offset presses.

Book of Psalms: First book published in North America, in 1640.

bubble jet printer (liquid thermal technology): An ink-jet printing technology in which heat causes the ink to vaporize into a large bubble. Pressure within the printing nozzle forces the bubble droplet on to a sheet of paper.

bugs: A term referring to modern day computer problems and software malfunctions. The term originated from the problems that occurred in ENIAC when insects were found to get stuck between the contacts of the switching terminals.

bump exposure: A bump exposure is taken to increase detail in the highlighted areas of the negative during the halftone photographic process. The bump is made with the halftone screen removed from the film, usually for a period of 3 to 5% of the main exposure time.

camera obscura: A dark room with a pinhole opening in one of the outside walls. Light from an object illuminated outside of the camera obscura passes through this small pinhole opening and is projected upside down on the opposite wall of the room.

camera-ready copy: Original copy ready to be photographed on the graphic arts process camera. Camera-ready copy requires high resolution images for both text and graphics to maintain quality in the printed image.

capstan imagesetter: A series of transport rollers to keep the film or plate media under tension, moving it from the supply cassette to a take-up cassette as the imaging takes place.

catalog disc: The Photo CD catalog format is set up to handle a large number of images at lower resolution for display on regular television sets.

CD-DA: Audio format compact discs (Compact Disc—Digital Audio).

CD-E: Eraseable CD format (Compact Disc—Eraseable).

CD-Plus: The CD-Plus, or enhanced format, enables the creation of multisession compact discs. This enables computers to read and play back both audio tracks and additional information on the disc, which is transparent to normal audio CD players.

CD-R: Recordable compact discs (Compact Disc—Recordable). CD-Rs are sold as blank discs and then recorded, using a compact disc recorder.

CD-ROM: The conventional CD (Compact Disc—Read Only Memory). These discs can only be written to only once. No further changes on the disc are possible after the initial writing.

CD-RW: Rewriteable compact discs (Compact Disc–Rewriteable). These discs can be recorded, erased and then recorded on again.

chain delivery system: The paper delivery system on offset printing presses that use two chains connected to a series of gripper bars that grabs the printed sheet as it leaves the press cylinders and then drops it onto the paper pile.

charge-couple-device: The light sensor converter used in most flat bed scanners.

Cinepak: Compression software developed by SuperMac® Technology.

clock speed: The speed that a computer chip processes instructions, measured in millions of cycles per second (MHz).

CMOS array: CMOS–complimentary metal oxide semi-conductors–are light sensitive devices arranged in special patterns to capture images in digital cameras and scanners.

CMYK: An abbreviation for the four colors used in conventional process color printing: cyan, magenta, yellow, and black.

cold scanner: Cold scanners typically use xenon cold cathode bulbs that limit light deterioration when working with color originals. Cold scanning also eliminates the need for cooling fans because the bulbs, sealed in dust-free enclosures, generate very little heat.

collating: Process of arranging pages into their sequential order. Collating machines are manufactured as stand-alone units as well as incorporated into conventional and digital printing presses.

color bars: Used in color separation negatives to give the press operator a visual indication of the colors resulting from the overlay of transparent color separation inks during printing.

comp: Short for "comprehensive dummy," the artwork used to present the general layout of a design project.

composing stick: A hand-held device that holds the individual letters of foundry type while it is being assembled.

computer-to-press (CTP): A process in which images are sent directly from a computer to the printing press. CTP eliminates all of the intermediate photographic, stripping and plate making steps associated with offset imaging.

constant linear velocity (CLV): To accurately read data on a compact disc, the CD drive must maintain a constant data rate moving under its data pick-up head. This rate is called constant linear velocity, and is achieved by the CD drive varying its rotational speed, which is dependent upon the specific location of the drive's pick-up head over the disc.

continuous ink jet printer: Ink jet process where a pump forces a continuous stream of ink through a nozzle under constant pressure, producing more than a million ink droplets each second.

continuous-tone copy: Continuous-tone copy contains blacks and whites as well as intermediate shades of gray, or a gradation of tonal ranges. Examples of continuous-tone copy include original black and white and color photographs, charcoal sketches, and airbrush renderings.

copyboard: The table on a graphic arts process camera that holds the copy to be photographed in position during the camera exposure sequence.

copyright: The legal right of an author, artist, photographer or other creator of an original work to protect that work against unauthorized use by someone else.

crash: A drive "crash" occurs if the drive heads come into contact with the drive platter. This type of hardware crash renders the drive inoperable and is usually accompanied by either a partial or complete loss of data stored on the drive.

creep: Describes the tendency of the center pages of a book, or series of pages in a large signature, to move, or creep, forward, resulting in an uneven edge before the signature is trimmed.

crop marks: Printed guidelines that show the paper cutter operator where to trim the finished sheet.

cropping: Eliminating unwanted areas from photographs, scans, etc. In a photographic darkroom, cropping is performed on an enlarger during the printing process; on a computer, cropping is accomplished through the use of a cropping tool, in an image editing program.

Daguerreotype: A glass photographic plate, coated with a light-sensitive chemical emulsion, and placed inside a light-tight box. After a long exposure, the plate is processed to hold and fix the image.

darkroom camera: A graphic arts process camera designed to be installed in a light-tight room such as a photographic darkroom.

daylight processors: Machines that process (develop) cassette-loaded film in normal room light.

deep-etch plates: The emulsion coating of the plate is etched into the surface of the plate material, making these plates more suitable for long press runs than other types of plates.

delivery cylinder: A cylinder sometimes incorporated on commercial offset presses, that routes the printed sheet around the cylinder and into a delivery tray, or onto a table.

densitometer: Device designed to measure the optical density of either reflection (print) or transmission (negative) materials. Although most densitometers are electronic devices, density can also be measured using optical densitometers to compare various shades of gray in original copy to calibrated patches on the densitometer.

densitometry: The process of determining how much light is reflected from, or is transmitted through, a photographic negative or print.

density: The ability of a substance (such as the developed silver particles in the emulsion layer of a piece of photographic film) to prevent light from passing through the film. Density is measured with a device called a "densitometer" using a scale numbered from 0 to 4.0.

descender: The portion of a letter that falls below the baseline, as in the letters g, j, p, q, and y.

descreening: Removing the halftone dots from a printed image during the scanning procedure.

die-cutting: Cutting shapes out of paper or cardboard using steel cutting die in a printing press.

diffusion transfer processing: Diffusion transfer uses special paper and chemistry to transfer an image from an intermediate transfer negative onto a sheet of photographic paper. This process is accomplished through the use of a special processor and chemistry resulting in prints that are often referred to as "velox" prints.

digital camera: A camera that records images in digital format on both discs or eraseable memory rather than conventional film.

digital color proofs: Digital color proofs, in order to be considered "contract" grade proofs, must be able to be matched on the printing press. Thus, many low-cost printers cannot be used for producing contract proofs. Most often, dye-sublimation printers are used to produce digital color proofs.

direct dampening system: A direct dampening system on an offset press delivers fountain solution to the printing plate using a roller delivery system that is separate from the ink delivery system.

direct image offset plates: Offset plates usually manufactured from paper, and prepared by either typing or drawing directly on the plate.

direct photographic plate processing: Process that uses a special camera system loaded with pre-sensitized plate media. The camera is also equipped with a processing unit to develop the plate material after exposure.

Director®: Software program developed by Macromedia, Inc. Director® is used for authoring interactive multimedia games and other Web-based materials.

doctor blade: A steel blade found on the ink-feed systems of offset printing presses that controls the amount of ink delivered to the ink rollers. This is accomplished by varying the distance between the doctor blade and the ink fountain.

dot gain: The tendency of halftone dots on an offset printing plate to become larger when they are printed. This is caused primarily by the pressure exerted by the rubber blanket on the press during printing as well as the ink and water used in the printing process.

dot matrix printer: Early-generation computer printers that used a series of steel pins to punch through a modified typewriter ribbon to produce both text and rudimentary graphics.

dots per inch (dpi): The measurement of resolution for page printers, imagesetters, and computer screens.

double sheet detector: The system on offset presses, collators, etc., used to detect double sheets and, if necessary, halt the paper feed until the double sheet can be eliminated.

drum scanners: Scanners that incorporate a spinning drum to hold original copy while a beam of light moves across the copy to digitize it.

drum-type imagesetters: During the imaging process, media is fed from a supply roll onto a drum where it remains during the exposure sequence. Drum-type imagesetters are configured as either internal or external systems.

dry offset (dryography): A modification of the wet offset process that works without the use of a dampening solution. Special silicone-based plates are employed to separate the image and nonimage areas.

ductor roller: A roller incoporated on the dampening and ink systems of offset presses that first picks up either ink or dampening solution, and then delivers it to the feed rollers.

duplexing: Printing on both sides of a sheet, or roll, of paper during one pass through the printing press.

duplicator (offset): Small format offset printing press.

DVD: Digital Versatile Disks. DVDs were originally called "digital video discs", because the format was intended to be the primary delivery system for digitized movies shown on home TVs. Since then, other applications have moved onto the disc. Due to its potentially huge storage capacity, the "video" has been changed to "versatile." The DVD specification calls for an eventual storage capacity of 17 GB.

DVD-R: Recording format for Digital Versatile Discs (DVDs).

dye sublimation: When the dye from a specially coated ribbon is heated, it changes from a solid to a gas in a chemical process called sublimation. When the gaseous dye comes into contact with specially coated paper, it changes back into solid form. The dye sublimation process is used by graphic designers to deliver high quality press proofs for customer approval prior to printing a job.

edition binding: Hardcover textbooks with which we are familiar are examples of edition bindings. The bindings consist of several signatures that are first sewn together, after which a hardcover is glued on to end sheets that hold the cover in place. Edition bindings are the most expensive types of bindings, and are usually reserved for text books and other relatively expensive books with high page counts.

electron beam (EB) printer: EB printers (sometimes referred to as ion deposition printers) employ four steps to produce an image: generating the image on the drum with electron beams; developing the image; transferring and fusing the image on to paper; and cleaning the drum.

electrostatic plate: The image to be printed is projected onto an electrostatic plate master in a procedure similar to making a photocopy. As the plate is processed, toner is applied and fused to the plate surface. The fused toner becomes the grease-receptive image area on the plate.

em: Typographic term for the unit of measurement equal to the width and height of the type being set (approximately the size of the uppercase M in the face).

embossing: Embossing produces a raised image on a sheet of paper, accomplished with the use of an embossing die in the printing press.

emulsion layer: The layer in film that holds the light sensitive silver-halide emulsion.

en: A unit of typographic measurement equal to one-half the width of the type bing set. An en is one-half the width of an em.

ENIAC computer: Electronic Numerical Integrator and Computer—first-generation computer built at the Moore School of Engineering, University of Pennsylvania to calculate ballistic tables for the United States Navy during World War II.

external drum imagesetter: Film is cut and held on the outside of the imagesetter drum during exposure.

family: See "type family."

file transfer protocol (FTP): On the Internet, the protocol which allows a host user to access and transfer files to and from another host over a network.

film sensitivity: The degree to which photographic film reacts to light conditions. The more sensitive the film is to light, the less light is needed to produce a correct exposure. Film sensitivity is expressed as either ASA or ISO numbers; the higher the number, the more sensitive the film is to light.

Firewire®: High-speed data transfer port operating at speeds of up to 400 Mbps.

flag: The designed title of a newspaper or magazine as it appears on the first page or on the cover.

Flash®: Software produced by Macromedia, Inc., designed to produce animations and applications for the World Wide Web.

flash exposure: Performed in the halftone photography process by exposing the ortho film/halftone screen sandwich to a yellow filter lamp located above the camera, usually mounted on the ceiling of the darkroom. The flash exposure is designed to bring up detail in the shadow areas on the negative (the clearer areas on the halftone negative).

flat: Name given to the goldenrod sheet after all of the negatives have been stripped in and it is ready for platemaking.

flatbed scanner: Scanners that operate with the original material placed on a flat glass plate. During operation, the scanning head moves horizontally across the bed of the scanner to capture and digitize the image.

floppy disks: Widely used device for storing small files in computers. Floppy disks started out as 8-inch disks used in first-generation typesetters. They then moved to 5 1/4-inch disks, and finally to the 3 1/2-inch format currently available. With the advent of newer, high-capacity drives using flexible media, the venerable floppy drive is being phased out by most computer manufacturers.

flowchart: Used in multimedia programs and sometimes referred to as "navigation charts," flowcharts illustrate the major elements of the multimedia program and how they interract with other elements in the program.

flowline: Material organization used in certain multimedia authoring programs. In flowline logic, all of the elements that will appear on the screen are placed in a linear sequence, or flowline, on the screen.

font: A font of type is the smallest unit of packaged type, consisting of a complete assortment of type of one size and family. A traditional font of foundry type consists of three packages: lower case, upper case and figures. Computer fonts are electronically packaged in the same configuration and stored in suitcases residing on the computer's hard drive.

foundry type: type cast from molten metal (lead, tin and antimony) in a type foundry. All of the letters in this process are individually cast.

fountain solution: The dampening solution used in small-format offset presses and duplicators to wet the printing plate and repel ink from nonimage areas.

Fourdrinier papermaking machines: Developed by the Fourdrinier brothers who built the first commercially successful papermaking machine in 1804 in England. Modern papermaking machines still bear their name as well as a close resemblance to the original Fourdrinier machines.

frequency modulation (FM) screening: Also referred to as stochastic screening, FM screening relies on varying the spacing between the dot patterns of same-size dots to reproduce a continuous tone color or black-and-white printed image.

gallery camera: A graphic arts process camera that can be used in a lighted room. Gallery cameras contain a removable film holder which is taken into a darkroom where the film is either loaded or processed after exposure.

general purpose interface board (GPIB): An add-on computer board that operates a peripheral computer device and is installed into one of the expansion slots on the computer's motherboard.

gigabyte (GB): One gigabyte is equivalent to 1,000 megabytes.

goldenrod: Sheet of specially-prepared paper on which all of the negatives that make up a page are positioned. The sheet of paper is known as "goldenrod" because of its yellow color.

graphic arts process cameras: Large-format cameras used to photograph original copy for subsequent platemaking and printing.

gravure printing: Printing from a recessed surface. The image to be printed is cut into, and below, the surface of the printing plate.

gray contact screens: The standard contact screen, which contains vignetted dots, lighter in the center and darker toward the outer areas of the dot. Gray screens are used in direct-screen halftone exposures for both black-and-white and color separation work.

grayscale images: Images that contain black and white as well as intermediate shades of gray.

gripper margin: The margin, or space incorporated into a goldenrod flat, that represents the non-printing area on a sheet of paper created by the gripper fingers on the feed system of an offset printing press. This margin is usually between 1/4 and 3/8-inch.

GUI: Graphic User Interface, incorporated by most present-day computers, that allows a person to use the various functions of the computer without having to navigate the computer's operating system (OS).

halftone screen rulings: The method used to classify halftone screens, based on the number of dots-per-inch incorporated into the screen.

halftone screens: Sheets of glass or plastic that contain a built-in series of dots. The screens are placed over a sheet of film in a process camera when photographing continuous-tone originals, to break up the picture in to a series of halftone dots. The dot structure enables the continuous tone illustration to be printed on conventional printing presses.

HFS: The hierarchal file system used by Macintosh® computers.

hickey: Hickeys are small blemishes or dots that print in either image or nonimage areas, and are caused by small pieces of paper or ink that adhere to the plate or blanket cylinder during the press run.

hieroglyphics: Pictures and symbols that represent ideas, objects, and symbols in a formalized writing system, used by the Egyptians around 3,000 B.C.

High Sierra format: Part of the ISO 9660 format for CD-ROMs.

hot scanners: Fluorescent or xenon light source, coupled to a cooling fan, to regulate the temperature of the light source.

imagesetter: Computer-output device used for producing images on either paper, film, or plate media.

imposition: The placement of each image on a flat so that it will print in the right order and position on the page.

impression cylinder: The cylinder of an offset press that creates a solid backing for a sheet, or roll, of paper during printing.

Indeo®: Video software compression developed by the Intel® Corporation.

indirect dampening systems: Indirect dampening systems on offset presses carry both the ink and fountain solution on the same set of rollers; there is no need for a separate set of dampening rollers as used in a direct dampening system.

ink fountain: The ink fountain is a reservoir from which ink is fed to the press. The ink fountain, consisting of a shallow tray and a "doctor" blade, enables ink to be evenly metered out to the ink system during each rotation of the printing press.

ink jet printers: A variety of highly sophisticated printing technologies that rely on liquid-based colored inks.

intaglio: See "engraving."

integrated dampening systems: See "indirect dampening system."

interactivity: The amount of control that can be exercised by the user of a multimedia program.

interlaced monitor: An interlaced monitor refreshes, or redisplays, only half of the lines on the screen during each refresh cycle.

internal drum imagesetter: On internal drum imagesetters, the media must first be cut, then held in place on the inside of the drum during exposure.

interpolated (software interpreted) resolution: A software program to boost the optical resolution of a scanner. Interpolated resolution relies on software that uses a mathematical formula called an algorithm. The algorithm analyzes the original scan and then adds pixels to fill in the spaces between the original and final scan requirements.

ion-deposition imaging: A method of printing utilizing an electrostatically charged image area on a drum, belt or paper, as a vehicle to attract oppositely charged toner and transfer it to a substrate to create an image.

ISO 9660: The International Standards Organization (ISO) file format for CD-ROM discs.

italic typeface: Using graceful, slanting letters to mimic handwritten characters. Italic type was originally designed by Venetian type designer Aldus Manutius.

jogging: Process of quickly vibrating a stack of paper to line up all of the edges of the paper stack.

Joliet file structure: An extension of the ISO 9660, and the basis for the CD-Plus specification that allows the use of multisession compact discs in conventional audio CD players by placing audio tracks on the first session of the disc.

JPEG: JPEG is an acronym for "joint photographic experts group." JPEG images use what is called a "codec" (for coding/decoding) that removes repeated elements between frames to compress the file size of the image. JPEG is the common format used for illustrations on the Web.

kerning: To adjust the space between two characters to improve readability or achieve balanced, proportional type.

Kilobytes (KB): 1,000 bytes of information. 1,000 kilobytes is equivalent to one megabyte (MB) of information storage.

laminating: Laminating is a process in which a film of plastic is adhered to a sheet of paper or similar stock after it has been printed. This plastic coating also adds stability to the thinner papers used in ink jet and electrostatic printers.

lands: Lands are the untouched surface areas between the pits burned into a compact disc during production.

latent image: In photography, exposing film to light causes a chemical change in the emulsion of the film, producing what is known as a "latent image." The term latent image refers to the fact that the light striking the film has been recorded by the emulsion of the film but requires further chemical processing in order for the image to become visible. Latent images also exist on electrostatic copiers and imagesetters after the imaging drum has been sensitized and before the toner has been applied.

leading: The horiontal space between lines of type, measured from the baseline of one line to the baseline. of the next.

LED: Light emitting diode that requires only small amounts of power to operate. LEDs are often used as power and status indicating lights on everything from hand-held electronic devices to large industrial machining applications. LEDs are also used as exposure light sources in imagesetters.

line copy: Copy consisting only of black lines, with no intermediate shades of gray.

line negative: Photographic negative produced on a graphic arts process camera, that contains only line copy.

linen tester: High quality magnifying lens, sometimes called a "loupe," for close inspection of photographic negatives and prints.

lines per inch (lpi): The rating of mechanical tint and halftone screens. The higher the number, the higher the resolution of the screen.

Lingo®: The scripting language used in Macromedia's Director®. Lingo® controls many of the interactive and other powerful functions associated with Director®.

Linotype machine: Invented by Ottmar Merganthaler and first used commercially in 1886 to set lines of type by a process of machine casting. The Linotype machine was the standard of typesetting from its invention until it was finally replaced by photographic typesetters in the 1950s.

litho stone: Polished piece of cut stone, usually limestone, on which an image is drawn using special grease-based materials, for printing in a lithography press.

local area network (LAN): A computer network that serves a specified, delimited area, e.g., a series of corporate offices within a large office complex.

lowercase: Term used to define the uncapitalized letters in a typeface.

Ludlow typesetting machine: A machine used to set display type for headlines and large captions. Often used together with the Linotype machine in setting type for newspapers and magazines.

magenta contact screen: Magenta contact screens are used for black-and-white halftone screening. They are not used for making color separations, because the magenta color of the screen interferes with the color filters used in the color separation photographic process.

magnetic/optical (MO) drives: Available in different removable cartridge sizes for backing up or storing large files, MO cartridges resemble thick floppy disks. During the data recording process, a laser heats a magnetic alloy recording layer on the disk to approximately 150 degrees. At this temperature, the alloy can be magnetized for data storage.

main exposure: The main exposure captures the majority of the detail, highlight, and middle tones of the original in the halftone photographic process.

makeready: Press preparation time including all of the steps required to be performed prior to an actual press run.

masking sheet: See "goldenrod."

mechanical: The traditional method of preparing copy for photographing. Mechanicals consist of all of the elements of the job adhered to a heavy piece of mat or illustration board. While text and line copy can be photographed on the process camera directly from the mechanical, continuous tone illustrations must be photographed separately and later added to the flat for final plating and printing.

medical photo-CD format: This format allows data from CAT and MRI scans to be stored on the Photo-CD for later analysis, or for archival purposes.

megabytes (MB): One megabyte (Mb) is equivalent to 1,000 kilobytes.

Mesolithic: Middle Stone Age period.

microprocessor: The central microprocessor chip was introduced by the Intel® Corporation in 1971. Microprocessors combine thousands of individual electronic circuit components onto one small chip to process the instruction sets of the software programs during computer operation. The speed with which microprocessors carry out the processing of instruction sets is measured in millions of cycles per second (MHz).

MIDI: MIDI is an acronym for "musical instrument digital interface." The MIDI process is often used to enhance compact disc products and programs by adding computer-generated music and musical effects.

moiré pattern: A pattern, generally objectionable, produced by the improper alignment of halftone dots. Moiré patterns occur most frequently in re-screened scans and prints. These patterns can be minimized by selecting the "de-screening" option available in most scanner software programs.

MP3: MP3 is an audio file format compression, an extension of the MPEG file format. MP3 offers much smaller files (about 1/10th the size) than traditional MPEG files for reproducing CD-quality audio.

MPC specification: MPC (multimedia personal computer) level of specifications that detail the computer hardware configurations necessary to deliver base-level performance characteristics for most software, game, and entertainment titles.

MPEG: MPEG is an acronym for "motion pictures experts group." MPEG compression uses an algorithm that creates one compressed "interframe," and then removes repeated elements from succeeding frames and codes only the differences.

multimedia: The combination of text, audio, graphics and video combined into one application presented to the viewer.

multi-platform: Computer programs authored, or developed, on one computer platform or operating system (for example, a Macintosh) that will run on a different platform, for example a Windows® PC.

multisession CD: A multisession CD has more than one lead-in area, program area and lead-out area. Multisession discs can be written either during one writing session or at different times, depending on the features of the CD-recorder.

navigation chart: See "flowchart."

negative acting plates: Plates that use standard photographic negatives stripped on to a flat to produce positive images on the plate.

nonimpact printing: Digital and electronic printing techniques that rely on electrostatic charges, rather than physical contact, to transfer images to the printed sheet.

non-interlaced monitors: Monitors that refresh, or redisplay, all of the lines on the screen during each refresh cycle.

NTSC standard: NTSC is an acronym for the "National Television Systems Committee." This system, based on 30-frame-per-second video, is the color television standard for the United States, Japan, Canada, Mexico, Taiwan, and other countries.

object-oriented/vector images: Images generated on the computer screen and stored as a series of connected lines and shapes. Vector graphics are the type generated in CAD and drawing programs.

Occupational Safety and Health Administration (OSHA): The federal agency responsible for legislation and enforcement of environmental regulations in the workplace.

offset lithography (offset printing): A lithographic printing process in which an image is transferred from the printing plate to a rubber blanket and then "offset" on to a sheet of paper.

oil and water principle: Scientific principle underlying lithographic printing: oil and water don't mix. This principle separates the image and nonimage areas on an offset printing plate or litho stone.

opacity: Opacity is the same thing as density (the light stopping ability of the emulsion layer of film). Opacity is measured on a decimal scale from 1 to 100.

opaque proofs: Opaque proofs incorporate a heavy paper or plastic support base on top of which sensitized color sheets or toners are added to create progressive proofs of a job. After all of the exposures have been made, the finished proof results in a high quality representation of the finished job.

opaque solution: Liquid applied to photographic film using either a brush or special applicator, to cover small pinholes and unwanted image areas in the negative.

optical character recognition (OCR): Optical character recognition software enables the computer to compare the letters of scanned text to predefined patterns for letters of the alphabet stored in the OCR software program. This enables the computer to generate pages of text from scanned material.

optical scanning resolution: Actual, or mechanical resolution ability, of the scanner using its built-in optical and hardware power for distinguishing the number of lines, or dots, per inch in the scan.

ortho film: Photographic film sensitive to the blue and green portion of the visible spectrum. Ortho film is red-blind, enabling the use of dim red safelights, when handling this film in the darkroom.

page description language (PDL): Program that contains the commands for a printer to take the text and graphics generated on the computer and properly place this information onto a printed page.

PAL standard: The phase alteration line (PAL) standard is based on 25-frames-per-second video and used in most of Europe and South America.

panchromatic film: Film sensitive to the entire visible spectrum.

papyrus: Writing material made from a tropical reed, once used by ancient Egyptian societies.

parchment: Writing material made from dried animal skins.

perfect binding: The paperback book, phone book, and Yellow Pages® are examples of perfect bound documents. In the binding operation, the spine of the book is first trimmed and then inserted into a machine where a flexible binding adhesive is heated and applied to the spine. While the glue is still wet, the cover is adhered.

perfecting: The process of printing on both sides of a sheet, or roll of paper, during a single press run.

perforating: Perforating, or "perfing," is often performed during the printing process. When in contact with the paper, perfing rule presses a series of holes through the sheet. While not cutting completely through the paper, perfing enables a sheet of paper to be easily torn along the rule marks.

phase-change ink jet (solid ink jet) printers: Ink is supplied in solid form, resembling crayon sticks. During the printing process, the ink in the stick is heated and quickly melts while the print head travels across the paper, spraying ink droplets onto the paper.

photo CD master disc: The original photo-CD format for the consumer photographer. The disc can hold 100 images at high resolution.

photographic gray scale: The gray scale is a small (1/2x3-inch) strip of photographic paper divided into twelve steps. Step one is bright white, step twelve is solid black, and the steps in-between are the intermediate shades of gray the represent the overall contrast range in a convenient wedge format. The gray scale is used as a quality control device when exposing and developing line and halftone negatives, and offset printing plates. Gray scales are also used to ensure the output quality of imagesetters and platesetters.

photomechanical proofs: Inexpensive photosensitive materials, exposed through the flat and developed, to offer a rendition of what a finished job will look like without the expense of using the actual papers and printing inks.

photomultiplier tube (PMT): Drum scanners typically use photomultiplier tubes to sense light reflected from original copy and digitize the scan.

photoreceptor drum: The drum on photocopiers and laser printers on which the pattern of charges created by the laser beam leaves an electrostatic latent image. Toner particles are attracted to the image areas of the drum that make up the final printed image.

photoresist layer: The layer on a glass master compact disc through which a laser burns pits onto the glass surface below. During manufacture, the photoresist layer prevents the etching of the disc in all areas other than those exposed to the laser to produce the data "pits" on the disc.

Photoshop®: Market-dominant photo-editing software program, produced by Adobe Systems, Inc.®

pictograph: Literally means "writing with pictures." Prehistoric cave paintings are pictographs, which are limited to communicating simple messages.

pits: Indentations of varying lengths burned into the spiral data tracks on a CD by a laser, during the initial manufacture of the disc master.

pixel: A shortening of the term "picture element," which computer monitors use to display images.

planographic (planography): Printing process in which both the image and nonimage areas are located on the same plane, or height, on the printing plate.

plastic binding: A system of book and pamphlet binding that uses plastic honeycombs to fasten the pages together. Plastic binding is associated with the square holes punched into the sheets of paper through which the plastic honeycombs are inserted.

plate cylinder: The cylinder on an offset printing press that holds the printing plate.

platemaker: Device used to expose printing plates. Platemakers consist of a high intensity ultra-violet light source coupled to a vacuum frame. Offset flats of stripped goldenrod sheets are placed in contact with the printing plate and exposed in the platemaker.

platesetter: Computer driven device that images offset printing plates directly from the computer. Platesetters are composed of two parts; the raster image processor (RIP) and the imaging section that exposes, or generates, the image onto the printing plate.

plug-in applications: Software applications that reside and work within larger software programs. Scanner software and special effects filters for Adobe Photoshop®, Illustrator®, and QuarkXPress® are examples of plug-in applications.

PMT gray contact screens: Screens used in the diffusion process transfer, or photomechanical transfer (PMT) process, for making screened paper prints from continuous tone originals. These prints are referred to as "velox" prints.

positive acting plates: Printing plates made using photographic positives rather than photographic negatives to produce the positive image on the plate surface.

pre-mastering: Before the actual mastering process of a CD can begin, original data must first be converted into one of the standard CD-ROM formats (ISO 9660, High Sierra, Apple HFS, or DVD). This data conversion is referred to as pre-mastering.

presensitized additive plates: A special chemical solution that adds a lacquer, or long-run coating, to the image areas of the plate during the development.

presensitized subtractive plates: Processing solution that removes all of the image coating from the nonimage areas of the plate, thus "subtracting" the image coating from the plate during processing.

press proofs: Proofs made on the printing press, taken at the beginning of the press run. These proofs ensure that the job is set up correctly and that registration and image quality are as specified.

print engine: Imaging devices incorporated in laser printers, black and white and color electrostatic copiers, and digital printing presses.

print photo CD disc: Developed for the color electronic prepress industry, storing color originals in the CMYK (cyan, magenta, yellow, and black) format necessary for producing color separations.

printer control language (PCL): Printers are accompanied by a corresponding page description language known as its printer control language (PCL). PCLs enable the printer to take the text and graphics generated on the computer and properly place this information onto the printed page.

printing primaries: The four ink colors of cyan, magenta, yellow and black used in offset printing.

pro-photo CD master disc: The pro disc offers a higher level of resolution than can be found on the CD master disc storing pictures at a resolution level of 4096 x 6144 pixels.

proportion scale (proportion wheel): Small hand-held device, consisting of two rotating cardboard wheels, used to determine the percentage of enlargement or reduction required for a specific job, based on the size of the original and finished copy.

QuarkXPress®: Page layout program manufactured by Quark, Inc. QuarkXPress® is the standard layout program used in the design and publishing industry.

QuickTake® camera: Early generation, single exposure point-and-shoot camera released by Apple Computer® in the mid 1990s. The QuickTake® was the first digital camera to open up the market to the desktop publishing industry.

Quicktime VR®: Software developed by Apple Computer® for developing and playing back virtual reality applications.

QWERTY: The modern keyboard configuration found on typewriters and computers, credited to inventor Christopher Sholes.

RAID array: A redundant array of independent (or inexpensive) disks. Using multiple hard drives, RAID systems are installed where data-intensive applications such as high-speed video, image processing, and other disk-intensive operations are the primary system functions.

raster image processor (RIP): A RIP interprets data from a computer and sends this information to an imagesetter, platesetter, or digital printing press.

recto: The right-hand page of a book, magazine or other publication.

recto-verso: Two-sided printing.

reflectance: Reflectance, or reflection, is the percentage of incidental light that reflects off copy (a photographic print, for example) in a particular tonal area.

register pins: Metal pins used to line up multiple flats on a light table during the stripping process. The use of register pins helps to ensure proper registration of multiple colors and images during printing.

registration marks: Registration marks are placed in pairs at each corner of the printed piece and allow for the printing and alignment of successive colors in multi-color printing applications.

relief printing: Printing from a raised surface. The image areas are raised in relief from the non-printing surfaces of the printing plate.

replica casting: Type is cast in a mold from molten metal, one letter at a time. The mold is reusable, so many letters of type can be cast from the same mold, each identical to, and a replica of, the other.

re-screening: The process of taking a picture that has already been screened, and either scanning, or photographing it again to produce a different halftone pattern in the print. When re-screening, care must be taken to prevent moiré patterns from occurring in the re-screened print.

Risograph: Digital printing press, incorporating a built-in scanner and quick change ink cartridges to produce multi-color prints.

Rosetta Stone: The Rosetta Stone provided the major key to deciphering ancient Egyptian hieroglyphic texts. The stone was deciphered by a French scholar, Jean Champollion, in 1822.

rotogravure: The process historically used to print the color sections of Sunday newspapers.

rubber blanket: The blanket attached to the blanket cylinder of an offset printing press. This blanket accepts the image from the plate cylinder and "offsets" the image onto a sheet of paper, thus the term "offset lithography."

ruby masking film: Masking film, whose name comes from its color, is often used for preparing multicolor printing jobs where only one flat is used for making multiple exposures on to a printing plate. Ruby film is cut by hand to expose window areas on a flat for separate exposures during platemaking.

saddle stitching: Stapling a series of signatures or a complete book, through the center fold, or spine, of the pages.

safelight: Low-intensity light source that will not affect, or expose, specific types of photographic films. The color of the safelight will vary, based on the type of film being handled in the darkroom.

sans-serif: Term used to categorize typfaces without finishing strokes at the end of their letterforms; French meaning "without serifs."

scoring: Scoring rule is set up in a special form, similar to die-cutting rule. Scoring rule does not cut through the sheet but rather, creases it. This enables the end user to make folds at pre-determined places on a sheet of paper.

screen tint: Adding screening or shading effects to a job during the platemaking process. Commercial tint screens are stripped into a flat for subsequent exposure.

scribes: Monastic scholars who transcribed books and other materials by hand.

SCSI: High-speed "small computer systems interface" (pronounced scuzzy). The revised SCSI-2 format enables data transfer at speeds up to 10 megabytes (MBs).

scumming: A printing condition in which the printing plate picks up and prints ink in nonimage areas of the print.

SECAM: The television standard used in France.

sectors: The data tracks on a computer disk are divided into individual sectors. The sectors on a disk are likened to individual file folders within the drawer of a file cabinet.

serif: The finishing stoke found at the end of the main stroke of letterforms within a family of type.

sheeter: Device used on the output side of web-fed presses to cut the web, or roll, of paper into individual sheets.

sheetwise layout: Printing both sides of a sheet of paper with two different images, using two separate printing plates.

side stitching: Stapling the pages of a signature, or book, through the side of the sheets.

signature: One sheet of paper on which many different pages are printed. After printing, the sheet moves to a folding machine where it is folded and then trimmed, so that all of the pages are arranged in proper position and sequence.

silver-emulsion-based photography: Photographic process that relies on developer, stop bath, and fixer to develop an image in a silver halide photographic film emulsion.

single-session CD: A single-session disc contains one lead-in area, the program area, and a lead-out area. The data in the program area of the disc can be written either all at one time or at different writing times.

stamper: Stampers are the production discs used to make an actual compact disc. Using an injection molding process similar to the one used to produce traditional long-playing vinyl records, the stamper creates the pit and land structures on the polycarbonate compact disc (CD).

star targets: Printed at diagonal corners of the printed sheet, the star target shows the amount of ink spread; as ink spread increases, the center wedge of the star target begins to fill with ink. In addition to ink spread, the target will also show the amount of ink slur, or line doubling on the print.

step and repeat: Process used when the same image is to be printed many times on the same sheet of paper. Most often, multiple exposures at exact locations on the plate are made, as determined by the technician during the plating process.

stochastic screening: See "frequency modulation screening."

stop bath: Mild acidic chemical, usually acetic acid, used when developing film, to stop the action of the developer at a specified time during the development cycle. The acidic stop bath chemically neutralizes the chemically basic developing solution.

storyboards: A thumbnail sketch of a multimedia project, to help visualize all sections and interactions of the program.

streaming: Streaming technology divides a multimedia piece into segments that are downloaded to the user's individual computer. The advantage of streaming is that the program can begin to play as soon as the first segment is downloaded, without the need to wait for the entire program to be downloaded.

stripping: Cutting windows into a goldenrod flat to precisely locate and place line and halftone negatives, in preparation for plating.

subtractive primaries: The primary colors of reflected light: red, yellow and blue. In offset printing, cyan, magenta, yellow, plus black are used—also known as *printing primaries*.

surface-coated plates: Offset printing plate in which the presensitized photographic emulsion sits directly on top of the surface of the plate.

tabloid: Paper format that uses 11x17-inch paper.

thermography: Produces a raised surface on conventionally printed material. For this reason, thermography is sometimes referred to as "imitation engraving."

thumbnail sketches: Small preliminay sketches done to explore a variety of design concepts.

toner: Extremely small particles of carbon-based powder, available in different colors, used in laser printers, color copiers and digital printing presses.

tracking: The overall letterspacing as applied to a paragraph of type.

tracks: As the disk rotates in a drive mechanism, the drive head produces circles of information on the disk. These circles on the disk are called tracks. The tracks on the disk can be likened to the drawers in a file cabinet.

transistor: A small electronic semiconductor used in electronic equipment. It was invented by Bell Laboratory physicists Walter Brattain, John Bardeen and William Shockley in 1948. The invention of the transistor was one of the key technological enabling events in human history.

transmittance: Proportion of light striking a photographic negative that penetrates the emulsion layer of the film in any particular area.

Tsai Lun: Chinese court official credited with the invention of paper in 105 A.D.

TWAIN software protocol: The TWAIN software protocol eliminates the need for special software drivers for each type of hardware platform by ensuring compatibility of devices produced by a variety of manufacturers.

type family: The major grouping of specific typefaces having similar characteristics but specfic differences, e.g., Futura Light, Futura Book, Futura Italic, etc.

type-high: The standard height of all material printed on a letterpress. Type high is .918".

uniform resource locator (URL): Address system used to find specific addresses on the World Wide Web.

UNIVAC: The Universal Automatic Computer was delivered by the Remington Rand Corporation to the United States Census Bureau in 1951.

universal serial bus: High-speed data port operating at 12 megabits-per-second (Mbps), for connecting external scanners, drives, video cameras, and a variety of other peripheral devices to the computer.

unsharp masking (USM): Creates an invisible outline around an image, giving it a greater sense of detail.

uppercase: Term used to describe the capital letters of a typeface.

variable data printing: Customized printing applications on digital presses, that can vary the information being printed from one copy to another.

velox print: A black and white halftone-screened print, usually produced through rapid chemical processing, or diffusion transfer processing. Screened velox prints are often used in the preparation of mechanicals, and can be photographed alongside traditional line copy, since the photograph has already been screened.

washed-out copy: Copy that prints with a gray tone, reducing the contrast and quality of the image.

waterless printing: See "dry offset" and/or "dryography."

wax thermal printer: Elements in a print head melt a ribbon coated with a wax-based color ink which is then transferred from the ribbon on to a specially coated paper stock.

web-fed: Printing presses fed from a continuous roll of paper.

Windows®: The operating system, produced by Microsoft Corporation®, installed on most personal computers (PCs). (Apple Macintosh® computers do not run under the Windows® operating system without the installation of special emulation software or special add-on boards installed in the computer).

Wintel: An acronym describing computers that run under the Windows® operating system, with an Intel® corporation, or compatible, microprocessor.

work and tumble: Work and tumble uses one plate for printing both sides of a sheet. In this format, the paper pile is tumbled so that the opposite end of the sheet serves as the leading edge during the second press run.

work and turn: One printing plate is used to print both sides of the same sheet of paper. After the first press run, the pile of paper is turned over and fed into the press using the same leading edge on the sheets during the second press run.

x-height: The height of the lower case "x" in any given typeface.

Xeikon®: Manufacturer of digital printing presses.

Xerography: Generic term used to describe all electrostatic printing, developed by Chester Carlson and sold to the Xerox® Corporation in 1938.

zinc line cut: Line or halftone engraving, etched onto a zinc plate and mounted on a piece of type high wood (.918"). Zinc line cuts have largely been replaced by magnesium line cuts, and are printed on conventional letterpresses.

ZIP drive®: ZIP® drives, first appearing in the mid 1990s, have quickly become the standard flexible-media storage system. Zip® drives utilize a flexible plastic 3 1/2-inch disk housed within a rigid plastic case, and feature both 100 and 250 MB of data storage.

INDEX